Memories

of Opportunities,
Family & Adventures

Memories
of Opportunities, Family & Adventures

1 9 5 4 - 2 0 0 4

AN AUTOBIOGRAPHY
Inge E. Stanneck Gross

VOLUME TWO

Inge E. Stanneck Gross

Island In the Sky Publishing Co.
Eastsound, Washington
www.MemoriesOfWWII.com

ABOUT THE PHOTOGRAPHS, MAPS AND ILLUSTRATIONS
The vast majority of photographs in this book were taken by the author or her family members and are used by permission. Every effort has been made by the author and publisher to locate and secure permission from the copyright owners of historical photographs, maps and illustrations from the World War II era that may be still protected under copyright. A few such images from the author's scrapbook are used pursuant to the fair use doctrine or because they are apparently now in the public domain. However, if any reader is able to provide further information on the origin of any of these images, the author would appreciate being contacted through the Publisher at the offices listed below.

Published by Island In The Sky Publishing Co.
P.O. Box 139, Eastsound, Washington 98245-0139

Publisher's Cataloging-in-Publication Data

Gross, Inge Erika.
    Memories of opportunities, family and adventures 1954 to 2004 : an autobiography
volume two / Inge E. Stanneck Gross.
    p. cm.
    ISBN 13: 978-0-97603-287-8
    ISBN 10: 0-9760328-7-2

1. Gross, Inge Erika. 2. German–Americans—Biography. 3. Berlin Wall, Berlin, Germany, 1961-1989. 4. Soviet Union—Description and Travel—1945–1969. 5. Grand Canyon (Ariz.)–Description and Travel. 6. Ross Island (Ross Sea, Antarctica)—Description and Travel. I. Title.

E184.G3 G7 2005
921—dd22   LC#2004099726

Jacket design by Linda Griffith, Portland, Oregon
Printed in the United States of America by Patterson Printing Co.

Contents

Preface

This is the second volume of my autobiography which begins with the day I left Berlin and immigrated to the United States, and it covers the next fifty years. It is the story of an immigrant who took advantage of opportunities, raised a wonderful family, and who had many adventures along the way. It is a story repeated over and over again by generations of immigrants, yet each is unique and deserves to be told.

The first volume, *Memories of World War II and its Aftermath, by a Little Girl Growing up in Berlin,* covers the very difficult years from 1940 to 1954 before I immigrated to the United States. It has been published separately from the rest of my autobiography because I believe it covers a period of history that needs to be recorded, and is unique. As time goes by there are fewer and fewer people left from that era, and even fewer still who have written about those times particularly from the vantage point of a young child, and in English.

This second volume is intended primarily for my family and friends, and those readers of *Memories of World War II and its Aftermath* who may be interested in finding out what happened to that "little girl" who was just starting the greatest adventure of her life.

Memories have a way of blurring over time. I am fortunate to have a precise memory of life experiences, and I did write down my impressions of some of our many travel adventures. In several of the chapters I have included accounts of these travels as written at the time or immediately afterward. The account of our pioneering automobile trip to the Soviet Union in 1960 at the height of the Cold War, and the detailed letter I wrote to Mal just three days after two of my cousins escaped from East Berlin after The Wall had been built could only have been written at that time. These writings have been included in this volume.

The two volumes have been a long project which was precipitated by the birth of my first grandchild—Meagen Moser—thirteen years ago. I suddenly recognized that neither of my children, and to a lesser extent my husband—Mal—really knew what my life was like as a child growing up in wartime Berlin. The project started out solely to provide this information for my family, and perhaps my friends. Over the years

I shared parts of the manuscript with a number of friends, and all have encouraged me to continue and to expand it.

The manuscript has grown far beyond what I had originally intended. I hope that not only my family and friends, but others as well, get enjoyment from reading both this and the earlier volume.

I thank my husband, Malvern Gross, for his encouragement and support, as well as his technical help in laying out the book in an electronic document that my printer could use. I thank my book coach, Joyce Griffith, and the design artist, Linda Griffith, for their invaluable help in making these books happen. Special thanks go to Sylvia Cole of Tricor Press for her unselfish assistance in providing her insights as well as her editing skills.

These books have also allowed me to acknowledge the contributions many people have made in my life without whom I would not be here today. More than any other person, my mother, Johanna Stanneck, has been the guiding light in my life. Her legacy lives on in my brother Peter and me.

Above all I hope that this autobiography expresses my love of this great country of ours, and the freedom and opportunities that we enjoy which too often so many seem to take for granted.

Inge E. Stanneck Gross
Eastsound, WA
February 2005

Dedicated to the Memory of
Our Mother

Johanna M. Stanneck

Peter and I would not be here today
but for her unselfish devotion, common sense,
innate intuition, and the ability to find humor
in the most bleak of circumstances.

PROLOGUE

The Beginning

On June 14, 1929, Erich August Paul Stanneck married Johanna Magdalene Elisabeth Hinniger. They had met at a soccer game. Papa's love was soccer. He was on a team which played regularly on weekends. Mom's oldest sister, Hilda (Hildegard) was engaged to Hans Grau, who was also on the team. Tante Hilda had invited her sister *Hannchen* (Johanna) to go with her and watch the soccer game. During intermission, Hans and his friend Erich stopped to say hello to Hilda, and Erich met Johanna. They fell in love.

I was born on September 13, 1934, in Berlin–Schöneberg and christened Inge Erika.

Johanna and Erich Stanneck

1

I am at 8 months old

Mom told me that Papa was a typesetter with a publishing company, and during the Depression he had been without a job for five years. He held a number of temporary jobs until the last one just before my birth had turned into a permanent one. Thus, Papa happened to fall into becoming a salesman for tobacco goods. The job did not pay well, but it was a job, and it was desperately needed.

Mom loved children and happily expected my birth. She did some occasional cleaning work to earn pocket money with which to buy some things for her expected baby. Mom was a certified tailor, but jobs in that line were nearly nonexistent. A high priority item on her list of things to buy was a camera. This was very important to her. She wanted to be able to take pictures of her baby, and she had a lot of fun with a Brownie–type camera which she bought at Woolworth's for five *Reichsmarks*. Today I feel lucky. Thanks to Mom's little luxury I have pictures of my early years, and twice–lucky that those pictures survived the turmoil of the war. Many of them are in this book.

We lived in Berlin–Lichterfelde–West, Dürerstraße 9, in an apartment on the ground floor. The apartment consisted of one room and a kitchen.

Some of my memories from early childhood start at about age two. One was of a steamship trip on the *Teltow Kanal*, where I wanted to sit by the bell. I have a photo of that trip, and I remember the bell and reaching for it, wanting to gong it. Mom would not let me. Obviously, that bell was there for a purpose, and not for little kids to play with.

Two major German rivers, the Spree and the Havel, flow through Berlin, and a network of canals connects the rivers for shipping purposes. I liked water and loved it when Mom took me for walks along the canal so I could watch the ducks and the boats. There were steamships which cruised the rivers, lakes, and canals of Berlin for sightseeing purposes, and there were barges. Most of Berlin's goods, and especially coal, arrived by waterway.

The footpath in the park by the canal was at higher ground and a steep embankment went down to the water. I remember always wanting to get near the water and Mom having to watch me closely so that I would not try and then perhaps tumble down the embankment. Below, along-side the canal, was the tow-path which had tracks for engines that towed the

I loved picking buttercups and little daisies, and enjoyed outings in nearby parks.

barges. Sometimes we saw an engine towing a barge and I wanted to get down there to watch at a closer distance.

There were several nice little parks near the canal which we visited often. I remember one with the Lilienthal Monument. It always impressed me because the man had wings. Mom liked taking me to different city parks where there were lawns, wildflowers, benches for people to sit, and usually a sandbox for the children. I loved picking buttercups and little daisies.

My Papa

Music was very much a part of my parents' life. They liked the music from musical films and shows, as well as operas and operettas, Johann Strauss waltzes, and just any music one could dance to. With his first earned money, Papa had purchased a gramophone which was his pride and joy. It was the old Victrola type where the needle had to be changed for each record, which was the only kind that existed in the early 1920's.

Papa also liked to dance. He was a good dancer. Some of my favorite memories of my parents are occasional Sunday afternoons when Papa would play some dance music on his gramophone, and Mom and Papa would dance together.

Very few people owned cars at that time, unless they needed one for business. Onkel Martin and Tante Lotte (Charlotte), Mom's middle sister, had a car because they had a butcher shop and needed it to make deliveries. Most of the population of Berlin used the excellent network of public transportation, and many people owned bicycles. Germans also love to walk.

Papa served his clients by bicycle. He not only had to bring in the orders, but also deliver the merchandise. Sometimes on a Saturday, when Papa worked a shorter day, he would take me with him as he called on his customers. This was always a special treat for me. I loved having time alone with my Papa. I remember a feeling of importance

to be allowed to go to work with him.

On Sundays, Papa often worked on his bicycle. He cleaned it, as well as oiled and repaired it to keep it in good condition. After all, he depended on it for transportation. Papa was a handyman. He owned most of the common tools and was very proud of his tool collection. He could repair anything around the house and could even put new soles on our shoes. I loved to hang around and watch when Papa worked on his bicycle.

I am 15 months old, standing on a bench

Christmas 1936

I remember the following happening, mostly from Mom and Tante Hilda reminiscing about the hilarious evening during the next couple of years. Being only a little over two years old, I would not have remembered the details, but I do remember the Christmas trees and the laughter. Here is the story:

It was a Friday and Christmas was only about a week away. As usual, Mom with me, of course, and Tante Hilda (Mom's oldest sister) went to the bi-weekly market together to do some grocery shopping. Tante Hilda and Onkel Hans lived upstairs in the same apartment house. There were Christmas trees for sale at the market, and the two women discussed buying trees, since their husbands had not yet done anything about it. According to Mom, Papa always selected our Christmas tree because he wanted to be sure we had one that was as perfect as possible. (I know from whom I inherited my cursed perfectionism!)

Tante Hilda and Mom decided to buy their trees and dragged them home. That evening, Onkel Hans came home from work and brought two Christmas trees, one for us and one for themselves. We all stood around with tears running down our faces from laughing so much. Before long, Papa arrived with a Christmas tree for us. I still see all of them doubling up with laughter. Now we had five Christmas trees between our two families.

Mom was the first one to recover and to decide that something had to be done. I remember her going up to the next floors to try and sell Christmas trees to some of the neighbors. It was close enough to Christmas so that most people had already bought their trees, and I do not remember whether or not Mom and Tante Hilda sold any of the three extras. Even if they didn't, they had more than enough fun for the money.

That Christmas was also a very special one. Papa had built a dollhouse for me, complete with wallpapered walls. Mom had made a bedspread, pillows, tablecloths and kitchen towels. The dollhouse had three rooms—a kitchen, living room, and a bedroom. Its special feature was a fancy ceiling lamp which could light up. It had a green silk shade. Due to lack of space the dollhouse was left out for me to play with for only a month or so after Christmas, then it was put away until the following year. I remember each Christmas looking forward to getting my dollhouse back to play with. Something new had usually been added to it, such as a piece of furniture, a rug, or even a tiny doll.

Ready to ride down the snow mountain with Papa

During that winter we had a lot of snow. One weekend the men got together and shoveled some of the snow into one big pile to make a little mountain so that we children could ride our sleds downhill. This had been Onkel Hans' idea. He just loved children. I climbed up onto the snow mountain and was too scared to ride down because the "mountain" was so big and I was so little. I went to get Papa and he rode down with me on my tiny little sled, while Mom took pictures with her camera, of course.

Mom loved having a little girl. She knitted and crocheted the cutest outfits for me. Being a tailor, she also made all of my clothes, as well as hers. The only limitation was the lack of money for fabrics and yarns.

My favorite Time with Mom

In the evenings when dinner was cooked—at that time it was always vegetable and potato stew with perhaps a little bit of meat, or at

Catching some fresh air by the kitchen window from which Mom and I watched Papa come home in the evenings.

least soup bones in it for flavoring—Mom and I set out to wait for Papa's arrival from work. Papa's arrival time fluctuated, sometimes by as much as forty–five minutes, because he was calling on customers and riding a bicycle. Most evenings, Mom and I would wait for Papa by the open kitchen window from where we could see the street. We lived on the ground floor. During the time of the year when it was already dark outside, we enjoyed what we called *Dunkelstündchen* (hour in the dark) together. This "hour" was mostly only ten or fifteen minutes, or even less, and the dark kitchen was necessary for us to be able to see Papa outside in the dark. For me it was special, personal time spent with Mom before she got busy again. I loved sitting in the dark and waiting for the moment when I would catch the first glimpse of Papa. Knowing that we would sit by the window, he would wave to us as he rode by. This *Dunkelstündchen* is one of my fondest memories from my early childhood.

Sunday Excursions

Sunday outings were excursions to the Berlin Zoo, the Botanical Garden, to parks, walks in the forest, or in the summer to one of the lakes for swimming, as well as visits with relatives and friends who lived in the city. My grandparents Hinniger lived in Berlin and so did Grandma Stanneck, her brother Karl and niece Else, and Mom's two brothers and two sisters.

I remember Sundays as being special in Berlin. The Berliners love being outdoors, and all recreational facilities would be crowded, especially Berlin's much beloved *Grunewald* (Green Forest).

My Onkel Hans

Tante Hilda and Onkel Hans lived in an apartment just two floors above us, and we often went on Sunday excursions with them. Onkel Hans loved children. They did not yet have any, and according to Mom, Onkel Hans liked to pretend that I was his child whenever we went out together. If we rode the city train or the streetcar, he would go into another car with me. I remember riding in the *S–Bahn* one time and looking through the window into the next car where

My second birthday. From left: Papa, Grandma Stanneck, Onkel Hans and Tante Hilda. The doll carriage was my birthday present from Onkel Hans and Tante Hilda.

my parents and Tante Hilda sat. We were all waving to each other. It sounds silly, but for a two–year–old it was fun.

Unfortunately, Onkel Hans died at the age of 33, just before I was three years old, but I remember him well. He would sometimes take me to a toy store and buy me toys. Had I been a boy, he would have liked it even better because he bought me a ship, little soldiers, and a car, as well as girls toys. For my second birthday I received a doll carriage and a doll from Onkel Hans and Tante Hilda.

Onkel Hans also spent time playing with me. Mom told me that every evening after work he would first stop at our apartment and play with me before going upstairs to his and Tante Hilda's place. One of the games he played with me, which I remember well because I especially liked it, was "airplane." On outstretched arms he would fly me through the air and eventually let me fall out of the "sky" and onto the bed. I loved it and the excuse of jumping on the bed a bit before he took me off. According to house rules, I was not allowed to jump around on the beds, but it was different when Onkel Hans had dropped me there.

Less than a year after his death when my brother was born, he was named Peter Hans in honor of Onkel Hans. I remember Mom and Tante

Hilda wishing that Onkel Hans could have lived to see our little boy, and how much he would have loved to buy toys for him and to play rough games with him.

I do not remember being told that Onkel Hans was gone forever when he died; I do remember Tante Hilda sitting in our kitchen all day long, wearing black clothes and crying all of the time. She also slept in our apartment at night. I suppose I must have missed Onkel Hans, however, I do not have any particular memories of it.

Tante Hilda in mourning, sitting in our kitchen.

"Lieber Leierkastenmann"

Lieber Leierkastenmann	Dearest Organ–grinder
fang nochmal von vorne an	start once more from the beginning
mit den alten Melodien	play the old familiar tunes
von der schönen Stadt Berlin	about our beautiful city Berlin
Stehste unten uff 'n Hof	as you're standing in the back yard .....

The *Leierkastenmann* is a relic belonging mostly to the dreary back yards of Berlin's inner city tenements, who is remembered by older Berliners with much affection. Grinding out the cheerful old and familiar melodies, the organ–grinder was always a welcome sight—and sound—especially for the people whose apartments looked down on those desolate yards which were mere light shafts. No matter how meager the budget, a five or ten–penny piece could always be spared for the beloved *Leierkastenmann.* Many people just threw the coins down from their windows when children were playing in the yard. They would pick the money up and drop it into the organ–grinder's pockets.

The big attraction for us young children was not so much the music, but the live monkey which inevitably sat on top of the organ like a decoration. We lived on the outskirts of the city where the apartment houses were only two or three stories high. Our back yards were spacious, and therefore open and airy. There were trees and lilac bushes growing. Whenever the beloved *Leierkastenmann* showed up, it was like a festive occasion for us children. We loved watching the monkey. Standing out in my memory is one particular time when the monkey was not a happy one, and he tried to jump at me when I attempted to put my coins into the man's pockets. Being only three years old, I was scared and did not want to go near again. Reinhard, a little boy who was a year older, offered to put my money in along with his. Though being on a leash, the monkey jumped at the boy and scratched his face, barely missing his eye. Mom had come outside just before it happened and she received quite a shock. There was much commotion caused by this incident, however, the *Leierkastenmann* remained a part of our lives until the seriousness of war removed him. Today he stands at major tourist sites as an attraction, and a memento of Berlin's past.

Gypsies

On several occasions during the pre–war years, groups of gypsies would come around in the neighborhood and beg for money. I remember mothers excitedly yelling for their children to quickly come inside. "The gypsies are here—hurry up and come inside—quickly—hurry!" It was said that the gypsies would steal children, hence the frantic cries of the mothers, including mine. Once I was safely inside, Mom would lock and bolt the door. She had already closed the windows since we lived on the ground level. In answer to my questions, Mom told me that the gypsies would like to come inside and steal household items, and that they would take just about anything, especially jewelry.

I liked seeing the gypsies. They were dressed in colorful swirling skirts, red or yellow blouses, and they wore big hoop earrings and lots of bangles. I remember that they conversed with each other in a foreign language, but they spoke some German to us, pronouncing it differently than we did. One time Mom let me take a quick look out of the window and I saw a wagon drawn by horses in which they lived. It looked like one of the circus wagons I had seen, and I thought it must be wonderful to live in a wagon and move to different places all of the time.

To me it was always a highlight of the day when the gypsies came. They would sing cheerful songs for us. It made me sad when people turned away because they were afraid of them.

On Becoming Independent (or, My first "gypsy" travels)

It was a week before Easter and I was three years old. Mom was six months pregnant with Peter. It was a sunny and somewhat warm day for Germany, and Mom let me be outside with my doll carriage for awhile before lunch. Soon Ursula, one of my little friends, came by and asked me to accompany her to the *Hindenburgdamm* (Hindenburg Boulevard) to see the birds in the pet shop. Oh, I remembered the parakeets and all the little animals that one could see in the window. The pet shop was by the streetcar stop and Mom never let me spend enough time there. Whenever the streetcar came we had to leave because she did not want to have to wait for the next one.

That day, Ursula tried to talk me into going with her. I was tempted. However, Mom had told me to stay on the sidewalk with my doll carriage, opposite our kitchen window so that she could keep an eye on me. Ursula was persuasive. She was used to being left somewhat unsupervised when her mother and grandparents, who lived in the neighboring house and had a fruit and vegetable business, went to market. This was a day on which they had a stand at one of the markets in the area.

Ursula argued against my indecision. She said we would not be gone very long and that Mom would not even miss my absence. We'll walk real fast, she told me. The pet shop drew me so powerfully that I became disobedient and went with Ursula.

We did walk as fast as we could, still, the pet shop was about half a mile away. We stood by that window and looked. Not only were there parakeets and a parrot, but also a couple of puppy dogs and a number of baby rabbits and chicks for the upcoming Easter holiday. It was wonderful to spend all the time we wanted, while streetcar after streetcar came by (probably ten or fifteen minutes apart). What a wonderful feeling not to have to hurry up and get on the streetcar with Mom!

Mom! Oh, I hoped she had not noticed my absence. We really had hurried on the way to the pet shop, but now it was time to turn back.

Ursula then suggested we go just a little bit further to another store where she remembered seeing a large Easter bunny. I said we had to go home. She assured me that it was not very far, and since we had come all that way we might as well see the other shop, too. This made sense to me, but I began to have guilt feelings. Mom had said: "Don't move out of view."

We walked—and walked—and walked—and every time I said we should turn around, Ursula insisted that it was just ahead. So we went on, all the way to the end of *Hindenburgdamm*, which I would guess was another half a mile. Then we turned into *Schloßstraße*, the main thoroughfare of the district of Steglitz. We lived in the district of Lichterfelde–West, but we did not know that. We walked about another half a mile and came to the intersection with *Albrechtstraße*, another large and busy street. There, Ursula saw the shop she had been looking for, all the way across the busy intersection. We managed to cross by following closely behind other people. This was another major shopping street and the sidewalks were packed with shoppers, as well as businessmen out for lunch. The *Rathaus Steglitz* (City Hall for the district of Steglitz) was way across the wide *Schloßstraße*, which had streetcars running down the center of it, at the corner of *Grunewaldstraße*.

Breathless from excitement (and also a little exhaustion), we stood and looked, awed by the enormous store window which had an Easter bunny as tall as the window. It was a magnificent one, and it carried two baskets filled with eggs and sweets—one strapped to its back like a big knapsack, and one strapped to its chest. The whole window was filled with Easter displays, but I remember only the detail of the big Easter bunny, and some small mechanical bunnies who were moving around.

It was time to go home now. Mom would be waiting—and angry? We crossed the big intersection again, staying closely behind adult people so that the policeman, who was directing the traffic, would not see us. He might ask where our mothers were. Was our conscience stirring? We had no idea of time. The big tower of the City Hall across the street had a clock, but we were three years old and could not yet tell time. Neither could we read street signs nor did we know the name of the street we were on now, or the one on which we lived. Our navigation was strictly by dead reckoning.

Ursula and I marched on, endlessly. We were getting very tired, but we had to get home. At one point we noticed that the street no longer looked familiar, even though we had not turned anywhere. Not having turned was the problem—we just did not know it. There were hardly any people walking in that section of the wide avenue. (We were near the Botanical Garden). I was extremely tired now. Ursula was a fat little girl and had some potential energy stored away, which I did not have. Being too tired to go on, we laid down on the front lawn of one of the apartment buildings and slept. We don't know how long. When we awoke, we were cold and also damp from lying in the grass. As we looked around, wondering what we did to get to this unfamiliar area, a man came walking along. Ursula asked him to take us home, despite my telling her that we could not ask him. Mom had instructed me never to talk to, or go anywhere with a strange man. The man asked where we lived, but we did not know our street address. "Just take us to Tante Hilda" I told him, and could not believe it when he said that he did not know where Tante Hilda lives. Everybody knew my Tante Hilda! I thought. But that man didn't and after asking us a few questions which we could not answer, he said he could not help us and walked away.

Discouraged, we continued on for awhile and suddenly Ursula recognized a landmark along that street—it could have been the Botanical Garden—and she told me that we'll go to the market where her mother and grandparents were. I distrusted her idea, but had no choice. We were lost and I wanted my mommy, even if she would be angry about my disobedience. Ursula insisted that today was a market day, and that her family would be at the market which was ahead, somewhere.

After another seemingly endless walk, Ursula began to recognize more and more of the area, and then we saw the market. Yes, it was market day at *Drakemarkt*, and her family was there. They, of course, had no idea that Ursula was missing, but my Mom was in a state of hysteria when Ursula's grandmother delivered me home. Realizing how frozen we were, she had taken us home immediately on the bus rather than making us wait another hour until the market closed, and then riding home in their truck.

What had happened was simple. On the return walk, we had crossed the *Hindenburgdamm* rather than turning into it. It forks off *Schloßstraße* like the left part of a Y, and we must not have recognized that we had even turned into another street on the way coming. Returning, we had continued on the right side of the Y rather than taking the left fork.

How many miles we had trekked I do not know. It must have been at least four. On a recent visit to Berlin I told this story to my friend Gerda and her husband. They live not far from the intersection of *Schloß* and *Albrechtstraße*, and were speechless about the distance we three–year–olds had walked. Gerhard, the husband, asked if I received a good spanking afterwards. I told him that Ursula did from her mother as soon as we got to the market, but I did not. Mom was so happy to have me back unhurt, and no amount of spanking could have made up for the six hours of agony I had caused her. Gerhard said: "That's why you have not learned your lesson and are still running away from home," referring to my camping and hiking trips.

Mom's Ordeal

Meanwhile, my poor Mom had become a wreck. Working in the kitchen and watching me from the window, she had taken her eyes away for only a moment. My doll carriage was there and I had disappeared.

Without putting on a sweater, Mom went outside and checked all of the obvious places in the neighborhood where I might be, before she hurried to the canal. Naturally, she assumed I would go for the water that I loved so much and always wanted to get to. While she was running to the canal about half a mile away, she pictured a little body floating in the canal. When she did not find me there she went to the

police, but they had not found us or even knew that we were missing. She ran all over the neighboring streets and little squares, checking, and checking again, all afternoon, until she nearly collapsed. She was six months pregnant and had not eaten since breakfast. I was gone for six hours!

That day took a lot out of Mom and she became sick with a bad cold and fever. So did I. Grandma Stanneck came and took care of us. I remember being wrapped in damp, hot towels and blankets to make me sweat, so that the fever would break.

I don't remember Easter, which would have been about a week later.

Mom and I at Easter

Mom and I were sick for almost two weeks, and the picture taken of us at Easter shows it.

The Happiest Day in my Young Life—the Birth of my Brother

It was Sunday, the tenth of July in 1938 and I was nearly four years old, when Grandma Stanneck told me that I had a baby brother. My excitement and joy were boundless.

As always during the warm summer months, my friends and I were playing outside. Grandma had called me in to tell me the good news. Very happy and excited, I went back out and proudly announced to my friends that from now on I would no longer play with them because I had a little brother, and I would play only with him.

I was taken to the hospital where I could talk to Mom by a window. A nurse came to the window and showed me a tiny bundle which had a baby in it with a wrinkled face. She told me it was my brother. The stork had brought him.

When Mom came home with this baby brother whose name was Peter, she put him into a beautiful basket that had curtains all around (a bassinet). Peter lay in there and slept all of the time.

Papa is holding two–week–old Peter. I am watching Mom take this picture.

Mom was in bed, too. Grandma took care of the family. She helped Mom bandage her legs. When I asked what happened to her legs, Mom told me that the stork had bitten her when he brought my brother. (Mom had varicose veins and carrying the extra weight during pregnancy had aggravated them.) I asked to see the wounds that the stork had made, but Mom did not want to show them to me.

I got discouraged after a few days of checking the basket many times a day to see if my brother had grown yet so that he could play with me. He was not growing. He did not even look at me or react to me in any way when I talked to him. All he did was sleep and eat. Mom said I had to be patient, that it takes time for a baby to grow. I kept checking and watching Peter, but he was making no progress at all. I decided that instead of not playing at all while waiting for him to grow, I would rather go back out to my friends and come inside now and then to check on Peter. When after what seemed to me to be an eternity, (another week, perhaps) he was still as small as he had been when he came to us, I gave up on him and went back to playing with my friends. For the time being, of course. I was still hoping for Peter to grow.

Measles

Just before Easter in 1939 I came down with the measles. Peter, being only eight months old, caught them from me. I loved my little brother very much, even though he was growing much too slowly, as far as I was concerned. I liked to hug him and hold him, and loved it when he smiled at me. Now with the measles, even though he had them too, I was not allowed to go near him, and I would not think of disobeying Mom again. I remember the dark room and seeing Peter's crib in the dim daylight, and occasionally catching a glimpse of him. I talked to him and sang to him, and was delighted when he would giggle and babble. Sometimes I could make words out of his babbling and excitedly told Mom that Peter was talking to me, and what he had said.

Two weeks in bed in a dark room seemed like two years in prison.

1939

Peter was a year old in July. He had finally grown and was no longer a baby, but an adorable little boy. I loved him dearly. Mom took a picture of him on his birthday with me and my friend Alice. Soon afterwards he started to walk, and I found out that before a little brother becomes a playmate he is a burden and a responsibility. It became my job to take Peter outside with me when I went out to play, to watch him and to make sure that he does not get hurt. This respon-

Peter on his first birthday with me (left) and my friend Alice.

sibility was to last for many years when Mom was working and I had to take care of my little brother. Despite all this, though, I adored Peter and was proud to have a brother. We grew close during the war years when we had to be alone at home, and this closeness has been a strength and joy to us all throughout life.

My Guardian Angel

In very early July, before Peter's first birthday, Grandma Stanneck came to take care of Peter and Papa while Mom took me with her on a short vacation trip to *Märke*, somewhere east of Berlin, where Grandma had relatives. Mom still had not quite recovered from a difficult birth, childbed fever, and a bout with her varicose veins. Everyone thought it would do her good to spend a couple of weeks in the country. The fresh air and farm food, as well as a rest from the household and the baby, would get her back on her feet. The only thing I remember about that trip is the big excitement after the ceiling had fallen down. Here is the story:

In bygone days, stables were attached to the farmhouse. At the place where we stayed, the people had recently built a separate building for their farm animals and renovated the former stables to be used as guest rooms. Stables usually had arched ceilings. To do away with this "typical stable" feature, the ceiling had been leveled out by filling the arches with plaster. We occupied one of the newly renovated rooms.

Mom's time of rest without me

Every day after lunch I was put to bed for a nap. On that particular day I could not fall asleep and pestered Mom about wanting to be outside with her. She was reclining in a chair out on the lawn. After I had been sent back into the room several times, Mom finally gave in and told me I could lie down on the grass next to her on my blanket, if I kept quiet. She wanted a peaceful rest and no chatter from me.

I was no sooner stretched out on my blanket when we heard a tremendous crash, like an explosion, coming from the building we were staying in. Nobody was in the house and now people came running towards it from all directions, expecting the worst. Upon entering, the plaster dust had not yet settled and initially there was nothing to see. As soon as the air cleared, we saw the room I had left only a few minutes before. All the plaster had fallen out of the arches in the ceiling and the room was covered with chunks of it. On my bed were several large chunks, one of which was about the size of me and it was on my pillow. Mom started to scream, visualizing that my head would have been underneath that ominous white rock.

It was a big job to clean up the room. Mom had misgivings about staying, but then decided that it was safe now with the ceiling being down to its original shape.

I certainly had a guardian angel. This incident contributed greatly to my lifelong belief that "when my time is up, I'm going to die no matter where I am." My time had not been up that day, nor on a number of other occasions which could have ended my life.

A Wedding

In October, Tante Hilda, who had been a widow for more than two years, married Rudolf Sawinski. He was a bachelor and lived in an apartment above Tante Hilda's. My friends and I had always liked him. He often talked to us when we were playing, and showed us interesting things such as little mica flakes in the sand, or pointed out to us the markings on butterflies.

I was so happy to be going to a wedding. I loved weddings. Being the youngest niece and close to Tante Hilda, I was to be the flower girl. My two older cousins, Erika and Heinz, were also at the wedding. Peter, being only fifteen months old, had been left with friends, and Heinz's little brother Klaus was also left at home. Mom made a beautiful sky blue taffeta dress for me and covered a basket for the flowers with the same fabric.

Wedding of Hildegard Grau and Rudolf Sawinski, with cousins Erika and Heinz. I have a big "propeller" in my hair.

The special thing about this wedding was that we still have a group photo of the whole family attending (see next page). World War II had started a month earlier, and this photo is the last one of the Hinniger family together before the war scattered or killed people, and before film was no longer available. The future brought other worries than to take pictures.

Moving

An apartment had become available at the other building. It was much nicer and about three times the size of our present one on the ground level. Mom, ever anxious to better herself or the circumstances surrounding her, applied for it and received the permit for occupation.

The new apartment was at the same address. It was across the yard from the house in which we lived, above the cow stables, where there were two apartments. Mom would rather not have lived above stables,

A rare photograph of the Hinniger family

Children sitting: (from left) Inge Stanneck, Heinz Tilch, Erika Hinniger
First row sitting: Great–Grandmother Schütz, Grandfather Hinniger, Tante Hilda
  and Onkel Rudolf, Grandmother Hinniger, Helmut Hinniger
Standing: Klara (youngest sister of Grandmother Hinniger), Johanna Hinniger (wife
  of Onkel Hans), Charlotte Tilch and Onkel Martin behind her, and next
  to him is an unknown person; Johanna and Erich Stanneck, Hedwig
  and Reinhold Sawinski with son Siegfried; Paula Sawinski (sister), Hedwig
  Munko (another sister) with son Horst and his father, and Grandma
  Hinniger's sister Lisbeth.

but this was the best we could do at the time, and it was quite an improvement over what we had. Papa teased Mom about her incessant desire to better our situation, but I feel it was a great asset of hers not to accept poor conditions, but rather to strive for improvement.

When Mom heard that the elderly gentleman who had lived in that apartment was dead, the wheels in her head immediately shifted into gear. She saw an opportunity to get out of the basement–type apartment consisting of only one room and a kitchen, and we did.

Our new apartment had two large rooms, a foyer, and a good sized live–in kitchen. The big bedroom was bright and sunny. It had ample room for all of our beds and for the huge wardrobe. The kitchen was also bright and, as was customary, we spent our waking hours in it. In the winter it was the only place that was heated. Our cooking was done on a wood/coal–fired stove, which heated the kitchen at the same time. There was enough room for Peter and me to play, as well as for Mom's sewing machine.

Mom, having learned tailoring which included design, was usually busy working on something. Peter and I always had nice clothes, despite our being on the poor side. Whether Mom bought fabric at Woolworth's or used the material from a garment that was no longer worn, she had a gift for turning out designer creations.

The living room was separate in that it was down the hall. It was not as bright as the kitchen and bedroom in the summertime. A large pear tree blocked out some of the light. However, living rooms in Berlin at that time were mostly used for special occasions only, such as celebrating birthdays and holidays, or when visitors came. As each room was separate with the door closed, using it meant that the coal stove would have to be fired up during most months of the year.

Mom and Papa renovated the whole apartment. It was old and badly needed sprucing up. I remember my parents working on it together and my wanting to help, but I was too young to help much. They were soaking off the old wallpaper and putting on nice, new wallpaper. Papa

We lived upstairs in this house, and below us were the cow stables (not obvious now). This picture was taken in 1960 after war damage had been partially repaired.

painted the kitchen walls. I remember a cream color on the top and green on the bottom half of the walls. Where the two colors joined, Papa made a beautiful border by dipping a piece of lace into paint and then rolling it onto the wall between two lines he had drawn. I loved his artistic paint job and remember a number of neighbors in the front building who asked Papa to paint their kitchens after they had seen ours. I was so proud of my Papa.

We lived in this wonderful apartment for about three years, at which time bombs destroyed it. By then we had been evacuated from Berlin.

World War II and its Aftermath

For me, the War started on Sunday August 25, 1940. I was not yet six years old and had been left to baby sit my little brother, then just age two. Mom had gone out for the evening to accompany Papa to the main railroad station to see him off. He had been drafted by the army to report to active duty and was leaving that evening. None of this I knew,

Peter and I at a farm near Berlin. Those were happy days.

or at least understood. What I did know was that Mom did not come back until very late that evening, and we had a terrible thunderstorm before she came back. I was scared. The next morning I learned from my friend, Reinhard, that the thunderstorm the previous evening was the first air raid by the British.

Volume I of this autobiography describes in considerable detail the fourteen–year–period from that night to Friday, May 21, 1954, the day I left Berlin to immigrate to the United States. Except for the several paragraphs below, I will not repeat them here. For those readers who have not seen Volume I, I would commend it to them (see page 371).

During the fall months of 1940 when the days were still fairly long there were only a few air raids, and we kids nearly forgot about them. However, with early winter the nightly terror resumed, sometimes twice a night. Once the sirens went off signaling the start of an air raid, we usually did not have more than five minutes before the bombing and flak fire started. Mom had to dress herself as fast as she could, help me, and, running out of time she just wrapped Peter into a blanket and carried him. Since our building had only the stables downstairs, we had to run across the yard to reach the cellar of the front house. By that time the bombs were already falling and the flak was barking. We could often hear shrapnel falling all around us on our mad dash to the other building.

After too many of those scary dashes, and wondering how long our luck would hold before one of us got hit by shrapnel, Mom went to bed at night only partially undressed. Later, Onkel Rudolf who lived in the front house came over to help Mom with us and he carried Peter for her. One of the things we needed to do at the start of each air raid was to unlatch all windows so that they could blow open during the bomb blasts. This saved the glass from getting broken. Onkel Rudolf would take care of that while Mom helped me dress. I always froze with terror as soon as the dreaded sound of the sirens started up. My heart would pound, and I shook so violently that I could not manage to get into my clothes. Mom had to help me.

These air raids continued all winter during the long nights, but as spring 1941 turned into summer, they decreased because the planes needed the cover of darkness to keep from being visible to the antiaircraft guns. By August 1941 Mom decided we needed to get out of Berlin before darkness once again brought nightly, or even twice–nightly raids.

She decided to move us to a village about fifty miles southeast of Berlin, to Straupitz. Straupitz is one of the largest villages in the Spreewald area, with a population then about six hundred. We knew about Straupitz because Tante Hilda had vacationed there and had friends in the area. She thought it would be a good town for us to move to. And it was. We did not get permission to leave Berlin; we just left. This presented us with many difficulties because as the war continued, there was an acute shortage of living space even in Straupitz, and since we did not have permission to be there, we were not entitled to housing. Through Mom's ingenuity, we were able to manage.

Early in December 1941 we received word from Papa that he had been released from active duty until further notice because he was sick with dysentery, and was recuperating in Berlin. We moved back to Berlin before Christmas to be with him, and then again experienced the horror of the nightly bombings. Early in 1943 Papa was ordered back to active duty on the Russian front. Initially we stayed in Berlin.

March 1, 1943—a night of horror that I will never erase from my memory—was my breaking point. I was only eight. I can't describe in one or two sentences what it was like, but two days later Mom moved us back to Straupitz and the relative tranquility of the countryside. We stayed in Straupitz until November 30, 1946. During that period Straupitz itself had come under attack by Russian aircraft and eventually, occupation by Russian soldiers.

Berlin in the meantime was destroyed, and after the war evacuees from Berlin were not allowed to return to Berlin unless they had a place to live (our apartment had been destroyed by bombs), did not need a job, and the husband had returned from being a Russian prisoner of war. Even then, they also had to have the permission of the commander of the Russian occupation zone. Grandma said she would share her two–room apartment, and Papa had returned in December 1945 from being a prisoner—captured at Stalingrad. He walked most of the way from Russia and was so emaciated that his mother did not recognize him. We were able to finally get permission from the Russians and returned to Berlin on the very last day they permitted people to leave Straupitz. A day later and it would have been too late; my life then would have taken a totally different turn.

The next four years were even more difficult than the war years. Starvation, constant Russian harassment, and eventually the blockade of Berlin designed to force Allies into leaving Berlin and abandoning the 2.2 million West Berliners. These were terrible times. We were saved by the heroic efforts of the Berlin Airlift which had to transport by air all of the food, supplies, coal and other goods. I have had a love affair ever since with anyone who participated in the Airlift, and saved us from Communism.

By 1950 things started to get better and little by little Berlin was recovering. In 1953 Papa died of a heart attack. Shortly afterwards I met a great aunt from the United States who visited Berlin. Subsequently she invited me to immigrate to the United States. I accepted, although with great reservations. I would be leaving my family behind with no guarantees that I would ever see them again. West Berlin was still like an island in the "middle of the red sea" and we had learned not to trust the Russians.

This book picks up my story as the *MS Italia* pulls out of Hamburg, and I start the greatest adventure of my life. It describes how I take advantage of opportunities, found a family, and engage in travel adventures that I could not have imagined in my wildest dreams.

PART I

OPPORTUNITIES

1

1954
The Start of the
Greatest Adventure of my Life
Age Nineteen

Leaving Berlin

On Friday, May 21, 1954, I said "farewell" to my beloved Berlin. Mom was accompanying me to the port city of Hamburg, about one hundred and seventy miles northwest of Berlin. We were flying to Hamburg with Pan American Airlines, and it was to be the first airplane flight for both of us. Mom did not want me to travel through the Russian occupation zone with an American visa in my passport. Knowing how unpredictable the Soviets were, she was afraid to take any chances on their getting nasty to someone who was "escaping" to America, and possibly delaying me so that I would miss the departure of my ship. We had had enough experience with Soviet harassment to justify our mistrust.

I enjoyed my first airplane flight and was relieved that we did not have to sweat it out with fear at the East German border crossings. This immigration adventure started out great. Back came my memories of being a six–year–old, and how fascinated I was after learning from a friend that houses seen from an airplane look as small as matchboxes. Now my wish to see the matchbox–size houses came true. I did see "matchboxes" down below. There were also little silver ribbons, which were rivers. It was wonderful to fly! The flight to Hamburg was much too short for me. Mom had enjoyed it as well.

Peter did not come with us. We could not afford the expenses for the three of us to travel to Hamburg. Mom had arranged for Peter to go to Tante Lotte's after work for the two nights that she would be away.

Not until a couple of years later did I find out what an awful time it was for Peter. It never occurred to me that my little brother would take my departure so hard. He went to pieces after I had left, and was devastated because we had not taken him to Hamburg with us to see me off. While at Tante Lotte's, Peter was also starting to suffer from terrifying nightmares in which he thought he was dying. This was a result of his having watched Papa die just nine months earlier. Peter's nightmares were to continue for years to come.

My Ocean Voyage

Saturday, May 22 was departure day. We were at the pier hours ahead of time, along with many other people. Finally it was time to

Mom and I walking up the gangway of the MS Italia

start the emigration process and the boarding. Mom was permitted to come on board and stay until a certain time before the ship sailed.

We were both shocked at how crowded and Spartan my accommodation was. We had noticed that the carpeting in the corridor stopped a ways back, and it looked as though the passenger area had already ended at that point. A sailor told us that the cabin I was in used to be crew quarters, housing two crew members. It had recently been modified to accommodate four passengers. Mom and I said to ourselves that we had booked the cheapest passage—other than a bunk in a dormitory for twenty—and that it would have to be my home for only eleven days. Except for sleeping, I would not spend any time in the room.

Mom and I enjoyed exploring the ship's facilities. It was luxurious, as ships have a reputation to be. I could not wait to get underway. Mom held up very well when the time came to say farewell. She pointed out to me where on the pier she would stand—underneath a certain sign on the building where I could easily spot her in the crowd. Also, since everybody would wave with a handkerchief—and it would be difficult to see who was who—she would wave with a newspaper instead. That way I would be able to identify her. It worked. Mom always had the best ideas. I would miss her so much.

Punctually at four o'clock, as the *MS Italia* slowly moved out of the harbor, the band played *Auf Wiedersehen*, and a number of the other tear–jerkers. While it was meant to be festive, we immigrants did not appreciate it. Ours was not a cruise to be followed by a happy return, but rather it marked a separation for an unknown period of time, and the start of life in a strange country.

For the time being the excitement of the trip took over. As dinner time approached, we had left the Elbe River and entered the North Sea. It was time to go and enjoy some of the legendary excellent and plentiful food which ships are known for. This was not a cruise ship, but rather more like an immigrant and commuter transport, although about two hundred of the one thousand passengers were in first class. There was also a cabin class for the more wealthy immigrants or frequent travelers. I thought the food was "out of this world," especially for those of us who could barely afford to be on board. I had never seen so much food being served, and mountains of it were left uneaten. I wondered what would happen to it. Why did they cook so much? There were not enough people to eat it all.

Earlier in the purser's office I had been assigned to a table in the dining room. At dinner time I found out that they had grouped the passengers in a certain way, so that I sat with people of approximately my age at a table for ten. There were eight young men, and my roommate and I. All of us were immigrants headed for the United States.

Life on Board

There were four of us in the little cabin which was outfitted with two sets of bunks and a sink. Annemarie, the girl who sat at my table in the dining room, was my bunk mate. She wanted the upper and I took the lower bunk. The porthole was by her bed, but the glass was thick and not clear enough to look out. We were both disappointed about that. A young woman and her four–year–old daughter occupied the other set of bunks. The first thing we found out about this community life was that there was no space for all four of us to stand up in the room at the same time. There was standing room for one person only. If all of us were "at home," three would have to sit on their bunks. This was fun when getting up in the morning. Only one person could use the sink and get dressed, then had to either go back to bed or get out of the room. We made a schedule.

Southampton, England

There were to be three stops before we arrived in New York: Southampton, England; Le Havre, France; and Halifax, Nova Scotia in Canada.

At one point during the night we awoke from the loud noise of banging and hammering. My upper bunk mate, Annemarie, and I wondered what they were building. Our cabin was the last one before the crew quarters and storage, and we just assumed there was a workshop on the other side of our wall. Annemarie stuck her head out of the door, hailed a crew member, and asked. He told her they were opening the holds in preparation for taking on freight and passengers in Southampton in the morning. The noise continued through the rest of the night, so that it was the end of our night's sleep. Annemarie and I were curious about everything that was going on and decided to get up early to watch the passengers board.

Sometime during the night we had entered the English Channel on our way to Southampton. Annemarie and I were up on deck by five in the morning and noticed that we were in port. To our disappointment nothing was happening this early, and we found that we were in for a long wait.

The new passengers started boarding at eight o'clock. It was more fun for us to watch the loading of the cargo than it was to watch the people board. Big cranes lifted huge crates, containers with boxes and baggage, as well as cars into the ship's holds.

Le Havre, France

After our ship left Southampton, the holds were closed again and the banging noise was once more heard in our cabin as they secured the ship. I never did understand why this took a number of hours. I also didn't know why they bothered since we were to approach Le Havre early in the evening and the whole process had to be repeated. It would have been a noisy day for us if we had spent more time in our cabin. However, there were so many activities on the ship which one could participate in, as well as nice facilities available for daytime use so that there was no reason for anyone to sit in a room. Besides, there was no place to sit in our cabin anyway.

The noise of closing up the holds after Le Havre went on until well after midnight. I was glad that there were to be no more stops until we reached Halifax. It was noisy enough hearing the ship's engines all of the time. We were on "D" Deck, which was the lowest passenger deck.

After leaving Le Havre, the English Channel lived up to its reputation in that the water was quite rough and the ship rolled much more than I liked. Annemarie and I had watched a movie in the afternoon before we reached Le Havre, and the Channel had been rough enough for me then. I remember several times during the movie when we nearly fell off our chairs, and my stomach was starting to feel just a bit queasy.

I felt better after a good dinner. Afterwards we went dancing, but then I started to feel queasy again. With the motion of the ship I found that dancing was even more of a balancing act than walking was. A lady at the table gave me a pill to take for seasickness, but it did not seem to take away the sick feeling. I was glad to get to bed that night. While trying to sleep, I kept hearing the waves crash against the bow of the ship and knew that we were in really rough water. It still seemed somewhat exciting for me to think that we were having a turbulent ocean voyage and I was not seasick—yet! I was sure that the little queasiness would be gone in the morning.

Earlier during the day I had thought that life on board ship was fun, and at that time I had wished the trip would take longer than the scheduled eleven days. Little did I know what was ahead!

The Atlantic Ocean

By the next morning we were in the North Atlantic. The sea was rough and our ship was pitching and rolling even worse than the night before. Dressing was extremely difficult, and I needed to get out of the stuffy cabin and breathe some fresh air. It was nearly impossible to keep one's balance while walking. This was an unknown feeling for me. The floor just seemed to drop away underneath the feet, and the corridor down to the staircase seemed endless. I managed to navigate the length of it and staggered up the stairs to the deck. The cold air felt good, but I still lost my stomach.

All throughout that day and part of the next I spent my time on deck. The weather was getting colder, the sunshine disappeared and the sea got more turbulent. I rented a lounge chair and a blanket, so that I could lie down outside during the day rather than staying in the cabin. Being inside the ship now became agony. I felt too sick to go to the dining room which was way down on the lowest deck, and just negotiating all those steps was difficult. One time I dragged myself down the several stairways to eat lunch in the dining room and I got as far as opening the door. As soon as I smelled food I had to turn away and run. From the one glance I took into the dining room I had noticed that it was nearly empty. I decided that they locate dining rooms of ships in such remote locations on purpose, to save on food.

I was so seasick that I ended up staying in bed on the third day out from Le Havre, and could not even find the strength to go up to the deck to be in fresh air. I stopped eating. So had many others. There was a storm system over the North Atlantic, and I later found out that eighty percent of the passengers were seasick. For the next several days I did not get out of bed at all. I lay there feeling so very sick, and listening to the waves crash against the ship while at the same time lifting it up

The MS Italia plying the North Atlantic

onto the tops of huge waves from where it lurched into seemingly bottomless depths. I kept hoping that the ship would break apart. At least I expected the porthole to be knocked out, which had been under water ever since we got into the Atlantic. I wanted to be put out of my misery. No longer caring about America, I rather wanted to die. Soon.

One of the young men who sat at our table came to visit me after I had not shown up for meals in three days. He brought me a couple of oranges and said he was concerned. He wondered if I had been given anything to eat—which I had not—and wanted to know how I was feeling. I was feeling awful and could not keep anything down, not even water. Annemarie was alright and so was the four–year–old girl, but her mother was sick, too, though not for as long as I was. I felt sorry for the young mother. The little girl kept pestering her about wanting to go out, but she had to stay in bed because mom was sick. There was no place in our tiny cabin for the child to sit but on the bed.

After four days I thought I was a little better because I felt hungry, which had not been the case until then. Getting dressed was exhausting, but I thought I would try to make it to the dining room. However, it was misery just trying to negotiate the seemingly endless aisle to the center of the ship where the stairs were. I did not get far before being sick again and having to turn back. There were others who clung to the handrails with all of their strength, just like I did. The ship was rolling so violently that it was impossible to keep one's balance without hanging onto something with the hands, while the feet left the floor and wanted to go elsewhere. Having been sick for so long I did not have the strength to hang on for any length of time. As I struggled to keep from landing on the floor, I was lucky to have a stewardess pass by who helped me back to my room and into bed. She asked me how long I had not eaten, and was shocked that nobody had looked in on me and brought me anything that I might have been able to keep down. She suggested some mashed potatoes, which appealed to me, and she went to get them for me.

The stewardess said that while the North Atlantic is stormy most of the time, she could not remember ever having had such a rough crossing. The ship was heaving, rolling, and creaking. In our cabin it sounded as if tree logs were slamming against the bow continuously. We kept expecting the ship to break up with each violent crash and shudder. Even Annemarie, who was not sick, was sure the ship would not survive this assault of tumultuous water.

The mashed potatoes did the trick and gave me the energy to stand up long enough to risk taking a shower. The shower and toilets were located next door to our cabin. I felt somewhat human again after washing up.

Less than two days out of Halifax we were in dense fog. The sea had quieted down somewhat and I began to feel better. I made it to the dining room for lunch, and was able to go to the "captain's dinner" in the evening. This was the dress up occasion at which pictures were taken while the ship's captain went from table to table to toast everyone.

The ominous blasts from the foghorn kept us awake during the night. The foghorn kept up all day long the next day, throughout the next night, and into the following morning. At that point we were told that we would get into New York one day later than scheduled. The ship had to proceed at reduced speed because of the dense fog. For me it meant one additional day of suffering. While on the mend, I was still extremely weak.

Halifax, Newfoundland, Canada

The angry sea had calmed down somewhat during the two days of fog. Once I had eaten and kept down a couple of meals, I felt better and

The "Captain's dinner" was my first full meal after having been sick for a week

stronger. By the time we got to Halifax in the afternoon of June 1, I definitely felt better, and I even enjoyed being on the ship.

Now there was the excitement of getting closer to New York. Less than two days to go! Suddenly the thought struck me that we were arriving a day late. Had my relatives been notified? The purser of the ship told me that this would have been done from New York. I was really getting nervous about it as I could just picture myself standing on the pier all alone, and nobody there to meet me.

The last two days were fun. Many passengers were immigrating into Canada and had disembarked at Halifax. It made quite a difference, and for me it was less overwhelming to have fewer people on board. Now that I felt better, I was even getting a bit sociable. Time passed much faster when one had interaction with others. This felt especially good after my long time of isolation when I was so sick.

New York, New York

The city that everyone dreams of seeing! We were scheduled to arrive the following morning, June 3. I had my best clothes all laid out in a handy space underneath my bunk in preparation for meeting Aunt Martha and Uncle Adolph.

During the night we were awakened by an ominous silence. The ship's engines had stopped. The silence scared us momentarily until Annemarie called out excitedly: "I think I see lights, there must be land nearby." She could see a glimmer through the porthole which was now above water. I climbed up onto her bunk to help her lift up the porthole. It was too heavy, even for the two of us. Together we could barely open it far enough to peek and verify that there were lights in the distance. New York at last!

It was three o'clock in the morning and dark outside. However, Annemarie and I decided to hurry up and get dressed so we could go outside and watch our ship glide into the harbor. We seemed to be stopped, but we figured that we would get going again, soon. We had been told that we must not miss the traditional greeting of welcome from the Great Lady, the Statue of Liberty, who greets all ships entering New York Harbor. It was dark outside, but perhaps *she* was lit up and we could see her after all.

Annemarie was gone in a flash, while I washed and carefully dressed up in my good suit. I was going to meet my relatives, whom I did not really know—and I had to look presentable. It was extremely hot and stuffy in the cabin and I was wet with perspiration before I finished dressing. I began to wonder whether Aunt and Uncle, who had to come from somewhere in New Jersey, knew that we were arriving in the middle of the night. They probably would not even be there this early. Thinking of arriving in a strange country while it was still dark, and being left alone and without any money to speak of, plus the oppressive heat in the cabin were enough to make me vomit right then. My stomach was still awfully touchy.

The thought of some cool, fresh air up on deck gave me the strength to walk that endless aisle to the center of the ship and up the stairs. At least the ship had stopped rolling and pitching, so the stairs were easier to negotiate. The heavy door to the outside was another challenge for someone who was emaciated. With great effort I got it open and was hit, literally, by hot, humid air and the foulest stench I have ever encountered. I barely had time to make it to the railing before I vomited again. Annemarie was there and said: "This can't be New York, we must be somewhere else." I said: "Yeah, Madagascar," thinking of a popular sailors' song about Madagascar and having the plague on board, which I recited. Annemarie thought I was funny. I did not feel funny at all, but rather quite miserable.

Soon other passengers were out on deck and some knew what was going on. We were stopped out in Lower New York Bay and had to wait until the tugboats started to work at seven, one of which would tow us into New York Harbor. So, this *is* New York. The lights we were seeing on both sides of us were those of Staten Island and Brooklyn, said one passenger who had been there before. The Statue of Liberty was still way in the distance, we were told. We were glad not to have missed it and would see it just before arrival in the morning. Nobody knew what the awful smell was. Somebody said it's probably from garbage being dumped regularly by ships waiting out in this area. There is the answer to the leftover food, I thought. "The hot, muggy air is normal for this time of the year," somebody else volunteered. I had not had any experience with excessive heat or humidity such as this. Somewhat deflated, Annemarie and I went inside and joined others who were sitting in one of the air conditioned day rooms, to pass some time.

Later on, back in our cabin, the air was too stuffy for breathing. Taking turns, we packed everything up in order to have our luggage ready for pickup by a certain time. They were banging and hammering again to open the cargo holds. I will not miss that racket, nor the tiny cabin.

Time for breakfast, our last meal on the ship. I did not feel like eating, but thought it would be wise to have something in my stomach. However, I could not keep it down. There was no getting away from the heat and humidity. It had never even entered my mind that the climate would be so different. For some reason I had pictured New York to be more or less at the same latitude as Berlin, but it was far further south. The thought of extremely hot weather such as this, and so early in June, was a matter of great concern to me. I never tolerated heat well.

The Arrival

7:10 a.m. The *Italia* was being towed now. Everyone was out on deck when, at 7:45 a.m., we passed by the Statue of Liberty, a symbol for all immigrants, and a welcome to the New World and a new life.

That moment was so powerful and I remember my emotions so vividly that I am in tears as I am typing this, almost fifty years later.

It was about 8 a.m., Thursday, June 3, 1954. We had arrived. Looking at the large crowd of people awaiting the ship's arrival, it seemed that there were far more people waiting than there were passengers on the ship. How would I ever find Aunt Martha? Would I recognize her? Would she recognize me? I had never met Uncle Adolph so that Aunt Martha was my only link. I was sick again. New York was not any cooler than it had been out in New York Bay; in fact, it seemed to get hotter all of the time. The humidity was intolerable. I was soaking wet and worried about meeting my relatives in this bedraggled condition, though I felt awful enough so that I was nearly beyond caring.

The immigration officials had set up an office area in the ballroom of the tourist class section. Here we were to get into line and have our papers processed for clearance into the United States of America. There was a long line, of course. First class passengers were being processed ahead of everyone else.

I caught a glimpse of the American officials at the table. They looked formidable in their official uniforms, and I was as scared as if I were about to be asked to take a difficult test. What if they did not let me in? I was feeling too sick to stand and wait in line, so I sat down in a lounge chair at the opposite end of the room and waited for the line to get shorter. I tried two more times but could not make it, then decided to wait until there was no longer a line, so that I could walk right up to the officials. Being sure that I looked as sick as I felt, or worse, I was convinced that they would not let sick people immigrate into the United States. My knees turned rubbery from fear.

I do not remember any of the details of the immigration process, but at one point one of the officials picked up my chest X–ray which was a part of my health record. He looked at me, looked at the X–ray, then looked at me again and conferred with the official next to him; then they both looked at me and again at my X–ray. I was just about in tears from anxiety, but managed to explain in a shaky voice that I had been very seasick and was still not feeling well. They cleared me for immigration. The way I looked—emaciated and all despite wearing the best outfit I owned—they must have thought that I had consumption or another serious illness.

Stepping onto U.S. Soil

Not walking, but rather staggering from weakness and the weight of my hand luggage, I was the last person to get off the ship. The waiting crowd had dissipated and there was no problem finding Aunt Martha. She was right at the bottom of the gangway looking as relieved as I was feeling. I managed to smile, and even my stomach felt a little better. She had been concerned when all the many passengers disembarked and I was not among them. By now it was one o'clock in the afternoon. Aunt Martha had been waiting for more than five hours! She explained to me that Uncle Adolph was expected to be along shortly with the car. Aunt Martha had come by bus. I later learned that she did not drive at all. Uncle had taken only half a day off

Here I am as I arrived in the United States—a prim and proper young lady facing the greatest adventure of my life.

from work. Since it was lunchtime, Aunt Martha suggested that we have a bite to eat while we waited for Uncle to arrive. Just at that moment he came towards us.

Adolph Timmann, Aunt Martha's husband, was introduced to me. Also a German, his family had immigrated from Hamburg when he and his brother were teenagers. He spoke a north German dialect, which is only slightly different in the pronunciation of the words. The main difference is that it does not sound as harsh as the Berliners' way of speaking. The "st" sound is pronounced the same as in English, whereas the Berliners pronounce it "sht." I was glad that I could understand Uncle. Had he been from Bavaria or from somewhere else in southern Germany, I could not even have understood him. The south German dialects are like different languages.

The Fun Begins

As Uncle turned around to lead the way towards a snack bar, Aunt Martha started to laugh hysterically. Uncle Adolph had bought a new sport coat for the occasion of my arrival. In the excitement of the day he had forgotten to cut off the labels and price tag which were on his back and on one of the sleeves. He was embarrassed but Aunt Martha thought it was funny, and when Uncle saw that I was laughing also, it broke the ice and he joined in.

My first new experience in America was getting a sandwich at the snack bar. Aunt Martha told me the choices were ham, cheese, ham and cheese combination, and turkey. I did not know what turkey was and Aunt Martha did not know the word for it in German. I chose ham. Now, this is a snack bar at the pier in New York City. Nothing fancy but still quite nice, I thought. I was not used to eating out. We had been glad to have food to eat at all.

I received my ham sandwich and my first lesson in the new country. The sandwich consisted of two slices of slightly sweet, but otherwise tasteless, white bread and a thin slice of ham, most likely cut with a razor blade. I took a bite and my face must have betrayed surprise. Aunt Martha questioned me, and I was honest and said that I did not expect to have to eat *dry* bread in America. We *had* to eat it during the many bad years, but now we had butter in Germany, or at least margarine, to spread on the bread. Aunt Martha told me that people in America don't want to get fat, so they don't eat butter on their sandwiches. But that was not all; there was not enough ham on that sandwich to even flavor the bread, and the bread turned to glue in my mouth. I was not impressed with American sandwiches. The dry bread brought back memories of times which all Germans tried to forget. I could not wait to write to Mom and tell her that people here voluntarily eat dry bread because they worry about getting fat. In Germany this was unheard of at that time. We were so happy to have food again and not to be starving any longer.

My First Impressions of America

My first impressions of America are still quite vivid in my memory, and there were many, especially in the first days and weeks. Aunt and Uncle lived in Cranford, New Jersey, about twenty miles southwest of

New York City. The trip can be a long one if there is a lot of traffic. This would usually be the case, especially since it is necessary to drive through one of the tunnels underneath the Hudson River to get to New Jersey. Most of the time there are backups at the tunnels which cause major delays.

Aunt Martha and Uncle Adolph

My luggage consisted of two large suitcases which held all of my worldly possessions, for the most part books and memorabilia. One of the suitcases was only half filled at that. After we walked out into the street I looked around and was shocked. I thought: "This is New York—the city that everyone longs to see?" Twelfth Avenue, where New York's piers are located, was far from being an impressive area and must have shocked many an immigrant into thinking that this was representative of America. I knew then that I would not like New York and hoped that New Jersey would be nicer.

I was amazed at the traffic. After leaving the parking area at the pier which was underneath a highway, we were immediately in backup traffic for the Lincoln Tunnel, perhaps a kilometer away—I did not yet know about miles. Slowly we inched our way towards the entrance of the tunnel. Streets from all directions were feeding into the entrance area, and we had already turned into several different streets to get into line. At no time did we drive through nice areas that looked anything like the pictures I had seen of Manhattan.

Finally we were at the tunnel entrance and on our way to New Jersey. On the other side I saw only factories and other industrial areas instead of the *Garden State* I expected to see. I had no map and did not know the location of our destination, but I hoped that it would be far away from this area. Until now I had not seen anyplace where people could live. I had the feeling that the whole area was unfit for human habitation, particularly with the extreme discomfort of the heat and humidity.

This was before air conditioned cars and homes. When both Aunt and Uncle had shed their jackets before getting into the steaming car in New York, I had done the same. Even then it was unbearable, and I found out that one could not open a window because Aunt Martha was sensitive to drafts.

More Lessons

As we were driving along and I was absorbed with the scenery which had not yet changed for the better, I became just vaguely aware of some arguing going on in the front of the car. Aunt and Uncle spoke a curious version of German which was a mix of English, German, and English words pronounced the German way. Some of the words even were half English and half German. It took me a while before I understood this unique language. However, at that point I heard Aunt Martha complain about the heat, and Uncle saying he heard on the radio that it was supposed to be above a hundred degrees. Aunt Martha's reply was that she did not think it was a hundred. Their conversation on the subject went back and forth a number of times, all the while I wondered about this hundred degree business, and whether or not I misunderstood something. I did not know the people who were my relatives, and I hesitated to interfere with their debate. When Aunt Martha made a comment to me about how hot it was, I told her that this was the worst heat I had ever experienced but that it could not possibly be a hundred degrees, because one hundred degrees is the boiling point.

Lesson number two for today: I was educated about Fahrenheit being different from Celsius, which is the measurement that I was used to. I was surprised. In school I had heard about Fahrenheit, it being an outdated way of measuring temperature, and last used in Germany about two hundred years earlier. Now I find that I am in the *New World* and ancient measurements are still in use. Puzzling.

Soon we drove through an area where the industrial plants along the highway were farther apart and nicer looking. I had still not seen any sign of places where people might live. We did come across a little restaurant along the highway which looked like an aluminum streetcar— it was a diner—and Uncle decided to stop. He suggested we eat a meal. The skimpy sandwich must not have been a big enough lunch for him. I was not really hungry—having been totally absorbed in the many new impressions—and would rather have kept going. Furthermore, I was afraid that another sandwich was about to come at me.

An American Chicken Dinner

Lesson number three was about to start. This was a restaurant and we were to order a hot meal. I did not want meat, but Aunt felt that I should eat something solid and nourishing containing protein. She also talked about vitamins, sounding like Mom. I obviously looked like I needed more food. The heat was really getting to me and all I wanted was cold water or milk. Maybe potatoes and vegetables. Aunt Martha strongly suggested a chicken dinner for me. I was alarmed. At home, chicken had been so expensive that we bought it only on special holidays, such as Easter or Christmas. I did not want them to spend money on something so extravagant as a chicken dinner when I was not even hungry. When I mentioned this, Aunt Martha told me that chicken was an everyday meal here. I liked chicken very much and told her that I was happy with her suggestion.

Back in Berlin, to prepare me for the upcoming trip and life with Aunt and Uncle, Mom had given me many lectures about situations I might have to handle. As always, she stressed the point of proper manners I needed to display, especially table manners. She did not want Aunt and Uncle to have to be embarrassed with me, lest they regret having sent for me. Knowing that I needed practice eating properly with knife and fork as the Europeans do, Mom had insisted on a lot of practice. Our fare at home consisted mostly of vegetable stews which were eaten with a tablespoon. Rare were the occasions on which we had a piece of meat large enough to have to cut it. Mom felt I needed more practice, especially with the left hand which has to hold the fork and get the food into the mouth—without spilling. She really drilled me in that skill. Even though for most of those drills we did not have any meat to cut, she would have me practice with bread, potato, or whatever it was we were eating.

Now it came to my chicken dinner at the restaurant. Of course, I knew how to eat properly. Soon I noticed that Aunt Martha was watching me. I got uneasy, wondering what I was doing wrong. After a few minutes she turned to me and said: "Put that knife down—this is not the way we eat in America." She proceeded to show me how I should cut off a piece of meat, put down the knife, change the fork into the right hand and eat the meat. I could not believe it. After all the hard work of practicing I was requested to do it the wrong, easier way. Furthermore, the left hand then is supposed to be under the table, which is really bad manners in Germany. I do not remember the rest of the meal, but I do remember telling Mom in my first letter that some bad manners are OK, and even required here.

As I am writing this I think of the many letters I wrote home in which I told Mom and Peter every detail of my new life here in America. Today I wish that those letters had been saved. They would have been a great diary. How interesting it would be to read in detail about my first impressions and experiences, and my reactions to them.

Summary of impressions so far: New York is ugly and smelly—sandwiches have no butter on them and the bread turns into glue when it gets chewed—it is brutally hot, but at least the boiling point has been moved up to be at 212 degrees, thanks to an ancient way of measuring—some things that are considered bad manners in Germany, are OK to do here, according to lesson number three.

I had already learned three lessons and we were not even home yet. With anticipation I looked forward to the next one.

Meanwhile, there were interesting things to be observed while driving along the highway. There were huge signs—billboards—which were obviously advertising consumer goods. Billboards such as these were totally unfamiliar to me. Germany did not have them at the time and did not need them. People needed everything, and they bought whatever goods became available. I found those large signs unattractive and disturbing.

As we got farther away from the industrial area immediately surrounding New York, I started to see what looked like apartment buildings, and finally, individual homes. The apartment buildings had unsightly iron stairways leading to the second and third floors. "Those are fire ladders," was the answer to my question. Two things were different: The homes were built out of wood, not brick or cement blocks with stucco as I was used to. Secondly, the houses in towns were spread out over larger areas rather than being clustered tightly together, as German villages would be. These were the impressions I had, as viewed from the road on this first day in America.

My New Home

Eventually we got off the autobahn–like road (Garden State Parkway) and turned onto a good–sized road. After driving about one kilometer we turned into a driveway. This was 1531 Raritan Road, which would be my home for the next two–and–a–half years.

The house was of modest size by American standards, a Cape Cod style with three bedrooms, one bath, and a finished basement which was used as dining room when Aunt and Uncle entertained. Upon entering the house, I was surprised at the impressive foyer which was quite large for the overall size of the house. There were oriental rugs, a sofa, chairs, and other furniture which at home we would have placed in a living room. Wow, this is elegant, I thought. We had something cold to drink—it was still dreadfully hot—and sat around talking for awhile. During all that time I wondered why we kept sitting in the foyer instead of going into the living room. Eventually I was shown the rest of the house and my room, of course. The unexpected thing was that the foyer we had been sitting in was the living room. I had never seen or heard of a house in which the front door led right into the living room. Even the smallest apartments in Berlin had at least a tiny foyer. This was so strange, and it took me years to get used to entering a living room directly from the outside.

The next strange thing was that all doors were always left open, even the bathroom door—except when it was being used. This was for circulation and more even heat distribution. In Germany, only one room could be heated and doors were always kept shut.

The house had two bedrooms on the main level, the smaller one of which was to be my room. The little bathroom was beautiful. There was a pretty shower curtain for the bathtub, and even a rug on the floor. This was the beginning of my falling in love with American bathrooms.

A large bedroom upstairs was occupied by Uncle Adolph's father, who was living with Aunt and Uncle. There was an attractive party room on the basement level. Its centerpiece was a large dining room table and chairs. Aunt Martha explained that the bedroom which is now mine used to be their dining room, but that it had been much too small all along. Aunt and Uncle loved to invite their German friends for dinner on special occasions, and had needed more space for enter-

1531 Raritan Road where I lived for two–and–a–half years with my Aunt and Uncle. Raritan Road was a busy street, particularly during rush hour. The Garden State Parkway entrance was less than a mile away. This Cape Cod house was modest by U.S. standards but to Aunt and Uncle, two immigrants, it was a home of their own—the American dream realized.

taining. Uncle and his father had therefore finished off the basement. I was soon to find out that Aunt Martha was an excellent cook and baker.

This was a day of learning endless lessons and I could no longer keep track of their numbers. Next, Uncle and I went outside while Aunt Martha busied herself in the kitchen. I wanted to admire Uncle Adolph's car. So far there had not been a chance to take a good close look at it. Having lived in the American–occupied sector of Berlin, I was well familiar with huge automobiles, so the size of it had not been a surprise. Uncle explained that it was a 1950 Mercury, manufactured by the Ford Motor Company. The color was two–tone gray.

Learning More About my New Home

It was hot standing out there in the sun, so I went into the shade hoping to find relief from the heat. For some reason this did not work and I mentioned it to Uncle. He told me that in high humidity such as this, there is not much difference between the temperature in the sun versus the shade. It was bad news for me because I did not like hot weather. On the evening news that night it was mentioned that the high temperature during the day had been one hundred and four degrees. Apparently it was unusual for the area to be so hot in early June. I surely hoped it was not normal, and that it would be cooler the next day.

While Uncle was showing me around the front yard, neighbors from next door and across the street were curious and stopped by to meet me. At that point I found out that my limited school English did not allow me to carry on even a simple conversation. People were talking much too fast, and I understood nothing. Each sentence sounded like one long word, and it did not sound like the British English I had learned in school. The people understood me, but the conversations were brief since I could not understand them.

Soon Uncle's father came home from work. He worked at construction jobs with a contractor friend of Aunt and Uncle's. We were still out on the front lawn. Looking up and down the street, I noticed that all houses were built of wood, though some had brickwork on part of the front as ours did. They were all about the same size and looked alike. I did not yet know about housing developments.

At one point I noticed that nearly each house had a huge arrangement of lightning rods on the roof. I was horrified and wondered how I would survive severe thunderstorms without Mom. In Berlin we had violent thunderstorms every afternoon or evening on hot summer days. Sometimes even Mom would be scared, and we would stand huddled together in the dark foyer of the apartment. Mom thought we would be protected from lightning bolts hitting us if we were in a place without windows. Thunderstorms also brought back memories of air raids for me.

This was the evening of a hot summer day, and those elaborate rods on the rooftops seemed to hint at something ominous. Carefully I asked Uncle's father if bad thunderstorms at night were common. He told me that occasionally there were some mild ones, but not at all every evening. When I questioned him about the reason for those lightning rods, he laughed and told me they were television antennas. Nobody can imagine my relief. This was the best lesson I had learned all day!

My next question was why none of the front yards were fenced in. I was told that this was not needed. People knew where their property lines were, and fences were neither needed nor desired. Not being used to this openness, I saw it as a lack of privacy. However, this was a matter of taste and getting used to.

It was rush hour and there was a lot of traffic on the road. Raritan Road was a major thoroughfare connecting with entrance and exit ramps of the recently completed Garden State Parkway which was less than a mile away. The traffic did not bother me since I was used to living on a busy street in Berlin. What bothered me was that except for the two neighbors I had not yet seen a single human being walking anywhere. There were sidewalks on both sides of the street, but no people. Having grown up in a big city, the total absence of pedestrians anywhere was one of the hardest things for me to get used to in this country.

For the evening meal we sat around a table in the small dining area in the kitchen. Aunt Martha told me that by the time I woke up in the morning they would all be away at work. Uncle was a toolmaker and Aunt Martha worked in a plastics factory (Monsanto). Mr. Timmann Sr. was a construction worker.

After dinner I was shown where things were, especially in the refrigerator, and I was told to help myself to anything I wanted. Aunt Martha opened the huge—by German standards—refrigerator and my eyes nearly popped out of my head. There were shelves filled with a variety of foods that to me were rare, or unknown. A whole drawer was filled with oranges. I had never seen so much food in one place except in a store, and I felt overwhelmed.

I was tired, having had a long and exceptionally exciting day. Tomorrow would be another day and I would have renewed energy. It did not take me long to get into bed. The mattress was strange. It was extremely soft and I sank into it, which I thought was luxurious. The next day I found out that it was foam rubber, which was unfamiliar to me. I drifted off to sleep almost immediately, but not before noticing that the whole room was rolling and I had the feeling of being on the ship again.

2

**1954
Beginning a New Life
Age Nineteen**

Exploring my New Surroundings

I awoke to a bright, sunny day, although the "ship" was rolling worse than the night before. After I got out of bed I had trouble keeping my balance. The house was very quiet. Everybody had left for work. Now I had time to look around, and to get familiar with my new surroundings.

After a refreshing bath—what luxury to have warm water available automatically—I took a closer look at my room. It was not large, but it was mine. This was the first time I ever had a room all to myself. Besides the bed, there was a small desk with a chair which Aunt and Uncle had purchased for me. The only other piece of furniture was an enclosed bookcase with glass doors. Both the desk and the bookcase were made of reddish brown, highly polished wood—mahogany, I learned later. It looked rather formal, but I found the dark color slightly depressing. In Germany at this time everything was contemporary and colorful. Not many people in Berlin had been able to save old furniture. Whatever was not destroyed during the war had been fed to the stove afterwards to keep from freezing to death.

The built–in closet was a new experience for me. I thought it was quite practical and eliminated the need for a bulky wardrobe. After

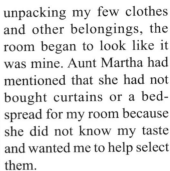

My room, above and below, after I made the curtains and bedspread.

unpacking my few clothes and other belongings, the room began to look like it was mine. Aunt Martha had mentioned that she had not bought curtains or a bedspread for my room because she did not know my taste and wanted me to help select them.

With all doors being open I could look into the other rooms. Aunt and Uncle's bedroom had light–colored furniture. It was maple, I learned upon questioning that night. The Colonial style was unfamiliar to me. The dining area in the kitchen had maple furniture as well. In the living room, all furniture was made of this dark mahogany as in my room.

I liked the idea of keeping all doors open. It made everything look more spacious and allowed the sunlight to be distributed throughout the house. However, I found it unusual that the living room and the kitchen did not have any doors at all. There was an archway leading from the living room into a tiny hallway, and opposite it, through another archway, was the entrance to the kitchen. The cheerful little bathroom was still my favorite. I could not get over having a rug in a bathroom. What a great idea! It was such a pretty touch—and a delight for the feet.

There was one disappointment in this bathroom—and I found out that I would have to put up with it for the rest of my life. It was the toilet paper. On the ship there had been this thin toilet paper, and I wrote it off to the cheap accommodations in what were really crew quarters. I was sure that once I got to my destination there would be *normal* toilet paper again. To my dismay I found that the awful toilet paper was regular American toilet paper, and that I would have to learn to live with it, and learn to use more than just one sheet at a time.

Next I became aware of being hungry. I went to the refrigerator and opened it. This was *Alice in Wonderland* time. I selected an orange and could not help but think of Mom and Peter. We each had an orange as a special treat for Christmas last year. Here, there were about a dozen of them in the refrigerator as well as some other, larger fruits which I did not know—grapefruits. Then I took out the rye bread and what I thought was butter. I was going to have some bread with butter on it. However, it said "cream cheese" on the package, so I decided to try that cheese. It was not like any cheese I had ever eaten, but rather more like deliciously flavored butter. Oh, was it good! I ate three slices of bread with that wonderful cheese, and worried that Aunt Martha would be angry because I had eaten so much.

During the afternoon I played the German records which I had brought with me from home, as well as some of Uncle's. All were the old, heavy, 78 RPM records. Fortunately, none of the ones I brought with me had broken during the long journey. Some of those had belonged to Papa. Uncle had shown me how to work his phonograph the night before when he saw that I had brought along some records. He knew that I would need a link with home on my first day alone in a strange country. At one point I opened the front door to find that it was another hot day outside, but not as uncomfortable as it had been the day before. Part of the house was shaded by a large linden tree which helped keep it somewhat comfortable, though still much warmer than I was used to.

There was a big wing chair by the picture window in the living room. I had never seen a chair that high. Sitting in it while listening to the music, I knew then that this chair would become my favorite. It is still in the family at this time.

Quite frequently during the day I looked outside, and I found it strange to never see any people. Now it was getting near the end of the day and I had yet to see a single person walk on the sidewalks. There were a lot of cars going by all day long, but no people.

I wondered where the town of Cranford was. Here were all these many homes close to each other, but as far down the street as I could see, there was not a single shop of any kind. Something had to be nearby. People would have to go out and shop somewhere, I thought. I would ask Aunt Martha tonight. Among a couple of other items, I needed to get postage stamps so that I could write home. I missed Mom and Peter, and wished that I could share my many new experiences with them.

Aunt Martha was the first one to arrive home at about five o'clock. I wondered where she had come from and how she had gotten here. There were no buses or any public transportation as far as I could tell, and people did not seem to walk. She told me that someone who works with her gives her a ride to and from work every day. Now I learned that public transportation in the rural areas of the United States is not as convenient as it is in Germany, this being such a large country with great distances between places.

How would I ever get to The Mennen Company? Aunt Martha told me not to worry about that yet. She wanted me to stay at home for a couple of weeks to rest up and get acclimated before I started to work. She also thought I had not eaten enough during the day. How could I recover from the ship voyage if I were not eating, she asked me. Feeling that I had done well, I told her about my fear of having eaten too much. She thought this was funny and she laughed. It was not funny to me. I was still used to being mindful of rations.

Aunt Martha's love was gardening. During the spring and summer, every evening after work and before starting to prepare dinner, she would spend about an hour in the garden in the back of the house. Unlike the front yard which was small, the back yard was quite deep and she kept a good–sized vegetable garden, as well as flowers everywhere.

The back yard was quite large. Aunt Martha grew vegetables and flowers. This is my second day in the U.S. and I am with Aunt Martha and Mr. Timmann Sr., Uncle's father.

Later when everyone was at home we ate dinner. I asked about a post office and was told that it was too far to walk there. Uncle said it was more than a mile to the center of town where the post office was located. At that point I learned about the measurement of miles instead of kilometers.

Now I knew that I had come to a prehistoric country instead of the *New World:* Fahrenheit and miles. In any case, I found out in which direction to walk to get to the post office. Uncle insisted that nobody walked here—which I had already noticed—and that he would drive me to the post office on Saturday. I argued, telling him that I loved to walk, and that even a mile was not too far for me; except of course, if the temperature were above the boiling point again. Aunt and Uncle were still laughing every time the temperature question came up. I did not know how to convert Fahrenheit into Celsius, and neither did they. Uncle pointed out there was no need for them to convert into Celsius since that measurement was not used in the United States, and, of course, I had not been taught how to convert into Fahrenheit for the same reason.

Visitors

The first set of visitors wanting to meet me arrived after dinner. In the course of the evening, two more couples stopped by and stayed for awhile. Everyone was curious and wanted to look me over. Aunt and Uncle's friends were mostly Germans who had immigrated sometime before World War II. Several couples lived in the general area, but a number of them were in the Allentown/Bethlehem area of Pennsylvania where Aunt and Uncle had lived before they married and settled in New Jersey. I was glad that nearly all of their friends spoke German.

When I first met them, I had been anxious to practice some of my really limited English, but I found that the Germans were not exactly forgiving or helpful when I made a mistake. Instead of correcting me, which I would have appreciated, they would laugh or make fun of my British English. Yet, even I noticed that their English was far from being perfect. There was a lot of German mixed in when they talked, and I was sure that one needed to know both languages to be able to understand them. In most cases both husband and wife were German, so that they spoke German at home, just as it was in Aunt and Uncle's household. They never really learned the language unless their jobs were such that they had to speak English all of the time, and correct usage was important.

The next day was a Saturday, and we were going to spend the weekend at Aunt and Uncle's vacation house, which was located at one of a group of lakes called Fayson Lakes. I was looking forward to riding in the car, which was such a novelty to me, and to seeing some of the countryside. It was a surprise for me to learn that nobody had to go to work on Saturdays. The schools were also closed.

Northern New Jersey is beautiful, hilly and wooded country with a lot of lakes. Aunt and Uncle told me that a year ago they had built a vacation home on a lake to have a getaway for spring and fall weekends. In July and August they usually rented it out. It was an hour's drive north of where they lived. I was excited about the trip, and especially about the lake. I loved to swim and the weather was so hot here. Unlike in northern Germany, here it was sunny and hot every day during the summer months.

Aunt and Uncle would usually leave for the lake house on Friday nights, but on this particular weekend the schedule was different. Having had visitors the night before, we could not go to the grocery store until Saturday morning. Uncle Adolph always had to take Aunt Martha shopping because she did not drive at all. Living in a big city I was used to walking to get groceries, and we would shop nearly every day for the foods we needed. We had no refrigerators in our apartments in Berlin at that time.

I accompanied Aunt and Uncle to the supermarket. It seemed to be a long ways away, at least two kilometers. No wonder they needed a car to go shopping. When we got there, I could not believe my eyes. I had never before seen a food store of that size. All of the foods that people needed could be purchased in one store. This was new to me. In Germany, bread and other baked goods were bought at the bakery, meats and sausages at the butcher, fruits and vegetables at the greengrocer, and dry goods at a grocery store.

The quantities of food they bought were unreal to me. Of course, they shopped only once a week, but still I wondered when we were going to eat all this. The refrigerator at home was still full. Aunt Martha explained that we were expecting guests at the lake house, and that she planned on cooking a big meal there. She bought more cream cheese so I would not run out. What else would I like? I said: "Pickles." Aunt and Uncle thought I was too thin and didn't think pickles were going to be helpful in their self–appointed mission to fatten me up.

Uncle had a sweet tooth and wanted several kinds of cookies and some ice cream. I had never seen people buy cookies. We always baked them, which was time–consuming and Mom baked them as a special treat for Christmas. Eating desserts after a big evening meal was another custom that was new to me. Not being keen on sweets, I always forgot to save room for dessert, and cake or cookies after dinner did not appeal to me. I had been living on ration cards up until recently and had not yet learned to eat unnecessary foods such as sugary desserts. My preference were foods that provided valuable nourishment.

My first Excursion

After dropping some of the groceries off at home and leaving others in the car to take with us, we were finally ready to leave. This was my third full day in the USA, and I was anxious to see the area in which I now lived. We drove through the town of Cranford and I was disappointed in the small center of the town. There was a hardware store, a small five–and–ten–cent store, a movie theater, a post office, and a few other small shops. I thought it did not look like much of a shopping facility for the population in the area. What stood out to me was that there were about half a dozen churches of different denominations in the town of Cranford, and more outside of town. Once again I was full of questions. With northern Germany having fewer than two percent Catholics, Berlin's churches are nearly all Lutheran. Aunt Martha explained that the people of the United States have come from so many different countries, and that they have brought their respective religions with them. It made sense to me.

Uncle explained things to me as we drove along while Aunt Martha was busy filing her fingernails. How could she do that instead of looking outside? To me, everything was new and I did not want to miss anything. I was amused that she did notice people's front yards along the road, and pointed out to Uncle wherever someone had planted a new shrub or a tree. Gardening was certainly a major interest of Aunt Martha's. I also remembered Uncle Karl's garden in Berlin. Uncle Karl was one of Aunt Martha's brothers. They were born on a farm in Germany, and the love for "digging in the soil" shows up in many family members of the Valten lineage, including Peter and me.

At one point we passed a roadside farm stand and Uncle pointed out a street sign to me, which was mounted just under the roof. This street sign stopped my breath. It was from Berlin and read *Unter den Linden*, which is the famous boulevard on the east side of the

Brandenburg Gate. The owner of the farm store had brought it with him as a souvenir from Berlin at the end of World War II. It may seem strange, but this sign was somehow a greeting from home. In the years to come, whenever I drove along that street I looked for the Berlin street sign which, with its rusty little impact holes from bomb fragments, was very special to me.

Next we entered a highway and stopped at a store called Channel Lumber, a forerunner of Home Depot. Uncle needed to buy a few things for the lake house which had been built only the year before, and some interior finishing was still going on. I found Channel Lumber to be a fascinating place—like a supermarket for handymen where they could buy everything they needed without having to go to several specialty shops. Channel Lumber was another unique experience to add to my list.

It was amazing how many new and different impressions and experiences I accumulated during only three days in the United States. This was such a different way of living from what I had known, and it looked like I still had much to learn. It was a good thing that I was just nineteen and not only could absorb it all, but was quite eager to learn more.

Down the road a ways we drove alongside a good–sized lake which was fenced in. Why would there be a fence around a lake? Wouldn't people want to go swimming? Here were two lessons at once: In this country most property is privately owned, including beaches and lakes. People who do not own a beach or a lake can swim only at a public beach. Secondly, the reason for the fence around this particular lake was that it was the reservoir for Jersey City's drinking water. From then on, the lake with the fence around it, commonly called the Jersey City Reservoir, became my two–thirds–way landmark for the trip to the lake house.

We were now in northern New Jersey's beautiful hill country. I was impressed with the steep streets in the town of Boonton which made me feel as though we were in the mountains. Berlin was so flat and I liked mountains. After Boonton we drove on country roads and were soon in a region of many small lakes nestled in a wooded area. It was pleasantly cool driving through the forest because we were in shade and at a higher elevation than we had been at home.

The House at Fayson Lakes

As soon as we arrived at the lake house, the neighbors came running out and were anxious to meet me. They were Mr. and Mrs. Seibert, who were Aunt Martha and Uncle Adolph's closest friends. The Seiberts had a daughter who was my age, Kay, but she was out with friends. I met her briefly later on when she and her friends stopped by for awhile. Mr. Seibert was the contractor for whom Uncle's father worked, and it was ob-

The house at Fayson Lakes

vious where the idea of building a vacation house at Fayson Lakes had come from.

I also met Mr. Seibert's sister and brother–in–law who were with them. The women were busy styling each other's hair and I received a lesson on how to do my own hair, which has been valuable to me all of my life.

We finally went into Aunt and Uncle's house. It was delightful! The paneled walls gave it a rustic look and there was a fireplace in the living room. Everything looked so comfortable, and I loved it. However, once I noticed the rowboat outside I was out there and ready to go. Either that or go swimming. The lake was the main attraction for me. I helped Uncle put the boat into the water, and off we went while Aunt Martha was busy squaring away the groceries.

This lake was not good for swimming, Uncle told me. It was shallow and had a lot of tree stumps in it. He would take me to the public beach at one of the larger lakes if I really wanted to swim. Well, for the moment I was interested in the boat. I had spotted some large rocks across the lake and had to go there to investigate. Uncle Adolph enjoyed my enthusiasm and was happy to see me have so much fun. He had brought along his camera and took pictures as I climbed around on the rocks. One huge rock was submerged in the water, except for a small part of it, which was perfect for me to stand on and look as though I was standing on the surface of the water. A great picture to send home! Uncle took quite a few pictures for me to send home to Mom and Peter. He knew that I was anxious to write to them and tell them all about my new life.

More Visitors

Suddenly I saw Aunt Martha by the lakeshore waving and motioning for us to return. There was a second car in the driveway. Company had arrived. I rowed back and we were greeted by a little boy who was waiting at the edge of the water. His parents and Aunt Martha were not far away. This was the Wehr family who were also close friends, and German, of course. I was introduced.

After being looked over and approved of by the Wehrs, the little boy was anxious for me to take him out in the boat. We were told we would have to wait until after lunch. The boy and I sat down on a log by the water's edge and I asked him what his name was. I had not understood the name when we were introduced. When he said "Raymond" and I still did not catch it, he wrote it in the sand for me. He was five years old and could write his name, and he told me that he was called "Ray" for short. Abbreviating names was not common in Germany, but here it made it easier for me.

Ray and I communicated quite well. Even though both of his parents were German and he understood the language, he did not speak it at all. Here was an example of a story which I was to hear often: German parents speak German at home, and when the child enters school he or she does not know enough English to get along in classes, especially when it is the first or an only child who does not play with others. At that point the parents are advised to speak English at home. At the same time the child refuses to speak anything but English because he needs to communicate with his peers at school. The

As "captain" of my yacht, I am waiting for passenger Raymond to board.

young child learns English in no time while the parents never really do. They tend to form friendships with other Germans and have therefore less occasion to speak English.

Little Ray seemed to have immediately adopted me to be his big sister. At lunch he insisted on sitting next to me, which surprised his parents. He wanted to eat exactly the same sandwich as I was making for myself although he normally would not eat certain things, cream cheese

My little friend Ray—a few years after I met him.

for one. He was even willing to try a pickle because I was having one. There was silence. Everyone watched in amazement as Ray ate the pickle. He did make all kinds of funny faces, then turned to me, smiled, and said "Picklefritz." All of us cracked up with laughter.

Ray and I were nearly inseparable whenever the Wehrs came to the lake, which was often. However, on that first day I met him he taught me a lessen which was to help me immensely in the following months— he taught me that children are infinitely patient teachers. Ray helped me with words, corrected or helped me complete sentences, taught me new words and—most importantly—he never laughed when I made a mistake. To him this was not funny but rather serious business, and with a lot of patience he would help me to get it right.

From that day on, wherever we went visiting I sought out the children and stuck with them. I was at an awkward age anyway. Most of Aunt and Uncle's friends were at least in their late forties, and mostly older. From children I learned a lot, and I felt comfortable with them. The older people were full of prophesy for my future. They just knew that I would lose my red cheeks and my healthy look once I rode in a car all of the time and no longer walked anywhere—they knew that I would get Americanized and not want to stick with the Germans, and so forth. Worst of all, I heard them talk about having to find a husband for me. That subject seemed to be on everybody's mind except mine.

The Wehr family left after dinner that night, and on Sunday Uncle took me to the biggest of the Fayson Lakes where there was a public beach. Nobody else was there, which I found unbelievable. Here was a perfectly nice lake with a beach and nobody used it. This would not

Aunt Martha and I at Fayson Lakes working on yard cleanup.

happen in Germany. I swam across the lake and back, which scared Uncle Adolph. He was not a swimmer and did not go into the water.

Aunt Martha was always busy with the house. Months later after having made many trips to the lake house, I decided that it was more work than relaxation to go there on weekends. We always brought enough groceries with us to be prepared for guests. After we arrived we put away the groceries, dusted the house, put up clean towels and sheets if guests had stayed overnight the last time or were expected to stay during this trip. If some of the many friends were staying overnight they usually let us know ahead of time, otherwise they might just stop by and spend the day, as the Wehrs always did. Aunt Martha, true to her reputation of being a good cook, was always prepared to cook a big meal for extra people. There was almost never a weekend when we were alone at the lake home.

After company left on Sundays, we would clean the house, pack up the leftover foods and dirty laundry and drive home, sometimes late in the evening. At home we had to unpack everything and square away the leftover foods. Once I was working and could no longer clean the house before we left on Fridays, we tried to get home early enough on Sunday evenings to do it then. With that hassle every weekend, the seed was sown for my lifelong aversion to owning a vacation home. In Aunt and Uncle's case they could not even enjoy their own vacations at the lake house because they rented it out during the two nicest summer months, July and August. On weekends in the spring and fall when they could go there, they mostly had a steady stream of friends visiting and enjoying it while Aunt Martha (and I) would work all weekend, taking care of the cooking and the cleanup.

Alone Again

It had been an eventful weekend for me with countless new experiences, however, on Monday morning I was glad to be alone again.

Nights and mornings were getting closer to normal as I was getting my land legs back. In other words, the "ship" was rolling less and less. It took longer than a week for this feeling to disappear completely.

We forgot to buy my postage stamps on Saturday. Now that I had seen where downtown Cranford was located, I did not have to march off into the unknown when I decided to walk to the post office. It was another hot day outside. A block away from home, as soon as I had turned the corner and was on a less busy street which led to Cranford, a lady stopped her car and offered me a ride. For the first time I was on my own and had to get along with my extremely limited English. I explained that I wanted to walk. She accepted this. Soon afterwards somebody else stopped and I declined again. People tried to tell me that it was too hot to walk and too far to walk to town, but I insisted on walking and was pleased that my English seemed adequate enough to get my point across. At least I think they understood. After turning down another offer of a ride, I got clever and crossed the street to walk against the traffic, and made it into Cranford. I had ambivalent feelings about the apparent custom of people offering rides. On one hand I resented not being able to walk without having to fend off well–meaning people, while on the other hand I was touched by their courteous gestures.

I got my stamps, then stopped at the five–and–ten–cent store to buy two items: ink for my fountain pen and a ruler so that I could get familiar with inches. I shall never forget the girl at the checkout. In my hand I held the cash ready. My purchases totaled thirty–five cents; twenty–five cents for the ink and ten cents for the ruler, no tax—but also no calculators. The girl wrote on a piece of paper twenty–five and ten, then added them together. I was stunned. I thought anyone could add that up in their head even without having gone to school. The cashier came up with forty–five cents. I told her that the total came to thirty–five cents. To my amazement she wrote again a twenty–five and a ten underneath, then added them up once more. At last she had the correct answer. I was puzzled. I had been told that in this country everybody automatically goes to high school, and parents do not have to pay for it as they do in Germany. This must be a different kind of high school here if a clerk needs paper and pencil to add two numbers together!

By walking on the sidewalk on the left side of the road opposing traffic, I reached home without being offered rides again. Now I could write to Mom and Peter. There was so much I wanted to tell them that the afternoon went by in a flash before I had finished my letter.

Aunt and Uncle usually watched television in the evenings, which in 1954 was still somewhat of a novelty. At first I would join them because I needed to learn English. Uncle's father always went back to his room after dinner. He had his own domain upstairs. Being a stamp collector, he enjoyed working with his collection and was active in trading with friends. I thought it was fun to have a television in the house. Televisions had come on the market more than a year ago in Germany, but we did not know anybody who owned one. Mom, Peter, and I had sometimes joined a crowd who stood outside a store window and watched a show when the store owner had been kind enough to put a television set on display. Aunt and Uncle told me they had had their television for only three years, and that they had been the first among their friends to own one. At that time they had company every night. Their friends would stop in after dinner to watch television, and they often stayed until late.

I found it difficult to understand the shows that Aunt Martha liked to watch. I remember one specifically, "I love Lucy." However, not understanding the particular type of humor, it did not seem funny to me but was rather silly, I thought. I did watch some programs and came away with the feeling that television helped me increase my English vocabulary. It was also important for me to become familiar with the sound of the language, since no English was being spoken at home or with friends.

One evening Uncle Adolph asked me if I had a dictionary. Proudly I showed him a set of two thick volumes, one book being German–English and the other English–German, which I had brought with me. They looked old, and used to belong to Papa. Uncle decided that I needed something more compact to be able to carry it with me daily during my early months in this country. I hesitated, but when he checked the publishing date and found that this set of books dated back to the late 1800's, I agreed that we needed to buy a new dictionary.

Uncle suggested we drive to Newark on Thursday evening when there was "shopping night," which meant that the stores would be open until nine o'clock in the evening. Aunt Martha welcomed the opportunity to do some shopping of her own at Bamberger's Department Store while Uncle and I went to the book department and found a dictionary which was handy, and comprehensive enough for my needs.

I was so exhilarated to be in Newark—a large city that had some life and reminded me of Berlin—that I started to skip along on the sidewalk. After watching the empty sidewalks in the suburbs, the life in the city was giving me a lift. Aunt Martha frowned when she saw me skipping, but Uncle understood.

Uncle Adolph seemed to have a talent for knowing what I needed. It was amazing how often he came up with helpful suggestions, or practical gifts for me. A few weeks after my arrival when I had not joined Aunt and Uncle on their weekly trip to the supermarket, Uncle came home with a pair of soft–soled Indian moccasins for me. He thought they might be more comfortable to wear around the house than the shoes I had been wearing. I found the moccasins to be the most comfortable footwear I had ever worn, and to this day—fifty years later—I wear moccasins around the house. I do not know how I would survive without them. I need my moccasins for comfort—and they have become a legacy of Uncle Adolph's thoughtfulness.

Life Gets Routine

As the days went by I began to get bored, and I kept asking how soon I could start to work. Aunt Martha, meaning well, said maybe in another week.

The big wing chair by the window had become my favorite place to sit and read. Every day I would sit there and watch the cars go by, but never did I see a pedestrian. Sometimes I would watch for an hour straight but the sidewalks were deserted. People lived in their houses, got into their cars, and drove away. Later they came back and went straight into their houses. No children played in the front yards. There was too much traffic on this road and the children were probably playing in fenced–in back yards. Having grown up in Berlin, I was used to watching out for traffic and to playing on the sidewalks. It had been a part of my childhood and one of my learning experiences.

I was always glad when Aunt Martha gave me little jobs to do. That way I could at least help her with something. She liked to do the cooking herself, and that was fine with me. I did not know how to cook any of the foods we ate here, but I always washed the dishes after dinner. On Fridays I cleaned the house, I dusted every day, and did all of the ironing, which made Aunt Martha happy. Later on when I was working, we divided up the chores. During the season when we were not going to the lake house, I would do the cleaning on Saturday mornings while Aunt Martha did the laundry. She had an old wringer style washing machine, and it took a long time to do the laundry for the four of us. In the meantime I cleaned the house, which was not that big a task. The agony for Aunt Martha was that I insisted on listening to the top ten "hits of the week" on WNEW, and the music had to be loud enough for me to hear it above the noise of the vacuum cleaner. She would often yell and complain about the noise I called music, just like I did twenty years later with my children when they were entering their teens.

Visiting in Pennsylvania

On my second weekend in America we drove to Pennsylvania and did some serious visiting there. After all, I had to be "shown off" to all of Aunt and Uncle's friends. Once again, the drive itself was a novelty for me and a learning experience. Now I had been in three of the forty–eight states—New York, New Jersey, and Pennsylvania.

We drove through the farm country of western New Jersey. I remember seeing several sets of Burma Shave signs along the way, for which I wanted translations, but those rhymes lost their humor in the translation. All Uncle could tell me was that the signs were advertising a particular brand of shaving cream. A red flag went up inside my head as I thought: "competition for Mennen." In comparison to the huge billboards alongside the highways I found the Burma Shave signs a more interesting and less objectionable way of advertising. Those signs were fun, especially once I knew enough English to understand what they said.

We visited several friends in Allentown and spent the night and the next day with Uncle's brother Bill and his wife Madeleine. They lived on the farm on which I was supposedly working, according to my visa application. Madeleine did not speak German and we had to speak English. I was unable to follow enough of a general conversation to be a part of it, though I had noticed that I could understand quite well when people spoke directly to me—if they spoke slowly. However, it was impossible for me to follow a group conversation, and I kept myself occupied and happy with some cats, a dog, and with washing their station wagon. I loved to wash cars, and unlike Uncle Adolph's, his brother's car was even more fun to wash because it was really dirty from being driven on farm roads. Besides, they did not wash it every week, as Uncle did. In fact, I was told that their station wagon had never been washed, and Madeleine

I was not able to follow conversations in English and kept busy with the pets.

and Bill were surprised and happy to see it look like new again. I had cleaned up the interior as well since it was unbelievably dusty from driving on unpaved roads with the windows open.

By now I was hoping that I had met all of Aunt and Uncle's friends. This visiting business was going on my nerves, and everywhere I had to explain why I did not drink coffee or eat cake. All Germans like coffee, I was told. Long after the war when coffee became available again in Germany, it was a luxury which we could not afford often. Mom had to prioritize, and we needed food more than coffee. At some point I had tried, but did not like it; and it would be another ten years before I drank coffee occasionally.

As for the cake, I was not used to having any except on special occasions such as holidays and birthdays. I was not particularly fond of sweets anyway, and I found American cakes and pastries to be excessively sweet.

I have a Job!

One evening when Aunt Martha came home from work, I sat in my favorite chair and had obviously been waiting for her. Having read most of the books they had, I told her that I was bored and eager to go to work. She said OK, I could go ahead and call Mr. Mennen.

The next day I telephoned Mr. Bill Mennen at his office, as he had told me to do when I met him in Berlin. I was worried about my English, but he understood my painstaking search for words. Mr. Mennen talked to me slowly enough so that I could understand him. He told me that he would call me back in a little while, and when he did, he had made all of the arrangements for me. He had even found someone who would give me a ride to and from work every day. This was something new to me, but necessary. How would I otherwise get from the town of Cranford which was more than a mile from my house, to the town of Morristown, from where it was still about two miles to the Mennen plant by non existing direct transportation? Morristown itself was eighteen miles from Cranford.

In the conversation Mr. Mennen told me that Mr. Jim Ford would pick me up at the house at eight o'clock on the following Monday morning, and that I would have a job in the office. Years later, Bill Mennen still laughed at my reaction to being told that a man would be driving me to and from work every day. While this was strange to me, it was quite ordinary in this country. I did not yet know about car pools.

This was the beginning of a lifelong friendship with Mr. William G. Mennen, Jr., Vice President of The Mennen Company. He personally involved himself in arranging for a job for me, and two years later for my brother. Peter worked for The Mennen Company until his retirement thirty–seven years later. I am eternally grateful to Bill Mennen for being given the opportunity to get off to a good start in a new country. I am also grateful to the "Mennen Family," as the employees of The Mennen Company were referred to; everyone who worked at Mennen played a personal role in my future as a Mennen employee, and helped me adjust to living in this wonderful country.

I was excited after my conversation with Bill Mennen that day, and could hardly wait for Aunt Martha to come home from work so I could tell her about my job, and that against my expectations I would be working in the office. I could not imagine what kind of work I could possibly perform there with my limited English, but I would find out.

The Mennen Company—Morristown, New Jersey

Aunt, Uncle, and Uncle's father were all happy for me and wished me good luck. They were especially pleased that I was getting an office job. Aunt Martha did manual labor in a factory, and she assured me that I would not learn much English while working on a production line. All three of them agreed. Uncle's father said: "Look at us, we never learned the language properly on our jobs. We can speak, yes, but we cannot write English adequately and correctly."

I was beaming with happiness and could not wait to go to work. Back in Berlin I had seen pictures of the beautiful new manufacturing plant which The Mennen Company had built near Morristown, New Jersey. One weekend on our way to the lake house we had made a detour to Morristown and driven by to take a look.

The Mennen Company

It was Monday, June 21st, and I was to start working for The Mennen Company. I dressed for work so early in the morning that I was ready to leave way ahead of time. Though filled with anticipation and some fear, my spirit of adventure was taking over. This would be a day to remember, packed with new impressions and experiences.

Mr. Jim Ford stopped in front of the house punctually at eight o'clock. He introduced himself and asked me to call him "Jim" and not "Mr. Ford." The custom of calling people by their first names upon meeting them for the first time was new to me. So far, I had called Aunt and Uncle's friends "Mr." and "Mrs." as was the custom in Germany, and because they were an older generation which demanded respect. Jim drove a station wagon, which I liked—I was getting quite interested in cars—and after a short trip on the Garden State Parkway we started driving through towns. A lady was waiting for us in the town of Springfield. She joined us for the ride to work. Her name was Alice. Next we picked up Beverly in Short Hills, and then another Alice in Summit.

So this was a car pool. Aunt and Uncle had approved of it when I told them about a man picking me up every day. This was perfectly normal to them. I just happened to be the first one on Jim's route. As I learned later on, there was no one else who came to work from that far away. Bill Mennen had done a super job in finding the only person in the company who traveled anywhere close to the area in which I lived.

Only a year before, The Mennen Company had moved from the city of Newark out to rural Morristown, and most of the employees had either relocated or had been hired from the local area.

We arrived at The Mennen Company's plant at 8:50 a.m., and I was guided into the Personnel Department. After a phone call made by the personnel manager, a middle–aged man arrived who introduced himself as Mr. Henry Oldenburg. He was the plant manager, and the only German at Mennen, having immigrated when he was a young man. Mr. Oldenburg had been assigned to be my lifeline in case I absolutely needed an interpreter. Initially he helped me fill out my job application form and told me all the things I needed to know about working there. This was vastly different than working in a small company in Berlin.

After entering the building in the morning, and again before exiting, all non–management employees punched time cards. There were set times for having lunch in the cafeteria and for morning and afternoon coffee breaks. Work hours were from 9:00 a.m. until 5:00 p.m., five days a week. My weekly salary would be $37.50, minus deductions. Mr. Oldenburg told me about holidays, vacation time, sick leave, etc, and that I needed to get a social security number. For this I had to go to the city of Newark, and he would arrange for The Mennen Company's driver to take me there on his next trip later in the week.

Before escorting me to my place of work in the Central Steno Pool, or the "Typing Pool" as it was referred to, Mr. Oldenburg gave me a piece of his wisdom which became a guideline for my new life in the United States. He told me: "The door of opportunity is open. We are not going to serve anything to you on a silver platter, but you can have whatever you want here, if you work for it." Most meaningful of all was his advice: "You can learn a lot if you keep your eyes and ears open, and your mouth shut." Those words became my *Golden Rule.*

As he ushered me upstairs to my new office, Mr. Oldenburg told me that the fastest way to learn English would be for me to speak it at every opportunity. He said he knew from his own home that it would not happen there when all family members speak German. I would therefore have to speak as much as possible at work. This floored me because I expected to be paid for *working* and not for *talking* in order to learn the language, though I realized that learning English quickly would benefit my productivity in the long run.

Mr. Oldenburg then told me that he would pretty much stay out of the picture so that I would not get used to relying on his translations. Instead, I should be on my own and therefore forced into having to communicate as best as I could. He assured me that he would always be glad to help me anytime I really needed his help. With that I was left in the care of the girls at the Typing Pool.

At the time there were only two girls, Virginia and Marilyn. I was told that Dottie, the supervisor of the Typing Pool, was absent because she was about to have a baby. Virginia was twenty–four and Marilyn was eighteen years old. They were both married, which surprised me, because I thought they were too young. I was nineteen and I certainly was a long ways from thinking that I ought to be married.

My First Day at Work

No sooner had I been shown to a desk at which I was to work when Bill Mennen stopped in to welcome me to The Mennen Company, or, as the Mennens traditionally liked to call it, the Mennen Family. Knowing from our conversation in Berlin that I was going to travel to the United States by ship, Bill Mennen asked how my boat trip had been, and I was faced with the first language hurdle. While he spoke clearly and I could understand him well—within the limits of my vocabulary— it took me a moment to make the connection between boat and ship. I had learned that an ocean liner is called a "ship" and was a little slow to get his question. During my moment of confusion I had to decide: "Does he mean the rowboat at the lake house which I had just used the day before? But then, how could he know about it? So, he must mean the ship on which I came from Germany—but, he did say boat, not ship." After some hesitation, I tried to explain that I really did not enjoy the boat trip very much because I had been quite seasick. We talked some more, and Bill Mennen laughed a lot. He seemed to be a very happy person, always having a smile on his face. Even his eyes were smiling.

Before I could settle in at my desk, it was break time. Marilyn was taking her break later so she could cover the phone while Virginia and I went downstairs to the cafeteria. I was surprised at how beautiful it was, and I could not help but think of my job in Berlin, where most of the time I could not find a moment to eat my sandwich at the desk. I could not have imagined such a lovely place for the employees to use, as I was still carrying the image that an employee was more or less a slave who was required to get the necessary work done regardless of conditions. Everything here was so beautifully decorated, bright and pleasant. Taking a break from work in this cafeteria was truly a revitalizing experience. The Mennen Company was a paradise to work in!

During break, several people were curious about me and stopped at our table to try and talk to me. I had brought along my dictionary, and with its help I could often get the gist of a sentence without needing to understand every word of it. The dictionary was my constant companion in the months ahead, and I was thankful to Uncle Adolph for his suggestion that we buy one I could carry with me.

My typewriter was an IBM Electric. Wow, what a machine—and what a change from the antiquated Olympia I worked with in Berlin. The keyboard of the typewriter was the same, as I knew it would be, except for the absence of the *Umlaut* symbols which the German language requires. The other difference was that two of the letters were transposed. The letter "Y" was located in the place where the "Z" is on the German typewriter. A "Y" is rarely used in the German language, whereas the "Z" gets a lot of use. The reverse is true in English. In the beginning, this difference caused me to automatically make a lot of typographical errors, which at that time required erasing. I learned to be extremely mindful because erasures took time, especially when multiple carbon copies were involved, and they did not look good.

To start with, my work consisted of typing purchase orders. The Typing Pool was a service office. We did any typing jobs that needed to be done anywhere in the company and out in the field. Some men did not have secretaries. In addition, we were there to help if someone's secretary had an overload. The Purchasing Department, which was next door to us, had us type their purchase orders regularly to take the load off their secretarial staff. The main part of our workload came from dictation. Our office had special equipment called dictaphones. Those machines could remotely record dictation onto disks. We inserted the disks into disk players, and with the help of headphones transcribed the dictation and typed the letters. The dictating equipment could be used within the company as well as by the salesmen out in the field who had portable dictating equipment. The salesmen would mail the disks to us and we, in turn, typed the correspondence for them.

Since I could not yet perform transcriptions because of my limited English, I was given copy work to do in addition to typing the purchase orders. Anything that needed to be copied or retyped was given to me. Since I wanted to know what I was typing, I made much good use of my dictionary. The copy work increased my vocabulary and greatly contributed to my learning the language.

There was one more thing I learned on my first day at the office, which was that I had been taught British English in school. My pronunciation of words was different than that of my coworkers, and at this point I could not even recognize some words as being the same. In addition, many of the English words that I knew were not American. For example, I learned that a "tram" was called a "streetcar" in American English. Then there were slang words which were not in my dictionary, and the girls had to try and explain those to me. However, I was confident that in time I would learn the language.

All day long now I had been meeting people, and nobody, except for Mr. Oldenburg and Bill Mennen, had made any motion to shake hands. This surprised me. In Germany, everyone shakes hands. I had already been made aware that this was not the custom here, but had difficulty believing it. Being so young, at least it was not up to me to initiate a handshake. Etiquette required for the younger person to wait until the hand is offered by the older or superior, which did not happen.

I was sorry when five o'clock came along and I had to leave this wonderful place. Everyone had been so nice and helpful, and had contributed so much towards making my first day at work a memorable experience. I was absolutely in love with The Mennen Company, and could not wait to return to work the next day.

Upon leaving the plant I got a shock. It had been another hot day. Being air conditioned, the Mennen plant had been pleasantly cool and comfortable. At the end of this highly eventful day I had totally forgotten about the awful heat. Stepping outside felt like walking into an oven, and inside the car it was unbearable. This was before most cars were air conditioned, and we had to ride in this stifling heat for almost an hour. I still felt nauseous when I got home and was even more anxious to go back to work the next day.

At home it was not any cooler in the house than it had been outside. Was this a sign of things to come during summers in New Jersey? Aunt Martha had prepared tuna fish salad, a cold meal for a hot day. I thought this was a splendid idea. Being used to herring, tuna tasted strange, and initially I did not particularly like it. However, as with other foods that were strange to me, eventually I learned to like almost everything. There was never anything that I would not eat, but, of course, I liked some foods better than others.

During dinner I told the family all the details of my extraordinary and eventful day. I was obviously enthusiastic about my job and my place of work. Aunt Martha could not help but comment once again when I told her about Virginia and Marilyn being married, and Marilyn being only eighteen years old. She told me that in this country everybody meets their sweethearts in high school, and that I would never meet anybody because I had "missed the boat" (or the ship??) by not having gone to school here. She pointed out that it was therefore important that people help find a husband for me since I was going to be twenty years old in a few months. At age twenty–one, I would officially be an old maid, and nobody would want me anymore. I did not argue with Aunt Martha or question her wisdom, but I did not quite believe this "old wives' tale" she was telling me. In any case, securing a husband was not on my list of priorities.

Working at Mennen is Fun

Each morning I looked forward to going to work, and every day brought new experiences. Soon I got used to the sound of the English language, and after I had asked people to "please speak slowly," everyone had made the effort willingly. It seemed that everybody in the whole company was anxious to talk to me. In the cafeteria, people would stop by the table at which I sat with Ginny—as Virginia was called—and

The Typing Pool. I am at the left side of the picture, standing.

Betty, the company's receptionist, and they always asked me questions. Often I had trouble, but people were extraordinarily helpful. They would then reword the question so that I might understand, which I did most of the time. Rarely did we get to a dead end. In that case my dictionary would help me out, which I carried with me at all times. What impressed me most was that everyone appreciated my attempt at speaking English, and was helpful. Unlike my Aunt and some of her German friends, nobody ever laughed if the sentence came out wrong, or if I used the wrong word to describe something. I was always thankful for any correction and help that people offered me.

Mr. Oldenburg was doing his part behind the scenes by telling people to stop by the Typing Pool and talk to me. It seemed like the whole Mennen Company was geared towards helping me learn English. Bill Mennen stopped in to talk to me every day; and his brother, George Mennen whose office was at the other end of the building, invariably took the time to talk to me whenever he saw me.

George Mennen was the Vice President of Manufacturing. He was a jolly fellow, always laughing and joking. When I met him and called him "Mr. Mennen," he looked behind himself as if searching for someone, then said: "Who is Mr. Mennen? I am George," adding: "You can call my father Mr. Mennen." It was difficult for me to call my superiors by their first names, and especially a head of the organization. However, George Mennen was such an informal person that I had to get used to it. He even asked me to call him *Georg* ("George" in German), as his German governess had done when he was a boy.

I was impressed with Mr. Mennen Sr., the president of The Mennen Company and son of the founder. I had always pictured heads of big corporations to be godlike and unreachable. At Mennen everyone was friendly and down–to–earth. I could feel that there was a close relationship between the top management and every employee in the company. Any time I met Mr. Mennen Sr. in the hall, he would stop and talk to me. He would ask questions about my family in Berlin, and if I liked living in the United States. There was obviously some personal interest on his part since he was the son of a German immigrant. Still, his kindness was special to me and I held him in high esteem.

As far as understanding people when they talked to me, especially in the beginning, I found that men were easier to understand than women. There must be something about the frequency of men's voices which makes the enunciation clearer. I have heard from other immigrants that they had the same experience. Nevertheless, within a few months I was doing quite well, thanks to everyone who gave me the chance to talk so that I had lots of practice. On my first day, Mr. Oldenburg had shown me where his office was located so that I could come to him for help. Amazingly I got along on my own thanks to his advice that I must fend for myself. He did stop by my office periodically to see how I was doing, and to ask if I had any questions. The conversion of Fahrenheit to centigrade was one problem he solved for me forever by giving me a temperature chart, which I still have—and use—today.

I was a fast typist, and despite the language problem I got a good deal of work done every day. I was quite good with spelling which was noticed quickly. Within two months of working there, the Typing Pool girls would ask me how to spell words rather than looking them up in the dictionary. This was difficult to believe. Here were Americans who had gone to school in this country, and they were not embarrassed to ask a foreigner how to spell their language? I did not know what to think about that. The cashier who could not add twenty–five plus ten came to my mind.

At home, when the family sat together at dinner we talked about things that happened during the day. One evening, while Uncle Adolph was still sitting at the table feeding his sweet tooth and I was helping Aunt Martha with the dishes, I learned that Uncle had problems understanding me. I had told a funny story about home (Berlin) and Aunt and I were cracking up with laughter, while Uncle was not even smiling a bit. Assuming that he did not think it was funny, I questioned him, and he told me that he had not understood me because I talk too fast. Berliners do talk exceedingly fast, yet it never occurred to me that he would have trouble following me. People in northern Germany (Hamburg, where he came from), do talk especially slowly. The Berliners have always been referred to as "fast troopers" in everything they do—tempo—tempo! After that incident I consciously made an effort to slow down when talking, and he had no more problems. In time he must have gotten used to my Berlin speed and to the sound of the German as well as to the slang that the Berliners speak.

Surviving the Hot Summer

This first summer was extremely hard on me not being used to such high temperatures, and especially the excessively high humidity. I suffered terribly from the heat. The temperatures in July and August were often in the high nineties, and a number of times it was above a hundred degrees. They said this was a bit unusual for northern New Jersey. There was no air conditioning except at work, and I was surprised when my nylons would not dry overnight. Each morning I would struggle trying to get into wet stockings. I could afford to buy only one pair at a time. It was hard to sleep at night, and in the morning I would feel sick from the heat and humidity. I remember having to sit down frequently while trying to get my clothes on. Everything was damp.

Aunt Martha started to worry about me. At some point it got so bad that I thought I could not live in this climate and would have to return to Germany. Some mornings I felt almost too sick to go to work, but I knew that once I survived the ordeal of dressing and the hour–long trip in the rear of the car, I would be in air conditioning and feel better. Mondays were the most difficult because the air conditioning had been shut off over the weekend. The company nurse would give me salt pills, but my stomach would still be upset and I did not feel better until I had cooled off.

At home, Uncle Adolph kept telling me that once I had experienced all of the seasons, I would be acclimated, and the second year would be easier to take. That wisdom did not help me much during this first miserably hot summer, and I was sure that I would not last until the end of it. I thought that New Jersey's climate was the pits and that it could not possibly be any worse elsewhere. Years later I told a friend who suffered as much as I had after immigrating from Germany, that if she could live in New Jersey, she could live *anywhere*. However, that was before I had been to Florida, New Orleans, Houston, or worse than that, lived in Washington, DC for eighteen years. How did people ever survive without air conditioning?

One day during Aunt Martha's vacation, we stopped by Mr. and Mrs. Winter's home. It was another very hot day and the living room looked dark and depressing with the drapes drawn shut to keep the room as cool as possible. In her living room, Mrs. Winter pointed to two especially decorative candles on the mantelpiece which were nearly the shape of question marks. She lamented that they had brought those candles all the way from Germany where they had visited recently, and now the beautiful candles were no longer straight because the heat was melting them. To me there was a simple explanation, and Mrs. Winter and Aunt Martha laughed so hard when I told them that those were

German candles and they just couldn't stand the climate in America. I was sympathetic with those candles.

My First Trip to the Seashore

After the lake house was rented out, Aunt and Uncle always planned for us to go to different places on weekends. We went to New York City, to Long Island, to Allentown, Bethlehem, and Philadelphia in Pennsylvania; to DuPont's Longwood Gardens in Delaware; and to Point Pleasant, Seaside Heights, Atlantic City, and Cape May on the New Jersey seashore, all during my first summer.

I loved to swim, and my favorite place to go to on summer weekends became the New Jersey seashore. It was a relief from the heat, although I had to be especially careful about sun exposure as I burn easily. The first time we went to the shore, I was quite excited to be going swimming in the Atlantic Ocean. To my big disappointment I found that there were lifeguards at the beach who would not let people swim just anywhere. There was a section of water roped off in which one could swim, but the area was not large enough for any serious swimming. I could not believe this. Here was a whole ocean full of water and people had to crowd into a tiny space which was too small for so many people. This reminded me of the Wannsee in Berlin in which one section was fenced off with barbed wire because it was the border between West Berlin and East Germany.

Aunt Martha and I at the New Jersey seashore

When Bill Mennen stopped by the Typing Pool the following Monday, he asked me what I had done on the weekend, and I told him the story of the roped off area reminding me of Berlin's Lake Wann–

see. He then told me about his own experience in Berlin. My former boss, Herr Heyn, had taken him to see this big lake, and it was packed with sailboats. When Bill Mennen had pointed out one area that was completely devoid of boats and asked why nobody went there, he was told that that part of the lake was in the Russian zone and there was barbed wire keeping boats from West Berlin out. It was awesome, he told me.

I said that it was appalling to me to have an ocean and then pack people into the space of a fish tank. He thought it was funny, but I was upset about not being able to swim freely in the ocean.

On this first trip to the New Jersey seashore I also found out about big traffic jams. Expecting heavy traffic, we had left at six o'clock on a Saturday morning. The entrance to the Garden State Parkway was less than a mile from our house, and we had not traveled long on the parkway before we were in extremely heavy traffic. "Everyone is heading for the seashore," Uncle said. We were in for a long, slow drive. The trip to Seaside Heights, which would normally take about ninety minutes, turned into a more than four–hour crawl. Aunt Martha was not a happy camper. She suffered from the heat nearly as much as I did, and the stop–and–go traffic did nothing to cool us off, even with the car windows open.

Besides the traffic tie–up, another new experience on that trip was the boardwalk. There were many little stores and snack shops. During the course of the day I tasted a candy apple, cotton candy, french fries, a hamburger, and salt water taffy, all for the first time. There were places with bumper cars and pinball machines. I felt like a child trying to make up for my lost childhood. There was so much action, and I just loved the seashore.

At the beach it was reasonably comfortable and we could cool off in the water, which was still quite cold throughout July. Once I got over my disappointment of being confined to a roped off area, I had a lot of fun with the big waves. I also got a painful sunburn on that trip. In the evening we walked on the boardwalk, and then had dinner before heading back. We tried to leave after most of the traffic was gone, and were successful. The reason Uncle had chosen to go to the shore on Saturday rather than on Sunday was that many people spent the whole weekend there, and everybody would head home on Sunday night. The Garden State Parkway was only one year old, and it was already overloaded.

I also learned about toll roads on that trip. The Garden State Parkway was one of them. Every few miles we had to stop at a tollgate and pay twenty–five cents. When I questioned this practice, I was told that the Parkway had just been built and that the money would be used towards the construction costs and ongoing maintenance.

My First 4th of July

I had worked for The Mennen Company just barely two weeks when I discovered that we had a long weekend coming up. What surprised me was that since July 4th was on a Sunday we were given Monday off. When I pointed out to those at the office that there was no reason for us to be off on Monday, I was told that when a major holiday falls on Sunday it is celebrated by giving employees off on Monday. American employers surely could learn how to economize from the Germans! At that time there were only four holidays in Germany for which people were off from work: Christmas, Easter, Whitsunday, and Labor Day which was on May first. There was no such thing as getting a weekday off if the holiday fell on a Sunday. Easter and Whitsunday were traditionally celebrated on Sunday and Monday, but there was no Saturday off from work or school because the holiday started on a Sunday.

Now we had a three–day weekend for celebrating America's Independence Day. We had been invited to Atlantic City which, at that time, was probably the most renowned seashore resort in New Jersey. A German friend of Aunt and Uncle's who lived in Allentown, worked for a wealthy lady who owned a vacation house in Atlantic City, as well as a good–sized boat. This friend, Käthe, had permission to spend the weekend at the vacation house with any friends she wanted to invite. We were among the lucky ones whom Käthe had asked to join her.

I was overjoyed about the prospect of spending two full days at an ocean beach, and was looking forward to a lot of swimming and walking on sandy beaches. Anticipation of this weekend brought back memories of how much I had enjoyed my two–week trip to the island of Sylt in the North Sea when I was still in school.

Expecting chaos on the Garden State Parkway because of the holiday weekend, Uncle Adolph suggested that we get on the road by two o'clock in the morning. It was a four–hour drive to Atlantic City, and we did it in just about that much time. Upon arrival in Atlantic City just after six o'clock, we stopped to eat breakfast and then went to locate the vacation house. It was huge, and we knew that Käthe had invited the whole Allentown gang for the weekend. Now that we knew where we were going to be, we needed to "kill" some time before we could reasonably show up at the door. We were not expected to arrive quite this early in the morning.

Seeing the beach only a block away, I was anxious to get into the water for a good swim after the long, hot trip. We stopped to take a look. There were no ropes in the water and no lifeguards watching. The beach was deserted. What was the matter with the people? It was Saturday morning and nearly eight o'clock, and people were not in the water enjoying a swim? This was unbelievable to me. What a waste of a beautiful beach. I had worn my swimsuit underneath my clothes, and was ready to peel and get into the water. Uncle Adolph said it was too early for swimming. I thought it would have been a perfect use for the time we had on hand, but Uncle had said "no." We drove around to see some of Atlantic City instead.

Eventually we drove back to the house at which we were to visit. The Maetjes from Allentown had already arrived. Lina Maetje was from Holland. Aunt Martha had known her during the six years she had worked in Holland before coming to the United States. She and Lina had immigrated together when both had been hired to work for the president of Lehigh University in Bethlehem, Pennsylvania—Lina as cook and Aunt Martha as general housekeeper.

Now we were visiting with the Maetjes and the others who soon arrived. After lunch we went for a boat ride which, with a crew of two, was available to Käthe and her friends. Then it was time for dinner, and I still had not been swimming in the ocean.

The next morning I was wide awake before six o'clock. The house was quiet. Nobody seemed to be awake yet. From the window I could look down the street and see the beach. I was going swimming!

I slipped into my swimsuit and quietly opened the door, trying not to wake up Käthe, who was my roommate. There was no sign of anyone. I snuck down the stairs hoping they would not creak, and was able to open the front door without making any noise, thanks to the custom of not locking doors in this country. In no time I was down by the beach and in the water. It was wonderfully refreshing after the hot night in an upstairs bedroom.

No ropes—and no lifeguards were whistling and telling me to get back. There was nobody else in the water and I had a great swim. The breakers were fun, and when I got past them I could really swim. Once I was in deep enough water I was careful not to swim out too far, but rather I would swim parallel to the beach. I was cautious since I knew nothing about the behavior of tides. Sometimes I would play in the surf for awhile, and then again go farther out and swim. This was wonderful—and time must have flown. At one point I looked towards the beach and there was Uncle Adolph, motioning frantically for me to come out of the water. When I reached him, he told me that they had been looking for me for more than an hour, and they were worried about my disappearance. Aunt Martha was upset. Remembering how much I had wanted to go swimming the day before, Uncle had the idea of checking the ocean. He insisted that we hurry, and that they were waiting with breakfast. I feared that Aunt Martha's wrath would descend upon me. When we got to the house she hollered quite a bit, but not any more so than she normally did. Everyone was tremendously relieved that I had returned unscathed. I was told, however, that it was dangerous to go swimming in an ocean all alone, and that I should not ever do that again.

What really seemed like punishment to me was that during the whole time we ate breakfast, there was nothing but talk about my little escapade. It was so embarrassing to me that I lost my appetite even though I had been quite hungry just minutes earlier. Nobody could get over how I had managed to get out of the house without anyone hearing me. I did not tell them that I had left at six o'clock when everybody was still asleep. It was past eight thirty when Uncle found me. Now I felt like I had been declared *sinner of the day*.

During the day, Aunt and Uncle were sitting around visiting with their friends and talking about "old times." There were no children or animals present, and I was more than a generation younger than anyone else. I was bored, but I did not dare ask to go swimming again. I sat and looked at magazines, and was glad when in the afternoon they decided to drive to the main beach of Atlantic City and take a walk on the boardwalk. There was not only the boardwalk with the many little shops and food stands, but also an amusement park. It was wonderful to ride the Ferris Wheel and have a great view of the vastness of the ocean from up high. Uncle always saw to it that I got to have some fun.

We had dinner at a seafood restaurant that night. Aunt and Uncle suggested I try shrimp or other shellfish. I did not know what shrimps or shellfish were, and nobody could translate it into German. At their suggestion I ordered shrimps, and ate the strange animals. Another new taste which eventually I would like. However, I got sick just before we got into the car and later on Uncle had to stop two more times on the way back to the house. Aunt Martha blamed it on my swim in the ocean, but I insisted it was the strange "fish" called shrimps. Aunt had also eaten shrimps and she had no problem. In any case, whatever it had been, I was fine the next day.

The sightseeing, swimming, and the boardwalk in Atlantic City had been fun, but I had been extremely bored most of the time during which the old people sat around and reminisced. I hoped that there would not be many more long weekends.

Back to Work

I was glad when the long weekend was over and I could go back to work. Being Tuesday already, this would unfortunately be a short week. I loved being at work. My friends at the office liked the story of my early morning swim in Atlantic City. Then Bill Mennen stopped by and asked me what I did on the weekend. When I told him my story about sneaking out for a swim, he frowned and had the same advice which I had already received all weekend: "Do not ever again go swimming *alone* in the ocean." I felt like I had yet another parent watching over me.

Other than my "ocean excursion"—which quickly circulated throughout the Mennen plant—the topic of the day was my dismay about something I had seen on the way to work. About two miles before we got to the Mennen plant, I had noticed a wooded area where workers were busy cutting down trees and bulldozing them into piles. Some of those piles were burning and more trees were being fed into the fires. Shocked about the obvious waste of firewood, I asked what was happening. I was told that the land was being cleared to make room for a housing development. This was extremely disturbing to me, so much so that my coworkers became concerned about my reaction. They could not know of the memories that came back to me, about sitting in bed wrapped in my feather blanket and hoping to keep from freezing to death—about the many people in Berlin who did freeze to death—about others who were burning heirloom furniture and precious books to get whatever warmth they could out of those possessions—the beautiful parquet floors that were fed into stoves—and how lucky we felt for having been able to save our featherbeds from the burning apartment building. I was glad that the Berliners could not see this insane waste of precious firewood. It was difficult for me to accept the fact that the trees were being burned rather than put to a useful purpose.

Eventually, fascination with the building process took over as I watched concrete foundations being poured. Then with amazing speed, almost like mushrooms sprouting up overnight, houses grew in this once wooded area. Up until now, the only construction I had seen in Germany was with brick or stone. I could not believe the speed with which the first one of those houses was framed, and within a few days the roof was on and it looked like a house. Meanwhile, the second house was framed and ready for the roof. This was the first time I saw the production line construction of a housing development.

Every day I looked forward to driving past that area and watching the progress. The development was at a corner tract of land at which two major roads intersected. We had to turn there, so that I could watch it from two sides. Within a couple of months, the first houses were finished and occupied, while the construction project kept going on. To me it was amazing. Wooden houses surely could be built fast. In Germany it took forever before the thick brick walls were up far enough for a building to look like it was going to be a place to live in.

Ten years later, we lived less than a mile from that particular intersection, and I drove past the development, sometimes several times a day. Looking at those houses still brought back the memory of the huge piles of trees being burned, and the shock I received about the waste of precious wood.

A Trip to New York City

Uncle Adolph and Aunt Martha loved to show me new places and to watch my reactions. One Saturday, we went to New York City to see a movie and a show at Radio City Music Hall. Aunt Martha just loved to go to Radio City and to Madison Square Garden. Over the years we would go there many times. I don't think she ever missed a Christmas program at Radio City Music Hall until near the end of her life.

It was my first trip to New York City, about a month after my arrival in the United States. This time I had a totally different impression of the city. We were where the action was. Just to be in the "canyons" between the tall buildings was breathtaking. Then there were the many taxicabs, the shops, the people. I felt exhilarated. It was wonderful to see crowds of people in the streets, like in Berlin. I loved the city. Aunt and Uncle had previously taken me to Newark to shop in the big department store called Bamberger's, which was the New Jersey division of Macy's at that time. Already then I had noticed how much I missed living in a big city. Aunt Martha liked the city, too. During the two–and–a–half years I lived with them, she and I went to New York often just to go shopping. On that particular day in New York we also visited the Statue of Liberty, and we walked the many stairs up to the top to look out of the windows from inside the crown. I remembered the day my ship arrived—not too many weeks before—and the impression the Statue of Liberty had made on me and on everybody else who saw her for the first time.

Our day in New York City had been a wonderful experience for me, packed with many new and exciting impressions. When I told the girls at the office where I had been, Marilyn said that she had never been to New York City. After my enthusiastic report, Marilyn happily told us a few days later that her husband had promised to take her there for her birthday. I was really surprised. Marilyn was only eighteen years old and already married, but she had never been to New York City. I could not believe it. This was another reason for me to not get married and tied down at such a young age.

Life at Home

Aunt and Uncle had many friends, and as soon as I thought I had met everyone, somebody else showed up from somewhere. Now it was the Asal family who visited one evening with the son I had been threatened with. Soon after they arrived, the parents suggested to their son that he take me out for a ride in the car, which he did. Luckily for me, he was as turned off about this obvious matchmaking business as I was. As we had been ordered to do, we drove around a bit. The boy mentioned the names of a couple of the neighboring towns through which we drove, and after about forty–five minutes we felt that we had stayed away long enough. We had a nice conversation within the range of my limited English, but he had no more personal interest in me than I had in him.

I still laugh when I think about the moment we entered the living room. There were four faces staring at us with anticipation. Simultaneously, Mrs. Asal and Aunt Martha said: "Well???" —as though they wanted to know when to send out the wedding invitations. I said: "We drove around. Now I know where Fanwood is, and Scotch Plains. Then we went as far as Rt. 22 and Plainfield, and came back through Westfield." They were speechless and nothing more was said.

Other Activities

Because many German people lived in our general area, there was a German Club which had picnics in the summer and dances on many Saturday nights throughout the year. Aunt and Uncle loved to go to these functions, just to get together with their many German friends. They did not dance, but I made up for it. While Uncle enjoyed a couple of beers with his friends, Aunt Martha caught up on the latest gossip with hers—and I danced my feet off. Most Germans love to dance, and there were quite a few young men who had immigrated and who went to the dances with their relatives. At least there was no shortage of dance partners, although I was still not interested in dating. There were too many new and interesting things going on in my life, and a time–consuming relationship was not one of them.

Several of my early dates, all from the German Club, arranged by Aunt Martha. Uncle Adolph (left) is chaperon.

The problem with going to picnics and dances at the

German Club was that young men would ask me for dates. Even though I told them that I was not dating, it did not keep them from coming and visiting my aunt and uncle. I had the feeling that Aunt Martha encouraged those visits. The German Club was like a big German family. People knew each other well, and these young men were relatives of people whom Aunt and Uncle knew. It was so embarrassing when Aunt Martha kept

I never could resist a swing

pushing me to decide on one of the boys, and to go out with him. She really was serious about trying to get me married off. She even told me that she had started a hope chest for me. I wondered whether it was her "parental role" which she took so seriously, or that she just wanted to give a wedding to a daughter, like some of her friends did at the time.

One day I asked Aunt Martha about her reason for the hurry, and she confessed to me that she did not want me to end up like herself. She did not get married until she was thirty–nine years old, and then it was too late to start a family. Uncle Adolph had waited ten years for her while she went to live in Minneapolis. Well, her concern was understandable, but not even being twenty yet, I did not feel that I was running out of time.

Of more immediate importance to me was the future of my job. I had been given a priceless opportunity by having been placed in an office job rather than in the factory. Now I needed to further myself by accumulating knowledge about the business procedures in this country so that I could feel I was earning the money I was being paid. I decided that after my English was more fluent, I wanted to find a business school which offered night courses in shorthand and business English. After realizing that my German shorthand could not be applied to the English language, I had to learn English shorthand to eventually become a secretary again. Business English also seemed of importance to me because the proper business language and phraseology is more formal than everyday conversation.

Uncle Adolph had already inquired, and had found out for me that Newark Preparatory School in downtown Newark offered the courses I was interested in, but I would need to wait another year before I was ready for it. In the meantime, Uncle found me a tutor who helped me once a week with general sentence structure and grammar.

My Room

At some point we went to a fabric store and selected a nice and cheerful fabric for me to make a bedspread and curtains for my room. Aunt Martha did not know how to sew even a button onto anything. Naturally, it was not easy to convince her that I could sew well enough to take on the project of making curtains and a bedspread. I had never done it, but I knew how to sew my own clothes. We bought a little booklet which gave instructions on how to measure, as well as hints and tricks of the trade, to make the fitted bedspread and pinch–pleated draperies. I felt entirely confident that I could do it. In the end Aunt Martha was amazed and pleased with the finished result.

To do this project, Uncle had put his mother's sewing machine, an old Singer Treadle, into working condition. I did not know this machine existed until we discussed the bedspread and curtains for my room, and I remarked that if I had a sewing machine I could make them myself. Aunt Martha told me about the Singer which was in the basement since the death of Uncle's mother sixteen years earlier, and that I was welcome to use it, if it still worked. I was positively delighted to have a sewing machine again, and down the road I could make clothes for myself.

I loved having my own little room and my desk. While initially I joined Aunt and Uncle in watching television, I would eventually spend the evenings at my desk. I wrote many letters to Mom and Peter, and to my friends. Once I went to night school, I had homework to do. It was then that the custom of having to leave the door open bothered me. When I was studying I found that the television was disturbing my concentration, and I convinced Aunt and Uncle to let me keep my door closed without their feeling insulted. This was not easy to do, since Aunt Martha had previously voiced her displeasure about my apparent wish to shut them out of my life. It was not always easy to do the right thing because I certainly did not want to hurt anybody's feelings, and I tried hard to fit in and not be a burden to the people who had kindly invited me to live in their home.

There were times when I missed Mom and Peter so much that I was sure I wanted to be back in Berlin. Everything was wonderful here, but I could no longer share all aspects of my life on a day–to–day basis, especially with Mom. I was living with relatives who had been strangers until recently, and I missed being a part of my own immediate family. Aunt and Uncle were good to me, and they enjoyed taking me to many places and exposing me to new experiences. However, Aunt Martha was often critical of things I did or did not do, and I would fear her anger when I had inadvertently done something that provoked her disapproval.

Naturally, there were times when I felt homesick for life in Berlin. Even though Cranford was still a part of the metropolitan area of New York City, to me it seemed like a really desolate place to live. Without a car, people could not go anywhere, and even when one did drive around, the streets were so empty without people. One of the most difficult things for me to get used to was seeing only cars and no human beings. My consolation during those times of homesickness would be that all I had to do was to pay off my present debt of the money I owed Aunt and Uncle for my fare to the United States, and save up for an airline ticket back to Berlin. Yes, it would be an airline ticket. No more ships for me! That thought usually made me laugh, and the momentary wave of homesickness would pass.

A Nightmare Returns

One night Aunt Martha came rushing into my room as a result of some commotion she had heard. It was the middle of the night and everybody had been asleep. She found me trying to get dressed, and while still not totally awake, I was urging her to hurry up, because we did not have much time. "We must hurry and get to the cellar," I told her. Aunt Martha did not understand what was going on, but I insisted that I heard the sirens and that the bombs would start falling momentarily. We must hurry. I was hysterical and shaking violently, while fumbling with my clothes. Uncle showed up, puzzled. I kept talking about the sirens and Aunt said there weren't any. I had heard them— they still rang in my ears. Aunt Martha then figured it out. Although she had not been awakened by the noise, an ambulance must have passed by with the sirens howling. In an effort to calm me down, she kept reassuring me that it had been only an ambulance and not an air raid. She warmed up some milk for me to drink, and told me to go back to sleep. I was still shaking and could not go to sleep for a long time, as I kept hearing the sirens and reliving the terror.

The sound of the ambulance's sirens evoked the dreadful memories of my childhood, even in my sleep. It was upsetting to me to think that nine years after the war, a sound can bring back so much terror. In Germany the sirens of emergency vehicles had been changed to other signals. People could not tolerate the oscillating whine of sirens. In this country I could not do anything about the sirens, but had to learn to live with them. However, each time I heard the dreaded sound of that particular siren signal, my body got a tremendous shot of adrenaline and then I would freeze or tremble.

Fires in a fireplace did that to me, too, and it was many years before I would not turn and run away from a fireplace. There is no question that the war had scarred people, perhaps for life.

Special Neighbors

There was a nice young couple living next door to us. Their name was Anderson and they had three young children, two girls and a boy. The tragedy was that both little girls had cystic fibrosis and were doomed to die. Gail, the oldest, was my special little friend. She often came to visit me with her sister Patti in tow. Aunt Martha always made sure to have some of her anise cookies on hand as treats for the little girls. They could eat only certain foods which did not contain any fat whatsoever, and just a minimum of sugar. Gail was six years old, and extremely thin and frail. She appeared smaller than her two–year–old sister, Patti, who was not yet as sick as Gail was. My bedroom window faced the Anderson's house, and at night I could hear Gail cough and gasp for air. She slept in an oxygen tent, and it was heartbreaking to listen to her whenever she had an especially bad night.

Gail was a thoughtful little girl. One time we came home from the beach and I was getting out of the car with a big beach ball. Gail came to me across the lawn and asked: "Do you have children?" I told her I did not. Only then did she ask me if I would give her the ball. I was touched by this little girl's considering the possibility of there being other children before asking for the ball for herself. I was devastated when Gail died a year later, and her sister two years after that. The boy did not have the disease, and when the Andersons took a chance by having another baby, the new baby girl was healthy, too. All of us had been anxiously awaiting the results of the tests, which could not be taken until the baby was six weeks old.

Cars

Spending two hours a day riding to and from work, I had nothing to do but to observe everything that was going on along the way. Being nineteen years old, my major focus was on cars, of course. I liked cars, and it did not take me long to know every make and model, as well as their original paint designs. I could tell at a glance which cars had been repainted. At that time, the United States had not as yet been invaded by foreign cars, so that getting to know all makes and models was much easier than it would be today. The color schemes were simpler, too. In 1954, cars sporting a two–tone paint design were still fairly rare.

A wonderful surprise happened to me one morning in the town of Springfield. I could hardly believe my eyes when I saw a Volkswagen Beetle going in the opposite direction. The sight of this familiar car was like a warm greeting from home. It touched me so much that I thought about it throughout the day. Of course, everybody at work and at home heard about the unusual event. Volkswagens and other foreign cars were not being imported at that time. Two days later I saw the same Volkswagen again. Since Alice was dropped off by her husband on the main street of Springfield where she joined our car pool, we sometimes had to wait a few minutes for her arrival. At that time I had fun watching for the Volkswagen which passed by at about the same time each morning, and I saw it fairly regularly two or three times a week. It was always a highlight in my day, and I wish the owner knew how happy he made me during my early months in a new country.

New Customs and Habits

As time went on, I learned new customs and habits as well as etiquette which applied here. One of the customs which really appealed to me was the idea of wearing informal clothing when going on trips. A couple of times we had occasion to stay overnight at a motel. Motels as they existed in the 1950's were totally unknown in Germany at that time. I thought it was wonderful to just drive up to a little cabin and walk into the room—no fancy hotel lobby to go through—no elegant luggage required to be carried by a formal bellboy—and, best of all, no need to dress up for the occasion. Here we could be in comfortable travel clothes—shorts and a T–shirt to befit the hot climate in the summer—and be acceptable. In Germany at the time, when people went on vacation they would travel in their best clothes, or even buy a new wardrobe for the occasion. While I had never stayed in a hotel in Germany, I had seen fancy hotels in movies and in the cities. They always looked so overwhelming to me.

Personal comfort seemed to be a way of life in America, and I took to it without hesitation. As soon as I had found out that sitting on the floor was not frowned upon, even by the German friends, I happily adopted the habit. Being so much younger than Aunt and Uncle's friends, and usually associating with children or animals, if present, I would sit on the floor with them and find it surprisingly comfortable. To my delight, nobody ever told me that it was not acceptable. Unlike what was left to us in Germany after the war, here the floors in people's homes were either covered with wall–to–wall carpeting—at that time not even known in Germany—or with beautiful area rugs. It was no hardship at all to sit on the floor, and I like it to this day.

A few years later when visiting my relatives in Berlin, I sat on the floor in front of a phonograph while listening to records. I will never forget the astonished look on Aunt Charlotte's face when she walked into the room and saw me. Shaking her head, she asked: "Don't you have chairs in America?" She found it unbelievable that anyone thought it was comfortable, and would want to sit on the floor. Besides, it was bad manners. Feet belonged on the floor, but people sat on chairs. That was the German way. However, I lived in America now, and while some behaviors may have been bad manners in Germany, they were quite acceptable here—according to lessons learned in my new country.

The Mennen Company's Annual Picnic

In early September, the extremely popular Mennen Company Picnic took place. Having heard much about it, I was looking forward to attending. I liked picnics and was particularly looking forward to this one because I would meet the families of some of the people I worked with. Whenever my coworkers talked about their husbands and children, it would be nice to picture the faces of their loved ones.

There was a lot of good food at the picnic, as well as games, swimming, and later in the afternoon, dancing. I thoroughly enjoyed the day, except for one incident. Marilyn, the eighteen–year–old who worked in my office, had mentioned to me that she and her husband were bringing the husband's brother to the picnic. They had apparently told him about me and, being single, he wanted to meet me. I later figured out that this was supposed to be a blind date, which I did not understand at the time, nor would I have agreed to. In any case, I went my own ways at the picnic, not realizing that I had been expected to spend all of my time with their brother. Marilyn was a bit sour about my behavior when they wanted to leave the picnic early and go to a drive–in movie, and I refused to go along as their brother's date. I did not want to go on any dates with the brother, especially since I was beginning to sense that matchmakers were at work, which turned me off once again.

A Birthday Party for Me

On September thirteenth I celebrated my twentieth birthday. Aunt Martha had fun inviting not only her friends, but also one of the young men from the German Club who occasionally came to visit at our home. She made an ice cream cake for me, and there were candles on the cake and balloons floating on the ceiling. I had never seen an ice cream cake, and was enchanted with it. However, it nearly crashed when I was asked to carry it downstairs to our party room. I did not know that the cake was slippery, and when I walked down the fairly steep stairs, I must have tilted the plate slightly and the cake came close to sliding off the plate. Aunt and Uncle had invited several of their friends for dinner, and it was a nice American–style birthday party.

Aunt Martha made a cake for my 20th birthday party, and invited some of her friends, as well as a boy from the German Club.

At the office, whenever someone had a birthday, got engaged, married, or had a baby, it was customary to buy a box of candy and pass it around in our department, as well as in the neighboring ones, where the question usually was: "What's the occasion?" My English was getting good enough so that I could express some of my humor. Not really liking the idea of having to say: "It's my birthday," I said instead: "My mother had a baby," and when everybody perked up with attention and curiosity, I added: "Twenty years ago." They loved it and we had a lot of laughs. Some people did not make the connection right away, but rather believed the first part of my announcement, which then caused even more laughs.

Emergency—I am Losing My Ride to Work!

My English was improving quite rapidly, but it was still not good enough to always follow a general conversation in a group, such as in the car pool. I might get the gist of it and know what they were talking about generally, though this was not always the case. One of those occasions on which I missed the point nearly left me stranded.

It was during the last week in September when I kept understanding bits and pieces of conversation about a move. As the other girls were asking Jim questions about a new house, and mentioned their worries about getting rides to work, I finally put some pieces together and realized that something was going on which would affect our car pool. Nobody had said anything directly to me or asked me any questions. Apparently no one realized that I had not understood what their discussions were all about. One evening when Jim dropped me off at home I asked him directly, and to my dismay he confirmed what I had feared. Jim was planning to move closer to Morristown in just three weeks! The question was how the four of us would get to work after Jim could no longer give us rides.

This came as a shock to me. I lived the farthest distance away. "How will you get to work after Jim moves?" Alice asked me the next day. I did not know. She suggested that I buy a car, and that she, Beverly, and Alice C. would ride with me and pay me for the gas. They asked *me* to buy a car? I had no means to do so. I was still paying off the money my relatives had advanced me for my trip to the United States. That plus room and board scarcely left me enough money for modest personal expenses such as postage stamps to write home, and for occasional small holiday gifts.

Reluctantly I told the family about my predicament and presented my plan. I suggested that I rent a room in Morristown and move there, so that I would be within close range of The Mennen Company and able to find a ride to work. Uncle said: "Absolutely not." Aunt Martha agreed. So did Uncle's father. Uncle's point was made from his own experience. As a young bachelor he had lived in a room in Philadelphia, and he said it had been very lonely for him. He could not afford to go out much, and except for an occasional movie, he spent a lot of time sitting in his room. He pointed out that being a girl, I would not want to go out alone, and Morristown was not that big a town with much going on anyway. Besides, the room I would find in somebody's home would not necessarily be within walking distance of the downtown area. Furthermore, during the winter months it would be dark at night and I should not be walking around anyway. All right, they made their point.

The result of the family conference was that Uncle Adolph would teach me how to drive. Then they would help me buy a car by advancing the money for it and just adding it onto my debt. That way I would not have to pay interest on a car loan. I was horrified about going into debt for a couple of years, having just about paid back all of the previous loan. However, they educated me about the common practice of buying not only homes, but also cars on time payments. The fact that sooner or later I would want or need to have a car had been clear to everyone—except me—and they felt that the time had come, albeit a little sooner than expected.

A Driver's License and a New Car

There was no time to lose. Jim was moving in less than three weeks. Uncle Adolph started to give me driving lessons immediately. At the same time he went out looking for a used car. Uncle had some good and practical ideas about the type of car he would like to find for me. Having always had good luck with Ford vehicles, he was looking for a small Ford, or else a Chevrolet. He told me that it would be wise to stay away from the big models because every repair, new tire, or whatever I might need would be more expensive, as would be the additional gasoline consumption for the forty–four mile round trip to work.

I knew what I would have liked. My very favorite, my dream car, was the Army Jeep, my old Love from the Berlin days since 1946. Somebody at work even told me about a special deal where I could buy one for one hundred dollars, if I sold a hundred of them. I thought that I could. Why, everybody on earth would just love to have one of those marvelous Jeeps, I was sure of that. Uncle told me that they would not, or people would already have bought them. This was hard for me to believe.

Uncle Adolph spent several evenings looking for a suitable car for me. The outcome was that at that particular point in time, the only cars he could find which were in reasonably good condition were the big ones, such as Cadillacs, Buicks, and Lincolns. However, it was early October and the end of the current model year. The 1955 models had just come out and looked real sporty after a change in body styling and two–tone paint designs. Some leftover 1954 models were now available at good discounts. Uncle suggested that we buy a brand new Ford. I went into shock.

While it was obvious that eventually I would save up to buy a car, never would I have dreamed of owning a new car to start out with. One

My first car, a 1954 Ford Mainline. I purchased this car when my car pool driver moved and I lost my ride. I actually owned the car before I had a driver's license. Aunt and Uncle lent me the money which I repaid over two years' time.

evening we went out and bought a plain Ford Mainline. I selected the spruce green color rather than the blue one, which was also available. It was plain all right—no chrome strips, no nice extras, dull gray interior, and of course manual transmission. The only extras Uncle insisted on were tubeless tires and a heater. The car cost eighteen hundred dollars plus the charge for the tires and heater.

I was as proud as a peacock. My brand new car was sitting in the driveway, and I did not even have a driver's license yet. That was to be the next step. After we brought the car home, some of the neighbors came to look at it. The men always want to see the engine—it was a V–8—and I was horror stricken when Uncle opened the hood and I looked inside. There was no floor below the engine and I could see the driveway. My beautiful new engine would get dirty in the rain! The only car engine I had ever seen was the Volkswagen Beetle's, and that one is inside. I insisted that Ford forgot to put the floor into my engine compartment, and I wanted to go and exchange the car. Everyone was amused, and I received my first lesson about cars.

At this point, I had less than a week's time to get my driver's license. The date for the test was set for the following Monday, and if I failed I would be unable to go to work on Tuesday. I had already told my three potential car pool riders that I wanted to drive alone during the first week, before I took on the responsibility of taking other people with me. They thought that was a good idea and made other temporary arrangements for themselves.

The written examination for the driver's license test worried me quite a bit. After being in the United States only four months, I wondered if my English would be good enough to understand the questions. It turned out that I did well, having only one wrong answer out of eighty questions. The examiner told me this was an unusually good score. The road test was easy, and I had my driver's license. The family was ecstatic. I still wonder how I could have been so lucky to have passed the written examination. I had studied the book thoroughly, of course, but I feared that I may not have understood the substance correctly. Uncle Adolph was especially proud of me for having learned how to drive in only three weeks. It never occurred to him that the credit was his for his patience and understanding during the driving lessons. Aunt Martha never drove a car at all, and Uncle always had to take her to wherever she wanted to go. It must have been quite a nuisance for him, though he never complained.

Nobody seemed surprised to see me at work on Tuesday. I had told everyone that I would not be able to show up if I did not pass the test, because I no longer had a ride. Bill Mennen was also proud of me, and he laughed when I told him that I had had serious doubts. He didn't have any. He was so pleased about my license, one could have thought I was his daughter. Everybody congratulated me wherever I went that day. The news had spread to every corner of the office area as well as to the manufacturing plant, and people really made me feel like a member of one big family. Everyone was enthusiastic about my being able to drive so soon after coming to this country, and proud of me for my accomplishment.

"Now you have wheels and can go places," said Bill Mennen. Yes I could, but there was the question of being able to afford to go anywhere. For the foreseeable future—I figured about two years—I was paying off the car. But I was happy. Having a car of my own did give me a feeling of freedom. I was able to stop and do little errands after work once I had dropped off my last rider. It also helped out Aunt Martha in that I could run errands for her, or take her to visit her friends without Uncle Adolph having all of the burden of chauffeuring her everywhere.

Financially it was not any more difficult than it had been in Berlin where I paid off my bicycle for a year and gave the rest of my earnings to Mom to help with the family expenses. Here in the United States, I cleared $34.50 a week from which I paid off twenty dollars for the car and ten dollars for room and board. Had I not had the three ladies riding with me, I could not have afforded the gas to drive to work for the forty–four miles round trip each day. Joyriding was not an option at that time.

On the fourth day after I received my driver's license, The Mennen Company's annual dinner dance took place and I ventured to go to it, now that I had a way of getting there. This was the first time I had to find my way to an unknown destination, going by the instructions that were given out on how to find the place in West Orange. Near the end of the evening, Bill Mennen asked me whether I would be able to find my way home. I told him that I thought so, and that all I had to do was to reverse the instructions to find the main street in Springfield. From there on it would be the same way I took to and from work every day.

Being somewhat concerned about leaving me on my own so late in the evening, he suggested that I let him know when I wanted to leave. I could then follow him to Springfield since he had to travel in the same direction. I was ready to leave at that time, and was grateful that I did not have to try and read directions in the reverse. I could not even begin to voice how much I appreciated his thoughtfulness.

A Letter from the Berlin Office

Sometime in the fall I received a note from Dr. Burmester. He told me how sad he was that I had not written a word to let him or the office know how I was faring in my chosen new home and country. "Everyone is asking me about you, and I cannot tell them anything. We are interested in your fate," he wrote. Then his humor broke through in that he told me about the many "emergencies" they have had to cope with at the office since I left. "Everything is in a terrible state of mess," and he blamed me for not being there to help them find things. "You need to return immediately," he teased.

There was also the possibility of a business trip to the United States on which he would accompany Herr Heyn and an architect on a visit to The Mennen Company's plant early the following year, wrote Dr. Burmester. Then he went on to say "since you are not writing to us, we just have to come over there ourselves and check up on you."

This got me going on a nice letter to dear old Dr. Burmester. In my enthusiasm about my new life in a new country I had obviously cut one too many ties. Now I feared that I had hurt his feelings. After all, Dr. Burmester had been exceedingly kind to me. Not only did I owe it to him to have a job at The Mennen Company, but I was sure he had strongly suggested to Bill Mennen that he find me a place in the office, and to look after me. I remembered that Dr. Burmester had not liked my idea of working on a production line.

The First Thanksgiving

Thanksgiving was a new holiday for me in the way it is celebrated in the United States. In Germany, by comparison, the farmers celebrate Thanksgiving at the end of September when their crops have been harvested and are safely stored to be used during the long winter. It is a

Thanksgiving dinner

time of giving thanks for the food that has been grown and ripened, and for the weather that had been beneficial to the growth of their crops. I remember the Sunday of Giving Thanks being celebrated in church when we lived in the village of Straupitz. People in the cities, however, were practically unaware of this holiday, as they were not growing anything.

When I first learned about the upcoming Thanksgiving holiday, I liked the idea of everyone celebrating Thanksgiving in appreciation of the food we are eating without normally giving much thought to where it comes from, and of who does the backbreaking work to grow it for us. I found the idea of the original Thanksgiving wonderful, and it is certainly appropriate that Thanksgiving became a traditional holiday. In addition, we have reason to be thankful that the pilgrims were successful in growing enough food for themselves so that they could survive in this new land to which they had come. They paved the way for all of us.

Aunt Martha decided to cook Thanksgiving dinner at our house. At The Mennen Company, every employee received a turkey for Thanksgiving. The one I brought home weighed nearly fifteen pounds. Aunt Martha was delighted and invited a German couple and Uncle's brother's family to help us eat it.

I could not ever have imagined what a feast Thanksgiving would be. Having eaten many outstanding dinners at our house, this one topped all of them. The quantities were unbelievable and the food preparation went on for days. Cranberry sauce was made from fresh cranberries, and the yams were not from cans. There was every condiment imaginable, and choices were nearly unlimited. I got filled up just looking at all the food. It was the first time I ever tasted turkey.

If one had not eaten enough during the scrumptious main meal, there was homemade mince pie, pumpkin pie, and apple pie—as well as whipped cream for all of them—for later on. It was an unforgettable feast!

While Aunt Martha was cooking, I polished the silver, washed the good china, and the crystal serving dishes because they had not been used since the year before.

Thanksgiving was certainly a memorable experience, especially for me personally, as I had much to be thankful for.

My First Christmas in America

Christmas was approaching, and overall it turned out to be a much happier experience than I was afraid it might be, considering that it was my first Christmas away from home, and that I missed Mom and Peter very much.

First, there were the Christmas carols. I was delighted with happy Jingle Bells, Rudolph's red nose, and a romantic walk in Winter Wonderland. Topping it off was crazy Alvin with his harmonica, and the other funny chipmunks. I found those cheerful songs to befit the happy, joyous Christmas season. To me, they were much more fun than "Silent Night" and many of the other German slow dragging church–type songs, which sound more sad than joyful. American Christmas carols are lively. One could dance to them, and I loved them!

Then there was a trip to New York City. Aunt and Uncle always went to Radio City Music Hall to see the Christmas Show. This year they had fun watching me enjoy the wonders of New York City during the Christmas season— Rockefeller Center's enormous Christmas tree, ice skaters, Macy's window decorations, and all. We ate out, shopped for Christmas presents, and enjoyed the holiday spirit of the big city. Naturally, I could not stop thinking of Berlin, and how much I missed living in a city. Aunt and Uncle bought me a dress for Christ-

Christmas shopping in New York City with Aunt Martha.

mas to supplement my meager wardrobe. We had fun shopping for it, and I really appreciated their thoughtfulness. They knew that there was no money at all in my budget for clothes since I paid nearly every cent I earned to reduce my debt.

While I found almost everything in America *wonderful,* the American Christmas tree became a matter of concern to me. There were several reasons.

Already starting in early December, I saw Christmas trees in people's windows which were all decorated and lit up. I found this strange. In Germany, it was the custom to decorate the tree on the day of Christmas Eve, or perhaps a day or two before, if it were a Sunday and the family was doing it together. Preceding Christmas were the four Sundays of Advent, during which a wreath made of balsam tree branches and decorated with red ribbons and red candles, adorned the family's dining table. Christmas music was not played anywhere until the first Sunday of Advent. Christmas decorations were not for sale until after the last Sunday in November, which is a memorial day for the dead.

I was most disturbed by the lights which I saw on these early Christmas trees. They were too odd to be Christmas tree lights; I thought they were either personal preferences or had a significance in another religion. The lights were colored light bulbs, much like the ones used on merry–go–rounds in Germany. I found them so strange that I never even asked any questions about them. I decided that the people who had them on their trees must be from some faraway countries where Christmas was not really celebrated as such, and that this was also most likely the reason for their having the trees up such a long time before our Christmas holiday. We, of course, would have candles on our Christmas tree, as has always been the custom in Germany.

Our Christmas Tree

As Christmas approached, Uncle realized that, even though I was no longer a child, I was not going to do without a Christmas tree. It turned out that Aunt Martha and Uncle Adolph no longer had any tree decorations. Being a childless couple, they were usually invited to the homes of their friends during the holidays, and saw no reason for putting up a tree in their home. They had therefore disposed of their Christmas tree decorations years ago. Noticing that I was devastated when I found out that they were not planning on having a tree, Uncle assured me that we would go out and buy a Christmas tree and ornaments for it.

We went shopping for a tree first. It was another learning experience for me. Those strange trees were not Christmas trees. I was used to balsam firs. Scotch pines were evergreen trees, but to me they were not Christmas trees. I did not see where one could hang ornaments because their branches were too dense to let anything hang on them.

Uncle and I searched at many lots which sold trees, and we finally found one that was at least similar to a *real* Christmas tree, and would do. It was a hemlock, and the branches were so soft and flexible that I expressed concern about whether or not they would be strong enough to hold up the candles. "Candles?" Uncle Adolph was aghast. "There will be no candles on any tree," he lectured me. "People here live in wooden houses which would burn down like matches. Nobody in America ever puts candles on a Christmas tree. It would be insane." That was Uncle's final word, and I knew that this time I could not do anything to change his mind.

I was heartbroken. When I asked him if we were going to have those "merry–go–round lights" I had seen, on our Christmas tree, I was told that they were the only kind existing. There were not even any electric candles available, as some people had in Germany. I felt dispirited. How can Christmas be the same without candles on the tree, at least electric ones? But then I was in a new land and had to learn, and put up with, new customs. It meant that Christmas would not be the same, not now, and not in the future. This greatly different Christmas tree tradition really hurt me. I wished Mom were here. She would have come up with an invention. Mom would have invented electric candles for American Christmas trees.

The cheerful Christmas carols made up for a lot, so that my Christmas spirit had not been snuffed out. Aunt Martha, true to her reputation among her friends, baked cookies as if she were a factory. I had never seen so many different varieties in a bakery, let alone in somebody's house. Uncle, who had quite a sweet tooth, bemoaned the fact that we wouldn't get to eat most of these wonderful cookies. "She gives them all away to the friends and neighbors," he whispered to me. "We get to eat only the 'cripples'," meaning the ones which did not look picture perfect. He made me laugh, but I found out that he was not too far off.

The Mennen Company Christmas Party
—and a Gift that Touched my Heart

The Mennen Company traditionally gave a Christmas party for all employees on the last workday before Christmas. We had received a generous Christmas bonus earlier, and now everyone was looking forward to the Christmas Dinner Dance.

At the office, I had been drawing Jingle Bells on my calendar each day to count down the days until the Christmas party, mainly because of the dance. Dancing was still my favorite recreation.

My friend Lois expressed concern that we might not be asked to dance by anyone since we were an all girl's department. We agreed, and created the "Christmas Dance List" to avoid the possibility of being wallflowers. Our Christmas Dance Lists became immensely popular. As the news of our dance lists spread throughout the company, the guys stopped by our office and eagerly signed up for dances. Even a number of sales managers who were attending a meeting at the company from different parts of the country signed up. We each collected dozens of signatures, even though there were not going to be enough dances to accommodate everyone. One of the men had the idea to sign up for intermission instead. We had much fun with our dance lists.

Every department had its own small party before the start of the big Christmas party which was held in the warehouse because of the space needed for about 350 employees. This was mainly a gift exchange among the people we immediately worked with. The office staff held this party in the cafeteria, where each office department used a couple of tables for their own little celebration. We had drawn names and bought a small gift for that person.

After all gifts had been distributed among the Typing Pool girls, there was one more gift left which had my name on it. Upon opening it, I found a lovely bracelet consisting of square, green stones in golden settings, perfect to go with the clothes I owned. The note read: "Merry Christmas, Inge" and was signed "John."

John who? There were many men named John at The Mennen Company, but I could not think of anyone who would give me a present. The girls were giggling and guessing. Even the girls from the neighboring offices joined in and verbalized their guesses. I was stunned and somewhat embarrassed. All of the men named John that I knew were married men, and there was no reason for any one of them to give me a present.

With the main party starting, my wish to thank someone for the gift had to be put on hold until after Christmas. I had to arrange for some detective work to be done. The girls were beginning to believe that I really had no clue as to who this mysterious John might be.

The Christmas party was a memorable affair. There was a sumptuous buffet dinner, drinks, entertainment, and dancing. There was even a photographer who took a group picture with one of those rotating cameras so that everybody could get into one picture. I kept thinking about the bracelet and wondering who the giver might be. The mystery had to be solved promptly.

My first priority after Christmas was to tell my coworkers that I really needed their help. I wanted to thank someone for the gift, and I also had to extinguish Aunt Martha's hopes of a possible suitor on the horizon. She had already started a hope chest for me—just in case. I am not kidding.

Back at work, my "detectives" pointed out that John, the cafeteria manager, always seemed to be especially interested in my welfare, which I had not particularly noticed, although he talked to me every chance there was. He was a man in his late fifties, and it was true that he said a few words to me every time I went through the line in the cafeteria. Aunt Martha always packed my lunch and I bought just a cup of tea, because I could not afford to spend money on lunches when I had a car to pay off. The girls teased me at times, suggesting that if I brought my own tea bags, John would probably be glad to give me the hot water so that I could save the five cents for the tea.

My first Christmas Eve in America, with my little admirer, Raymond, and Uncle's nephew Billy in the background.

Thinking about John's grandfatherly interest in me, I agreed that he might have given me the bracelet. Why he would do that I did not know, but we had no other lead. When I was in the cafeteria that morning, I approached John hesitantly and asked him. He acknowledged that he gave me the bracelet. "Why did you give me a present?" was my next question, and here is his touching story:

"A long time ago, I was an immigrant from Italy. When Christmas came, I had a job, but I did not yet have any close friends with whom I could spend Christmas. I was young, and homesick for my family. I could not afford to buy a Christmas tree. I spent Christmas all alone in my room—and I did not get a single present. I did not want *that* to happen to you."

I had tears in my eyes and so did John, but I was happy to assure him that I was living with relatives and had received many presents. He seemed relieved. I thought that everybody knew I lived with relatives, but apparently he did not.

I Survived my First Christmas away from Home

My fear of having a bout with homesickness had been real. This was my first Christmas away from Mom and Peter, and I had been dreading it. However, the many activities and new customs kept me occupied. A lot of credit goes to the cheerful American Christmas tunes, but mostly to Aunt Martha and Uncle Adolph who did everything they could to make me happy.

Since I enjoyed everything that was new and different, I did get used to our Christmas tree with the colored lights, and I thought that it was very American. My relatives and their German friends had kept up the custom of celebrating Christmas on Christmas Eve, so that I did not yet have to suffer the shortening of the celebration of Christmas to merely one day. That was in store for me years later. We had a wonderful Christmas. Uncle's brother and his family as well as the Wehr family joined us, and it was fun to have my special little friend, six–year–old Raymond, among us.

Mom and Peter sent me a painting of the *MS Italia,* the ship on which I immigrated. I had mailed a postcard to them during the voyage, and Mom had found someone who painted the ship from the postcard. It was a thoughtful surprise for me, and is a lifelong remembrance of the start of a venture which changed our lives forever. A photo of this painting is in Chapter One.

Aunt and Uncle gave me a starter set of silver–plated flatware with my initial engraved, for my hope chest, and Aunt Martha promised to keep adding items to this hope chest from now on. I did not know whether to be amused or not about the obvious hint. Aunt Martha was certainly hoping much more than I was.

New Year's Eve

To celebrate the end of 1954 and the arrival of 1955, we were trekking to Allentown and Philadelphia to visit the folks there.

Tony, one of the electricians at work who regularly repaired our dictating equipment, was always teasing me. Being in a new country and unfamiliar with many of the customs, I was pretty gullible, to the amusement of others. Just before New Year's Eve, Tony asked me where I would be celebrating. I told him that I would be in Allentown with my relatives and their friends. He then casually dropped the hint that he hoped there would be some nice young men present on New Year's Eve because it was the custom to kiss everyone at midnight. Noticing my expression of alarm, he went on to say that there was no way out; that it would really be rude if I did not kiss all of the men present. Tony knew, of course, that I would be stuck with only old people again, and he could already visualize my dismay at having to kiss them. He also knew that I believed him. To be sure, I checked with the Typing Pool girls after Tony had left, and was told that he was right. I did have to kiss everyone.

I tried to convince Aunt and Uncle that I wanted to stay at home while they went to Pennsylvania. That way I could be with Mom and Peter in my thoughts, and have time alone as well as some peace and quiet. I had had somewhat of a difficult time on Christmas Eve, thinking about Mom and Peter every minute of the day and knowing what they would be doing at certain times. My relatives did not want to hear of my staying at home alone. They knew that Christmas Eve had been hard on me, but Aunt and Uncle felt it would be better for me to be with people. They were also planning to take me to Philadelphia to see the traditional Mummers Parade on New Year's Day, which I really should not miss, according to them.

All right I tried, but I had no choice. The drive to Allentown was fun. I enjoyed seeing everybody's outdoor Christmas decorations. Uncle Adolph gave us a special treat by driving through the city of Bethlehem to see the spectacular decorations there.

Too soon we arrived at the Maetje's house. As the evening of New Year's Eve dragged on, I got more restless. As usual, it was boring without children or pets present, and Aunt and Uncle were reminiscing with their friends. Meanwhile I was dreading for midnight to come and having to kiss the old guys, especially Carl Maetje who was in his late fifties, had a hare lip, and who always made remarks which made me feel uncomfortable. By the time eleven o'clock came around, I had worried myself into a headache and used the excuse to go to bed. They argued and tried to get me to stay up, but I insisted that I was really feeling awful and needed to get some sleep. One of the women suggested that perhaps I felt a bit homesick. She had noticed that all evening I had been counting ahead the six hours to where it would be midnight in Germany. I loved her for that excuse and agreed that it was a part of my problem.

I must have gone to sleep immediately and was glad when it was morning and New Year's Eve was over with. We started out early in order to get to Philadelphia in time to secure good standing room at the curb for watching the Mummers Parade. It was bitterly cold as we stood lining the street all day, and watched as float after float, accompanied by bands playing marching music, passed by us. I don't remember the reason for the Mummers Parade, but vaguely recall that it was a Polish custom. The musicians played great music, and as always when I heard marches, polkas, or whatever music lends itself to dancing, I wanted to dance.

Back at work the next day, Tony stopped in to ask me whether I had kissed all the men, and I told him how I had gotten out of it. He roared with laughter, and then I found out that he had been "pulling my leg" once again.

3

1955
Starting to Fit In
Age Twenty

My Life in America

In time I began to feel that I was starting to fit in, and I was enjoying life in America. I loved my job and working at Mennen. It was the most cheerful of places at which to work. My English was developing rapidly, and having a car of my own gave me freedom. While I still missed the special "bounce" of city life in Berlin, I was learning to adapt to the ways of this country.

Bill Mennen and Mr. Oldenburg were still taking a personal interest in my overall progress. Bill Mennen was absolutely delighted that I had learned how to drive a car so soon. He lived in a neighboring town and occasionally asked me for a ride, either from the plant home, or from his home to the plant. The first time he wanted me to drop him off at his house, he asked me in to introduce me to his

With Bill Mennen at his home

family. He especially wanted me to meet his daughter, Stephanie, which pleased me because it would be nice to be able to put a face with her name. Bill Mennen always talked about her, but in the way he did I pictured a three or four–year–old. To my surprise, Stephanie was fifteen and taller than I was. I was praised and held up as an example to her because I had asked to use the phone to tell my aunt why I was delayed that evening so that she would not worry. Apparently, Mr. and Mrs. Mennen were trying to teach their daughter to always call them if she could not be home when expected.

Visitors from Berlin

In January we received word that my former boss, Herr Heyn, was planning to visit The Mennen Company in early February to discuss the feasibility of building a manufacturing plant for Mennen products in Berlin. He would be accompanied by an architect, Professor Noth, and, of course, by his old friend Dr. Burmester without whom no trip into a foreign country could take place. Dr. Burmester—diplomat, statesman, interpreter, and loyal friend! Neither Herr Heyn nor Professor Noth spoke any English.

I was excited to hear the news of their visit, which was brought to me personally by Bill Mennen. A few days before their arrival, Bill Mennen told me that I would be assigned the job of driving "my friends" around to wherever they wanted to go in their free time. This would give me the chance to spend a little time with them. I was delighted and appreciated his considerate arrangement.

I was told that I would have the use of the company's station wagon, and Bill Mennen took me out for a test drive to make sure I wouldn't have any questions about the car. He then gave me a credit card to charge the gas to, and told me to sign his name on the gas slips. He also told me that he had cleared my time away from the office with my supervisor, Dottie Smith.

It was wonderful to see my former employers again. Dr. Burmester was especially happy to see with his own eyes that I had adapted well to my new surroundings. I was proud to be their chauffeur, and I certainly knew my way around. While each of them had driver's licenses in Germany, a regular international driver's license was not valid in the United States at that time. The international traffic signs were not in use in this country, and one had to know English to drive here. For example, the way to mark a one–way street here was a sign saying "One Way—Do Not Enter," instead of the international symbol of a white circle with a red horizontal line, which is used in the rest of the world.

Visitors from Berlin—my former boss, Herr Heyn (left) and architect Professor Noth (right) with Bill Mennen.

Once their business at Mennen was finished I drove them to Philadelphia for an appointment to look at one other pharmaceutical manufacturing plant. The architect was collecting ideas for the design of the new plant in Berlin. Then we were free to sightsee a little bit of New Jersey.

Unfortunately, the weather was not at its best in February, but we did have a sunny day for a drive down to Atlantic City. I had been so enchanted with boardwalks and all of the activities there in the summertime that it never occurred to me that there would be just about nothing open during the winter months. It was pretty dreary and dead in Atlantic City, and my friends were not at all impressed. They probably wondered why we had driven a hundred miles each way to see what turned out to be a deserted boardwalk and closed little shops. Besides, they had seen elegant seaside resorts in Germany, Italy, and southern France, the likes of which I could not even imagine. I grew up knowing only the miseries of a horrible war and its aftermath. My friends did not show their disappointment, not wanting to thwart my enthusiasm.

But we did have a nice time together and lots of laughs and reminiscing about the office in Berlin. Dr. Burmester still had a cardboard box instead of a desk, and he was hoping to have his own office once the new plant was built and there was more office space. Herr Heyn teased his friend by telling him that it was wishful thinking on his part.

When I thanked Bill Mennen afterwards for arranging it so that I could spend time with my friends, he told me how happy he was that we had such a good time together. I felt that he was a very thoughtful person, and there was no way I could ever thank him enough for everything that he was always doing for me. All those little things meant a great deal to me as I tried to adjust to a new country as well as being on my own for the first time in my life.

I saw Dr. Burmester and Herr Heyn one more time in the United States, about three years later when I had my own apartment with Mom and Peter and they were our dinner guests. I also saw them twice on visits to Berlin in the early 1960's.

Both were deceased when I returned to Berlin next in 1980. However, not knowing this and trying to visit Dr. Burmester on the chance that he was still alive, even though he would have been about ninety, I met his much younger widow, Irmgard. She seemed to know me well from Dr. Burmester's talking about me. We became friends and our friendship lasted until her death ten years later. She visited me and my family in the Washington, DC area twice, for a month, and we always had a great time together. Irmgard kept alive my memory of Dr. Burmester as a treasured friend.

Mennen Hires Another German

One day in March, I was called down to the Personnel Department to help someone with filling out a job application. The applicant was a young German man by the name of Elmer Leibfried. He was two years younger than I, and was being hired to work in Production. After helping him with the application and telling him how wonderful it is to work for The Mennen Company, I also passed on to him the words of wisdom which I had received from Mr. Oldenburg less than a year earlier: "You can learn a lot if you keep your eyes and ears open, and your mouth shut."

It was a nice feeling to know that another German worked at Mennen. While our paths seldom crossed, it was comforting to know that someone else was there from my country of origin. Upon occasional meetings, a brief verbal exchange in German made it seem less lonely, even though I did have a lot of friends at Mennen.

Elmer worked in Production for a number of years before moving on to another job elsewhere. He and my brother became lifelong friends.

Elmer was the best man at Peter's wedding, and Peter had been an usher at Elmer's wedding. The two families kept up their friendship with each other until Elmer's death just a few years ago.

Driving a Cadillac

One beautiful day in late spring, Bill Mennen stopped by my desk to talk to me. He was beaming as he told me that he had bought his father's Cadillac convertible, and how much fun it was to drive it. He told me about all the automatic features of the car, including an automatic dimmer for the high beams. Everyone had always admired Mr. Mennen Senior's light green Cadillac convertible, and now Bill Mennen was happy to be the proud owner of it.

Bill Mennen was as excited about his "new" car as a little boy with a new toy. Then he surprised me by saying: "You have to drive that Cadillac and see what a wonderful car it is. Take it home with you tonight and have some fun with it. Go out for a good fast drive after dinner." I was speechless. I was still a fairly new driver and he trusted me with his beautiful new car, while he was going to go home with my plain old Ford! This was so much like him. He always enjoyed giving happiness and fun to other people.

Next we went out for a drive in the Cadillac for orientation about handling, and to introduce me to all the features. Power brakes and power steering were new to me, and so were power windows. There was power to raise and lower the convertible top. He showed me how it worked so that I could put it up if I wanted to. The car was awesome. During our drive we stopped at a gas station to top off the gas tank. He wanted to be sure that I would have plenty of gas to go riding around. Then I drove the car back and parked it in the employees' parking lot, while he put my Ford into his garage. I could hardly believe that Bill Mennen was letting me have that wonder of a car—but at five o'clock it was mine until the next morning.

My car pool riders went home in great style that night, and they enjoyed riding in the convertible as much as I enjoyed driving it. Aunt and Uncle were a little upset about the responsibility put upon me and did not want me to go out driving after dinner. However, it was still daylight then and I did go out. I drove it fast on the Garden State Parkway for about ten miles. I then drove through some of the nearby towns until it was getting dark and I could watch the automatic dim of the high beams.

Uncle wanted me to put the Cadillac into the garage at night, but it was too long and we could not close the garage door. I raised the convertible top and locked the car. Uncle was nervous about the Cadillac being partially outside. I was not. Nobody could steal it with Uncle's car parked right behind it. Aunt Martha was angry in the morning. She said that Uncle had sat by the window most of the night to watch the car. "Don't ever bring home a car like that again," I was told.

Bill Mennen, of course, was happy to hear my report about all the fun I had with his new Cadillac.

Being a Bridesmaid

As my first year in the United States came to an end, there were still new experiences awaiting me, even though I thought that I had been exposed to everything by then.

Kay, the Seibert's daughter, was getting married at the end of June and I was asked to be a bridesmaid in her wedding. This was something entirely new to me. There were no bridesmaids in German weddings, so that I first had to ask Aunt Martha what a bridesmaid is before I could accept Kay's request.

This was a wonderful experience for me. A few months before the

wedding, the bride with her mother, as well as all bridesmaids went shopping for gowns. We were happy with Kay's selection and thought our gowns were beautiful. Then came the fittings, and later the rest of the outfitting. Finally the important day arrived and I experienced the splendor of an American wedding.

Kay and I remain lifelong friends, even though we had not been that close during my first year in the United States. At that time Kay was dating her future husband, Bill, and she also had her own circle of friends from her school years.

In my bridesmaid dress for Kay Seibert's Wedding.

After her marriage and children, we saw each other only occasionally, since we did not live in close proximity. However, we have always kept in touch, even after the deaths of her parents and my relatives, who had been the points of connection up until then. Ours continues to be a warm friendship, albeit mostly by mail.

Later in the Year of 1955

Ever since I arrived in the United States, Uncle Adolph's words of wisdom had been: "Once you have experienced all four seasons in this country, you will be acclimated and everything will be easier and less uncomfortable for you." He had been right. The second summer did not bother me nearly as much as the first one had. Although I was still hot and miserable at times, I no longer had doubts about being able to stay in the United States. I knew that I could survive the summers, and I was staying. I liked living here. While I continued to criticize some of the things which did not make sense to me, the good things about life here outweighed the less desirable ones by far.

In September I became of age, as well as an "old maid," according to Aunt Martha. However, she had not quite given up hope as yet. There were three young men from the German Club who came to visit at the house occasionally. After one of them had been drafted into the Army, he still came back to visit during leave. One of these visits was on my birthday where he, with another one of the friends who was driving him back to Fort Dix that day, stopped by and they brought me a present. I did not date either of them, but Aunt Martha kept encouraging them to visit. She had invited another one of the boys from the German Club for my twenty–first birthday party, as well as German friends of theirs who lived nearby.

Mom had sent me a beautiful pillow on which the design of the Berlin Bear emblem was worked in wool. The other, most touching and very special present, was my first teddy bear. At last I had a teddy bear to comfort me in times of crisis. Teddy bears had obviously appeared on the market again. I never had one before the war, and later there weren't any available. Mom always had the most wonderful ideas. This one was tops!

I was now twenty–one years old and no longer a child; I had a car and with it some freedom. Occasionally I was dating, though not seriously, to Aunt Martha's continuing dismay. Uncle would tell her to leave me alone. However, even if she did, other well–meaning people did not. My coworkers constantly came up with some brother, brother–in–law, friend or son who wanted to meet me. Mr. Oldenburg not only tried to get me hooked up with his nephew who came from Germany for a few months to receive some business training in the United States, but also with either of his two sons. However, I still liked having my freedom and being unattached.

In the fall I had been dating a German fellow, Günter, a few times. He seemed to get serious about me and I was not. The military came to my rescue when Günter was drafted to serve his two years, and I stubbornly refused to continue a relationship. At Christmas, more silver–plated flatware was added to my hope chest.

Newark Preparatory School

I was doing well at work and loved my job. Near the end of September, I started night school at Newark Preparatory School in downtown Newark, taking shorthand and business English. It was a hard grind to go to school two nights a week, study the other nights, and then have to go places with my relatives on weekends. Shorthand took a lot of practice, but it was essential if I wanted to become a secretary again.

Business English was easy. By now my English vocabulary was more than adequate to get along. In fact, I did well, especially in spelling where I never made mistakes. Other students' business letters were full of spelling errors. The teacher was amazed and told the class that they ought to be ashamed to have gone to school in the United States and have a foreigner outdo them at spelling in every test.

I graduated from Newark Preparatory School at the end of January 1956. With this important accomplishment, I could consider 1955 to have been a successful year for me.

4

1956
Peter Immigrates to the United States
Age Twenty–one

A Snowstorm in Northern New Jersey

One night during the winter, sixteen inches of snow fell on northern New Jersey. I saw no reason not to go to work. Uncle Adolph had bought chains for my car, and we put them on. The streets were deserted because all schools and some businesses were closed. I picked up Alice on time, though neither of the other two girls were waiting for us at our meeting points. Assuming they had decided to take the day off, Alice and I continued our beautiful drive through a sunny winter wonderland.

When we reached The Mennen Company, we found the driveway and parking lot snowed in. Being less than half the age of Alice and very energetic, I was ready to drive into town and buy snow shovels so that we could get started on digging out the parking lot. Alice was dismayed at the thought, but I really believed that we could at least get started on clearing the driveway before the plows came.

Alice and I sat in the car at the entrance of The Mennen Company's driveway for perhaps forty–five minutes. There was no traffic at all on Hanover Avenue, which normally was quite a busy road. I kept insisting that we should at least get a start on digging the parking lot—of a plant employing 350 people—out of a major snowstorm, when one of Mennen's maintenance people who was responsible for arranging the plowing, came along. He told us the local radio station, WMTR, had announced that the Mennen plant was closed for the day. Alice and I lived out of range of that radio station. While Uncle had said something about the radio announcing school and plant closings, I did not believe that anything would close down because of snow. This, too, was unheard of in Germany.

After we were back at work the next day, news of my plan to help dig out the parking lot got around the office and plant. I suffered merciless teasing which went on for months afterward and continued the following winter. Only then did I realize how naive and unrealistic my idea had been. There was certainly nothing wrong with my dedication to The Mennen Company.

Bill Mennen comes to my Rescue

A couple of days later when most of the roads were clear again, my chains were still on the tires. Driving to work was slow because the ends of the chains had come loose when I was driving faster on bare payment than I should have, and they were banging against the outside of the fenders. When we were about five or six miles from the Mennen plant, I noticed Bill Mennen in the car behind me, trying to get my attention. He motioned for me to stop. When I did, he jumped out of his car, told me and Alice to get into it and said he would take care of my car. "Go to it so you won't be late—you can still make it," he told me. The deal was that we punched time clocks. If an employee had not been absent or late for two consecutive months, half a bonus day was awarded. Bill Mennen knew that I always got to work on time. The first time he needed a ride to work and I asked him at what time I should stop by his house, he told me that he had better be ready whenever I told him to be, and that he knew I would cut off his head if he made me late.

On that particular day he rescued Alice and me from being late and losing half a bonus day by giving us his car. Bill Mennen had told me to drive his car right up to the employees' entrance and to leave it there instead of driving it into his garage. The garages were located in a wing at right angles to the employees' entrance, but to save time, he wanted me to just pull up to the entrance and leave the car. I let Alice punch her card first, and as soon as I had done so, the clock changed to 9:01. We had both made it, thanks once again to Bill Mennen's thoughtfulness.

About forty–five minutes later, I received a phone call from the Personnel Manager. "Get that car of yours away from the employees' entrance before Mr. Mennen Senior gets angry," he pretended to yell at me. I tried to explain why my car might be there, and that Bill Mennen must have parked it there, when I heard George Mennen's familiar laugh—ha, ha, ha, ha, ha—in the background, and saying to the Personnel Manager: "I bet you scared her, Lowell." Then Lowell Wallace said to me: "Do you know who took the chains off your car? Two Vice Presidents and the Personnel Manger. Now come down and move that car of yours to the parking lot."

I flew down the stairs and into the personnel office, where George Mennen and Lowell were laughing even more when they saw my red face and frightened expression. Shaking with fear at the thought that the presence of my car blocking one of the Mennen's garages might have upset Mr. Mennen Senior, I thanked George and Lowell. Bill Mennen had already left, or those two would never have played this prank on me. Then I hurried out to remove my car.

This was not to be the only time at which Bill Mennen helped me out. When I got to the parking lot at the end of work one day, I found that my car had a flat tire. Never having changed a tire, I did not know how to go about it. Just as I approached the building wanting to use a telephone to call for help, Bill Mennen came walking out of the employees' entrance. He said: "Aren't you heading in the wrong direction?" I told him about my flat tire. "I know how to change a tire," he volunteered. Ignoring my protest, he walked over to his garage, grabbed a hydraulic jack, and wheeled it across the parking lot to my car. Soon he had changed my tire, and, extremely relieved, we were on our way. Any delays affected my riders as far as their connections with rides after they left my car pool.

Discussing Peter's Immigration

At one point near the end of 1955, Aunt and Uncle discussed with me the possibility of their sponsorship for Peter's immigration. I was elated! Peter was going to be eighteen years old the following July, which meant that he could legally work in the United States.

Peter at age eighteen

At this time he was still working at Tabak Erbach, the tobacco goods company at which our father had worked for twenty years. Peter was an apprentice there for three years, learning general business management and going to a trade school twice a week, which was part of the apprenticeship. He was now in his third year and earning only seventy–five Marks a month. To put this into perspective, a pair of shoes then cost sixty Marks. When Peter needed a pair of shoes, he paid them off in monthly installments of ten Marks. The German economy was recovering extremely slowly in some areas.

When talks about Peter's immigration became serious, I went to see Bill Mennen and asked him if there could be a job with The Mennen Company for Peter, if and when he came over. Bill Mennen told me that there would be, and I was delighted. I also asked him if he would write a letter to the American Consulate in Berlin to let them know that Peter would have a job, which he did. This letter alone was enough for the required sponsorship for Peter. My relatives were happy that all was set, and that Peter would have employment after his arrival.

My Brother Immigrates to the United States

Peter arrived on August 15, 1956, on the *SS United States*, and I was the happiest sister in the world. For the next couple of weeks I hardly left his side, needing to hang onto him or hold his hand, just to make sure that he was really with me. It was wonderful to be with close family. I had not realized how lonely I was without Peter and Mom.

Aunt Martha and Uncle Adolph were good to me, but the relationship was not the same as being with your own brother.

At the office, the story circulated that I had sent for my brother because I needed his help with shoveling The Mennen Company's parking lot in the coming winter.

Introducing Peter to Bill Mennen

Immediately after Peter's arrival in the United States, I took my two weeks vacation so that I could spend time with him. Having my own car, I was able to drive Peter around and show him the area.

We had a wonderful time together. Peter arrived just in time to attend the annual picnic of The Mennen Company with me, and I was so proud to introduce my handsome brother to everyone.

One of our first trips was to Morristown to show Peter The Mennen Company's plant, and to introduce him to Bill Mennen. I had been told that Peter would be working in the Mail Room, helping to distribute the mail to the different departments twice a day. When he met Bill Mennen, I wanted Peter to make as good an impression as possible so that he would not want to change his mind about hiring him. Peter had not had anywhere near as much English in school as I did, and even that was a few years in the past. I thought that Peter ought to be able to answer most of the questions asked him when I introduced him to Bill Mennen. Remembering the questions everybody had asked me after my arrival, I had tutored Peter, and we now rehearsed his lesson while we were on our way to The Mennen Company. I even drove through a stop sign without stopping because I was so busy rehearsing Peter's lines with him. We still laugh every time we think of that day. Many years later, Peter even told Bill Mennen about my English drills when he stopped into Peter's office for a visit after his retirement.

Here is how my lesson for Peter went:

Upon being introduced and while shaking hands, you say: "How do you do, Mr. Mennen."

Then Mr. Mennen will ask you how your trip was and if you had good weather. You say: "I had a good trip, and the weather was nice."

I told Peter that I would be doing most of the talking, trying to keep it simple and to a minimum. At some point, at my prompting, Peter was to say: "Thank you for giving me a job," as well as: "I am happy to meet you. Good–bye, Mr. Mennen."

I had really drilled Peter, and it went like clockwork. Bill Mennen asked all the right questions and Peter had all the right answers. Of course, at the time I had asked Bill Mennen about a job for Peter, I had told him that he knew almost no English. However, Bill Mennen knew that being only eighteen years old, Peter would pick it up in no time, as his sister had done.

Peter worked for The Mennen Company until his retirement thirty–seven years later, which nearly coincided with the sale of the firm to Colgate–Palmolive two years earlier.

5

1957
A Most Memorable Year
Age Twenty–Two

Looking for an Apartment of our Own

When Peter arrived, there was really no room for him in Aunt and Uncle's house. The only thing we could do to accommodate him was to have him sleep in the party room downstairs in the basement. Uncle bought an aluminum cot and a mattress for it, and although the setup was to be temporary, Peter seemed happy enough with his accommodations.

I was just about finished with paying off my car and would then have a chance to save a bit. As soon as Peter was settled into his job, we could think about renting a place of our own. There was no pressure from our relatives, although the house was quite crowded. After four months the situation began to wear not only on Aunt Martha's nerves, but on all of us.

After the Christmas holidays were over, Peter and I set out to find a small apartment in Morristown. We wanted to be close to work to cut out the long commute. Most of all, though, we had to have enough room to accommodate Mom when she came to join us. Peter and I had checked into immigration for her and had received some advice on how to go about sponsorship. Mom's letters had been full of loneliness. While she had many friends, she missed her children so much that she was willing to give up everything and start a new life in a strange country.

"There is no future for Berlin," she wrote, "the political situation is extremely unstable." The uprising against Communism in Hungary late in 1956 had been a bloody one, having been quenched by Russian tanks. The Berliners felt that West Berlin could be next. Mom spoke of her fear of the Communists taking over West Berlin, and then there would be no chance of ever being reunited. Her urgent plea to us was: "Please, get me out of here before we are cut off from each other forever." Peter and I decided that we had to take action immediately.

The result of our apartment search was that it was not much cheaper to rent a room in someone else's house than it was to rent an apartment in a complex of garden apartments in the town of Morristown. It was worth it to both of us to pay the extra eighteen dollars a month for the garden apartment and be totally independent, rather than living in somebody's home and having all kinds of restrictions, or having to walk through a part of their living area to get to the outside, as was the case in one place which we looked at.

By the end of the weekend, Peter and I had opted for a two–bed-room apartment at a garden apartment complex called Jacob Ford Village in Morristown, and planned on moving in on February first.

The family was not happy that we wanted to move out so soon, but in the long run it had to be. Peter and I were looking forward to having our own place. We told Aunt Martha and Uncle Adolph about our plans for Mom's immigration. Once Mom came to the United States, our little family would be intact again.

Peter and I could buy only the very minimum of furniture. I bought a bedroom suite and a dinette set, and Peter got a bed for his room to start with, and a television set for the living room. Otherwise the apart-ment would be quite empty, especially the living room. Aunt Martha helped with a bedspread, curtains and whatever she could spare in the way of household things. I was very touched by four sets of new bath towels which she gave to me with the words: "You might as well take these now—you'll never get married anyway." She had been accumu-lating those towels in my hope chest. Uncle Adolph decided it was time to buy a new phonograph and give the old one to us so that we had music in our empty living room. The phonograph and the sewing ma-chine—which was mine now—as well as Peter's television were the only furnishings in our living room. We had to sit on the floor to watch television, but we loved having our own place.

My Friend Adele

There was one woman working in the Typing Pool who guarded me with motherly interest. Her name was Adele Ericson and her parents had been immigrants from Germany. Adele, in her mid–forties, understood some German but did not speak it. She had told her parents about me and from then on, every time Adele went to New York State to visit them, her mother sent a jar of homemade bread and butter pickles back for me. Adele had noticed that I liked pickles and had told me about the homemade ones of her mother's.

I liked Adele very much. She was always cheerful, and her laughter came from the bottom of her heart. It was contagious. Her sense of humor was akin to that of the Berliners in that she would make fun of herself and laugh about it. In many ways she reminded me of Mom.

Adele, who lived in Whippany, was really excited about Peter and I moving to Morristown, and she promptly invited us to her home for dinner and to meet her husband, the "big Swede," as she called Mr. Ericson. Just after we had moved into our apartment, Adele brought several boxes to work which I was to take home. Those boxes contained all kinds of kitchen utensils, dishes, glasses, even dish towels and an apron. I was speechless. I would have had to buy all of those items almost immediately as we did not even have dinner plates, and here they were just given to us. Noticing how very touched I was, Adele said she just went through her kitchen and collected all duplicate utensils and dishes which she no longer needed or wanted, to give us a start. I found this idea so wonderful that I have done the same thing to a number of people over the years, and it was always much appreciated. To me, this act of kindness became "Adele's Tradition" perpetuated.

Once Mom was in the United States, Adele was quite anxious to meet her having heard so much about her. The two women, being about the same age, really took to each other. Adele and Mom understood the same kind of humor, and they laughed all of the time whenever we got together. Mr. Ericson's name was Arthur, but Mom always called him "Mr. Adele." We never stopped laughing when we visited the Ericson's.

Adele and I, as well as my family, remained friends for years to come, until her untimely death from asthma parted us.

Being on Our Own

We loved having our own place. For nearly three months Peter and I had this big, two–bedroom apartment all to ourselves. It was a good time, and also a time of bonding once again after Peter and I had been living separate lives for nearly three years. I suddenly found myself in the shoes of a housewife, being responsible for the household budget and having to do the cooking for the first time in my life. Surprisingly, it worked out well. I do not remember any catastrophe.

Peter and I had the chance to share some quality time before life separated us again. With much fondness I remember the times when I would be washing the dishes after dinner and Peter sat next to me on the stove top—there was no room for a chair in the kitchen—and entertained me with stories about his life in Berlin after I left, the dances and parties he went to, and the pranks he and his friends played. Those evenings together were a time of hearty laughter for Peter and me, and wonderful memories throughout the years to come.

Our Mom Immigrates

With suggestions from the German Travel Agency on sponsorship for our mother, and a temporary (less than a month) loan from Aunt

and Uncle to show a certain required balance in our bank account, there was no problem for Peter and me to sponsor Mom's immigration. Peter and I beamed with happiness, and once again the whole Mennen Company showed their interest and was delighted for us. Bill Mennen offered to be of help, if we needed any.

On April 16, 1957, Mom, still not quite recovered from a severe bout with seasickness—I sympathized greatly—set foot on American soil. Like Peter, she had come on the *SS United States*, which took only seven days to cross the Atlantic from Germany.

Mom arriving in New York

In preparation for Mom's arrival, Peter and I had purchased a chair which folded out to be a single bed. This chair was a welcomed addition to the meager furnishings in our good–sized living room. It was the best we could do to provide a bed for Mom, for the time being. On our salaries, Peter and I could just barely afford the apartment. We were living on a shoestring. I had had an automobile accident in a big snowstorm the day before we moved in, and the repair bill on my car had put me back financially. Besides that, I had my bedroom and kitchen furniture to pay off.

Our wonderful Mom! She was so much fun to be with and had happiness within herself.

Speaking of a shoestring—Mom arrived on a Wednesday and Peter and I took the day off to meet her in New York. Wednesdays were paydays at Mennen, which meant that we could not get our paychecks until the next day. We just barely had enough money for gas to get to New York and to pay the tolls for the Lincoln Tunnel. When we received our paychecks the next day, we had to drive into Morristown after work to cash them at the bank. Our car had been running on "empty" since that morning, and on the way into town we ran out of gas. Fortunately we were on top of a slight incline within sight of a gas station into which I was able to coast. Peter and I pooled our pennies, and we were successful in scraping together fifty cents between the two of us to buy gasoline to get us into Morristown (gas was only thirty cents a gallon in those days). We still laugh about it today, but that's how tough things were, though we did not feel then that it was a particularly tough time. Instead, Peter and I were grateful and so very happy to have our Mom with us.

We never told Mom that we had to struggle to show her a good time, and to support her until she knew enough English to get some kind of a job. The main thing was that our family was together, and we had fun and laughter once again. Mom had given up so much for us, and her whole life had been one big struggle and sacrifice. Now we wanted her to have a good life.

Peter and I were proud to have such a nice apartment in a good location. Mom loved it there, and spring was a beautiful time to start a new life in a new country. Even the forsythias had cooperated, and most of them were flowering to welcome Mom. Yellow was her favorite color, and Peter and I had talked to the forsythias and asked them to please bloom in time for our Mom's arrival.

During the daytime when Peter and I were at work, it must have been pretty lonely for Mom at times with not being able to speak the language. However, she has never been bashful and did not mind using a great deal of sign language to communicate. Somehow people understood her, and everybody liked her. She was always friendly and smiling, and people felt drawn to her and wanted to talk to her, even if it was difficult for both sides.

We had given Mom an English workbook so that she could learn some of the phrases she would need to be able to hold a conversation. Mom took her "studies" seriously and talked to us in some of her newly acquired English at night. Unfortunately, she had nobody to correct her pronunciation of the words, and we had many good laughs about Mom's German–pronounced English. On one of her walks around the neighborhood, Mom befriended a young mother who regularly took her baby out for a ride in the carriage. The woman lived in our building. She liked Mom's friendliness and good spirits so much that she volunteered to help her with pronunciation and conversation. This gave Mom something to do during the daytime and helped getting her started with learning English.

Overall, Mom had no problem fitting in. She had a talent for it. Eventually she learned English well enough to get along, and in time she even learned how to drive a car, and bought one. We were tremendously proud of her.

The Laundry Room and
Meeting my future Husband

My life seemed to settle in now that my family was back together again, and I even started dating more than before, though no serious prospects as yet. My favorite evenings out were social evenings once a week with Lois, my best friend at work, who belonged to a youth activities group at her church. As a group we played games, had discussions or went bowling. Now and then I dated someone.

With Aunt Martha at some distance now, I did not feel the pressure of needing "to decide" after I had gone out with someone. It was not until October of 1957, when I met a certain young man by the name of Malvern Gross, that I started to date regularly and seriously.

Initially we had met, of all places, in the laundry room of the apartment building. He and another young man who also worked for Price Waterhouse, had an apartment at the opposite end of the building in which we lived. Though much farther, I had been using the laundry facility at that end of the building because the one nearby was locked up at five o'clock on week nights, and on Saturdays it was always crowded. One evening when I approached the laundry room with my two baskets of laundry, I found that a young man was sitting on the steps outside, reading a newspaper. The washing machines at the apartment laundries were the Bendix front–loading type which had a pre–wash cycle. It was therefore necessary to wait ten minutes for that cycle to finish before the detergent for the wash cycle could be added. This delay had been the reason for his sitting there and reading the newspaper while waiting. He said: "Sorry, but I am using both machines," and I replied: "That's all right, I'll just come back later." This was the end of the conversation and I went away. Later on after dinner when I went back to do my laundry I was hoping that the young man would still be sitting there. He had impressed me with his politeness and good manner. However, there was no sign of him.

Malvern Gross, my future husband

Matchmaker At Work

I found out later that he, too, had been impressed, and wanted to find some way of being formally introduced. He knew just the person. Mal's hobby was private flying and through aviation activities he had met and become a friend of Mary and Noel Olmstead. Noel was also a pilot. Mary was the Welcome Wagon hostess for the Morristown area. She had already tried to call on us after Peter and I moved into the apartment, but had never found anyone at home. It was her intention to call on us one evening after work, which with Mal's urging, she now did.

One evening in early October, Mary Olmstead visited us in her capacity of Welcome Wagon hostess. She presented us with many coupons from merchants in the area, as well as the typical information which a newcomer to an area needs to know. Then she casually mentioned to me that she knew two young men who would like to meet me—she had included Mal's roommate, Larry Rice, who was also a bachelor. Not thinking of the young man I had seen at the laundry, I was my usual disinterested self and wondered why even a Welcome Wagon hostess made it her business to try and get me married off. Had Morristown not been twenty miles distant from Aunt Martha, I would have suspected her to be behind this.

The following details are important as they led up to my introduction to my future husband.

Before Mary Olmstead left that evening, she tried to get me to speak about Germany on the radio. Mary was involved with hosting a program on the local radio station, WMTR. I declined on the grounds that I had been away from Germany for over three years and had never been interested in politics anyway, so that I had nothing to say on the subject of what was going on in Germany.

Mom had been sitting at the table with us all that time and Mary, being an outgoing person, tried to talk to her despite Mom's extremely limited English. Earlier during introductions, Mary asked Mom to call her "Mary," and she wanted to know Mom's first name, then called her "Johanna." Except for children, calling strangers by their first names upon meeting was unheard of in Germany. Mom commented in her humorous way that they were now on a first–name basis like relatives or longtime friends. The two women laughed and had a great time together, with me being their interpreter.

Mary tried quite hard to get me to agree to be on her radio program, and Mom, of course, wanted her daughter to be on the radio. I firmly refused. Before Mary left she said that she would be in touch with me. After Mary was gone, Mom still tried to convince me that I should have agreed to the radio interview, but I insisted that I could not.

One evening about a week later, upon returning from an evening out, Mom told me that someone had telephoned and wanted to speak to me. Mom was not sure of the name, but thought it sounded like "Maril" or something similar to that. I told her I had no idea who it could have been and that this person would probably call back. A while later, Mom had the idea that it might have been this women who had asked to be called by her first name, Mary. Suddenly Mom was quite sure the name was Mary, and that she probably had called because of the radio program. I upheld that I did not want to be on any radio program. Period. Mom, however, insisted that I at least be courteous and return the call. Reluctantly I phoned the number on the Welcome Wagon folder which Mary Olmstead had left with us.

It turned out that Mary had not called me, but she was delighted that I happened to call her. The young man who had wanted to meet me had just arrived at their house for dinner, and before I realized what was happening I was introduced over the telephone to Malvern Gross. I did not know what to say to a stranger or how to handle this situation, but he mentioned that he had seen me at the laundry room. I had forgotten about him, and I certainly could not picture what he looked like. Meanwhile Mary, who already had two couples on her conscience by having been the matchmaker, waved a flyer in front of Mal which advertised an upcoming square and round dance at the Newcomer's Club. Mal asked me for a date. Loving to dance, I accepted.

It was not until after this introduction to Mal that I found out whose call Mom had answered on that particular evening. It had been a lady by the name of Marilyn who was in charge of the youth activities group at the church, and who eventually called me back.

About a year after Mal and I were married, I found out why we never went to any dances when we were dating. Mal hated to dance. Over the years, I had much fun teasing him about marrying me under false pretenses. Since our first date had been a dance, I just assumed that he liked to dance. As for my knowledge of advanced dance steps, I figured that I could teach those to him in no time. To my huge disappointment I had to forget about that, and it has been a real sadness in my life. Years later we hit on a compromise. Mary and Noel Olmstead were dedicated square dancers, and at their urging we took lessons and enjoyed square dancing for more than twenty years.

My First Date with Mal

Our first date was, as I said, a Square and Round Dance at the Morristown Area Newcomers' Club. He had borrowed his roommate's car for this date because he did not own a car. On the way back from the dance, Mal told me that he owned an airplane and asked if I would like to ride out to the airport to see it. Of course, I wanted to. I had never seen a small airplane up close. The Morristown Airport was less than three miles down the road from where we lived.

After we got to his plane, Mal showed me the inside and pointed out that it was not much different in size than the inside of a car. "Would you like to sit in it?" was the next question. Why yes, I wanted to sit in it. He helped me into the right front seat.

He must have untied the plane when he walked around to the other side, and then got in. He told me that since he did not own a car, he did not get out to the airport very often, and that he would like to take this opportunity to start the engine and run it for a few minutes. At the same time, I could hear what the engine of a small plane sounded like. I told him I had flown in an airplane only once before, from Berlin to Hamburg, at the time I immigrated to the United States.

Mal started the engine, and then began to taxi, pointing out that the plane "drives" just like a car. I was intrigued, of course. I cannot remember whether or not he mentioned that he would take off, but before I really became aware of what was happening, we were in the air!

It was a beautiful, clear night. Not long after we were off the ground we could see the lights of Manhattan, about twenty miles away. Above Manhattan was a full moon. What a beautiful night to go flying, and I have loved night flights ever since.

Those were the days before there were traffic restrictions over large cities, and it was permissible to fly right over Manhattan and sightsee. We did. I was enormously impressed. Next we flew out over the water from Long Island towards Connecticut, and with the moonlight reflecting on the water, it was a picture perfect sight and a most memorable experience. We landed back at Morristown Airport about forty–five minutes later. I could not believe that this had happened to me.

It was close to midnight when I returned home. Mom was tending to Peter who was seriously ill with the Asian Flu which was going around at the time. Peter was delirious and mostly unresponsive. Mom, as gravely concerned as she was about Peter, asked me if I had enjoyed my date. I told her that she would never, ever guess where I had just been. Then I told her that Mal had an airplane and had taken me flying over New York City.

Peter, who we thought was totally "out of it," said in a hoarse whisper: "you're crazy." To Mom and me, Peter's response was beautiful! It was a sign of life. He had heard and understood us when we thought that he was nearly gone. I stayed by Peter's bed with Mom until his fever broke about an hour later. Then Mom sent me to bed while she kept her vigil at Peter's bedside.

PART II

FAMILY

6

The Start of our Life Together

Mom, Peter and I enjoyed living in our own apartment. Our little family was together again, and we were very happy. No matter what might happen in Berlin or in Europe, we were in the United States, in a free country, and we had a deep appreciation for this freedom.

As time went by we felt more and more that we belonged and fit in, both at work and in the community. Even Mom felt at home in her new surroundings. She was still euphoric about being reunited with her children. After a summer job as a cook at a resort in the Catskill Mountains of New York State, she started to work at Morristown Memorial Hospital as a cleaning person in Pediatrics. Again, Bill Mennen had been instrumental in getting her the job. He was on the Board of Directors of the hospital, and later when I got married he even helped Mom obtain housing on the hospital grounds. Like a Guardian Angel he was watching over my family, and was always there to help whenever we needed it.

Mom loved working in Pediatrics because she had interaction with the children. With her great love for children this was a good job for her, though often sad. She would be sad when a child to which she had become especially attached got well and went home—because she missed it—but it was much worse when a child died. This did happen, and Mom would come home crying and telling us the heartbreaking news. Then Peter and I would cry with her.

Mal and I were married in Summit, New Jersey on June 28, 1958 in the Unitarian Church.

My Future is taking Shape

After my first date with Mal Gross in October 1957 we did not have another one until New Year's Eve. Price Waterhouse had sent him to the Dominican Republic to work in their office for two months. He returned just in time for Christmas, which he spent with his family in Winchester, Massachusetts. Mal called me up right after Christmas and asked me to go with him to visit friends on New Year's Eve. They had invited several couples to their apartment to celebrate the arrival of the new year 1958.

From then on my dating with Mal became regular and exclusive. He was a decisive young man, and on Valentine's Day we became engaged. We were married in June. Aunt Martha was happy that I had finally made a choice. She liked Mal and told me that she was glad I had waited until he came along.

Mal has always teased me, pointing out that ours was a "marriage of convenience." He had an airplane and no car, and I had a car and no airplane—as if I really needed an airplane! He said he needed my car to get to the airport whenever he wanted to fly. Until then he had been walking the three miles each way. Besides, he said he needed someone to do his laundry for him since he disliked that ten–minute wait for the pre–wash cycle before he could put in the detergent. This comment of his should have been a hint of his impatience and clearly a type A personality, but then he is saying the same of me.

The Start of our Trip Through Life Together

Mal had told me that an airplane would always be a part of our lives, so our honeymoon was a trip around the United States and southwestern Canada in his plane. We flew northwest via the Chicago area, Fargo, Bismarck, and Billings, heading for Yellowstone National Park. Billings, Montana, was to be our overnight stop on that particular day. We were glad, because as we approached Billings there were huge storm clouds in the vicinity. They looked menacing with streaks of green in them. We

After the wedding reception we went to the airport to include the plane in our happy day.

wondered about the brilliant green streaks in those clouds and were to find out very shortly what they meant.

The Billings Airport is located on a plateau overlooking the city. Mal's airplane was a Cessna 170A, a tail dragger, and upon landing the tail spring broke, disabling the plane. Mal informed the tower, and they sent a truck out to meet us on the runway. Just as the truck arrived, the tower informed us that a tornado had been sighted heading for the airport and that we had to immediately get to a protected area. The truck driver had me go with him to a small executive terminal. Mal, in the meantime, was told by the tower where to taxi, and with sparks flying from the broken tail spring as it was dragged along the pavement, went as fast as he could to find protection for the plane in between rows of T–hangars. The storm hit the airport scant minutes later.

Three men and I stood in the little terminal building and watched from behind the huge plate glass window as the storm unleashed its fury. Cherry–sized hailstones started to fall and were accumulating fast. The wind was ferocious and broke one of the tie–down chains which had been attached to a twin engine plane just outside the window on the ramp. This plane was then rocking like crazy, tugging on the remaining chain. One of the men said that we had better get away from the window and behind a sturdy wall before that plane came crashing through the floor–to–ceiling plate glass window. The terminal was small, and the only solid wall we could get behind was the one dividing the restrooms. I was semi–hysterical. The crashing, howling noises of the storm brought back memories of air raids. Where was Mal? Nobody knew, but one of the guys assured me he would be OK. But would he be? He was out there somewhere in that turmoil. All I could think of was that I did not want to be a widow at age twenty–three, and after only four days of marriage. As we were heading for the restroom area, the men told me to come with them. Mindlessly I did, not caring that they were going into the men's room. I certainly was not going to be taking shelter in the ladies room all by myself.

We waited until the storm calmed down considerably before we emerged from the men's room. Outside it looked like winter wonderland, except that it was hail instead of snow. Two inches of cherry–sized hail had fallen in only twenty–five minutes. We also found out that we had just survived the only tornado ever recorded in Billings. The wind velocity instrument had been knocked out when the winds hit one hundred fifteen miles an hour!

In the meantime, Mal had taken refuge between two rows of T–hangars, where he was able to partially shelter his plane by moving it as close as possible to one of the hangar doors. However, the plane was not tied down and if a good gust of wind had hit it, it would have been

badly damaged or destroyed. He was very lucky. Nothing happened to him or the plane, which was a miracle. The tornado had ripped right across the airport and turned some hangars and many airplanes upside down. Numerous other planes were badly damaged from the hail. We were awed by the damage. The area where Mal had been had escaped direct contact with the tornado. But, oh, so close it came!

This T–hangar was struck by the tornado, taking off part of the roof and then turning the aircraft upside down. It was just luck that Mal selected a space between the rows of T–hangars that escaped the brunt of the storm.

July 2, 1958, went down in history as a day to remember, not only by the Billings Airport, which was partially destroyed, but also in our minds. Every time we fly into Billings, which we do on most of our coast–to–coast flights, we remember that day. I will never forget the only time in my life when I've been in a men's room, with a bunch of men!

Yellowstone

With the airport in such a shambles, we could not get our tail spring repaired the next day. We had hotel reservations at Yellowstone Park and needed to get there somehow. After some checking we ended up taking a train from Billings to Livingston, Montana, and then a bus to Mammoth Hot Springs in Yellowstone, where we were staying that night. I was enchanted with the magnificent scenery we enjoyed from the observation car of the train—and that was only the beginning.

Visiting Yellowstone Park with its many geysers and hot bubbling pools was a memorable experience for me, and it was only the first one of the many natural wonders of this great country which I have had the privilege of seeing. Married life was starting out well for me. We even had an uneventful encounter with a bear on a hike to the Falls of the Yellowstone River in the Grand Canyon of Yellowstone. The highlight of a visit to Yellowstone Park, of course, is a stay at magnificent Yellowstone Lodge and viewing some of the regular eruptions of Old Faithful Geyser.

The Canadian Rockies and the Western United States

After our five–day Yellowstone tour was completed we returned to Billings where the tail wheel spring had been replaced. From Billings we flew north to Calgary, Alberta in Canada and stayed with a cousin of Mal's mother, Dorothy Wallace and her family. The Wallaces took us to the Calgary Stampede and then lent us a car to drive to Banff, Lake Louise, and the Columbia Icefields in Jasper National Park, which we toured. We stayed in a charming little log cabin at Moraine Lake near Lake Louise.

Calgary is a cold place. It was early July and snowing on the morning we left for Portland, Oregon. I was not prepared for this cold. Dorothy had lent me a warm jacket to wear in the mountains, and I did not return it to her until I sat in our plane. Three hours later we landed at Portland and the temperature there was 96 degrees. Between the temperature change and the bumpiness going across the Rockies, my stomach was queasy. I got sick after we landed while I was walking to a phone booth to call Grandma Gross to come and pick us up.

We were not only seeing some of the scenic wonders of the United States, but I was also meeting every one of Mal's relatives along the way. Grandma Gross, then eighty–three years old, drove a 1937 Chevrolet, which she herself had painted blue. I liked this practical German lady. She showed us Portland which I immediately declared my favorite city.

Next we flew to Corvallis, about eighty miles to the south of Portland. There we visited with Uncle Jim and Aunt Esther, cousins Susan, Jamie, and Wes, as well as Aunt Esther's mother, Grandma Strom, and Mal's Grandma Henderson. We took a day trip to the coast. Seeing the Pacific Ocean for the first time was another highlight of the trip for me.

Continuing our flying trip, we toured San Francisco, enjoyed the beach at Santa Barbara in California, and then turned inland towards Arizona and the Grand Canyon. I remember a flight across seemingly endless desert as we were following the "iron compass"—railroad tracks—which were paralleling Route 66. It was unbearably hot in the plane, even though we were flying at 10,000 ft. I did not like the desert. The heat bothered me very much.

The Grand Canyon was an incomparable, overwhelming sight, and beyond description. I could not believe that I was actually seeing this natural wonder of breathtaking scenery and grand proportions.

Next we headed for Kansas City to meet the last of Mal's relatives, the incredible "Aunties." Mary and Isla Henderson were the two sisters of Mal's late Grandfather Henderson. I formed a special bond with these grand old ladies. They both lived to be in their mid–nineties, and in the years to come we had many great visits with them. Anytime we crossed the county with our plane, we would stop for a visit in Kansas City. The Aunties—understandably they did not want to be called "aunts"—had a terrific sense of humor. For now, we had fun with their gullibility. Mal told them with a straight face that the Rocky Moun-

Aunt Isla (left) and Aunt Mary. Over the years we made many trips to Kansas City to visit with them. Their father was Mal's great grandfather, an immigrant from Scotland, and later a buffalo hunter, era 1870's.

tains in some of the highest places were too high for us to fly across, and therefore we flew through the railroad tunnels after first checking the train schedule to avoid meeting any trains in the tunnels. The Aunties believed him. Mal has always had a sense of humor and loved it when people fell for his tall tales.

Our first trip together had been so different, and much more than I had expected a wedding trip to be. I had seen the United States "from sea to shining sea," and in my mind I gained an overview of the vast distances and the incredible beauty of this magnificent country in a short period of time. This trip also reflected both our personalities and preferences for travel in that we did not spend a whole vacation sitting in one place somewhere, but rather moved around and saw the country. The airplane, of course, was an efficient time machine that helped us see more in a given time period.

Settling Down

After this wonderful month long vacation trip it was time for both of us to get back to work. Mal was an ambitious young CPA with Price

Waterhouse, one of the most prestigious public accounting firms. His office was in New York City, close to Wall Street, and he commuted daily by train and subway. Even during normal working hours it was a long day because of the commute. In addition, he worked countless evenings and Saturdays on his climb to success during the early years. It was not always easy to put up with these crazy hours, especially when there were children who did not see much of their dad during the week. Ten years later, the payoff came with his admittance to the partnership of the firm, and eventually, financial security.

At The Mennen Company, I became a secretary again when Mr. John Henze, the Plant Engineer, asked me to work for him.

1959 Brought Many Changes

We were starting to get bored in the apartment and were looking for a little house of our own. Early in the year Mal sold his beloved airplane. This helped with the down payment for a small house in Denville, New Jersey, which was within walking distance of the Mount Tabor railroad station. We always had to consider the proximity of the

Our first home in Denville. While small—it had 2 bedrooms—we were delighted to have our own home, and lived in it for six years. The car in the driveway is the Ford I bought soon after arriving in the United States.

railroad to avoid the need for a second car. I loved having a house of our own, and a garden. This was the American Dream.

Mom was still working at Morristown Memorial Hospital and was living in part of a small house on the hospital grounds, which she was able to rent—once again through the help of Bill Mennen. While working at the hospital, Mom met Jim Finan, a jovial Irishman about her age, and they were married in July. Jim was a lot of fun to

Mom with Jim Finan

be with, and Mom had been lonely and suffering from "empty nest syndrome" since I had married and Peter had gone into the Army soon after our wedding to get his mandatory military service over with.

About two years later, Mom and Jim took a trip to Florida and Mom loved it there. She ended up buying a trailer house and they moved to the Daytona Beach area. The trailer was small, but quite comfortable. It was on a foundation and had a living room added onto it. The lot was a nice deep one, and much larger than the one on which our house in Denville stood. In the years to come we had many good visits with Mom in Florida, especially when the children were young and we could spend vacations in Daytona with plenty of time at the beach.

Next was the immigration of my friend Evelyn Lesch, my adopted "twin sister." Evelyn and I had met while working at the of-

We helped Evelyn Lesch, my "twin sister," immigrate in 1959. She still lives in New Jersey and we see each other regularly.

fice in Berlin. After I left for the United States, we had become fast friends while writing long letters to each other. I knew that Evelyn wanted to emigrate to the United States, but I had told her that my family came first, and that perhaps I could help her sometime in the future. Then I got married and thought I would never be able to sponsor Evelyn's immigration. One evening I mentioned this to Mal, and he said it was our obligation to help someone, to pay back in kind the help I had received from my relatives. Evelyn arrived in September of 1959, and the United States gained another responsible person, and five years later a proud American citizen.

Becoming an American Citizen

The other important event of the year was that it had been five years since my immigration, which made me eligible to become a citizen of the United States of America. I was proud to be sworn in as a citizen of this great, free country, on November 9, 1959. Mal's grandmother Henderson sent me a forty–nine star American flag which had flown over the capitol, to mark the occasion. Alaska had become the forty–ninth State that year, and 1959 was the only year in which our flag had forty–nine stars. Hawaii joined in 1960. I prize Grandma's thoughtful and appropriate gift.

Our Trip to Europe—May 18 to September 13, 1960

While I was still working at Mennen, we saved my salary and went on a four–month trip to Europe. I wanted to go back to Berlin to visit my relatives and friends, and show Mal where I was born and raised. In addition, we wanted to travel in Germany to see some of the country which many Americans had seen and I knew nothing about. From this initial idea, the trip evolved into four months and fourteen countries. We had looked at a map of Europe and everything seemed so close. Our thought process was: As long as we are in Bavaria, we might as well see Austria and Switzerland—then Yugoslavia—Greece—and on it went.

Planning to start a family soon, we decided that we should see Europe before children tied us down. This was also likely to be the last year Mal could take a leave of absence during the summer months because he was advancing in his career with increasing responsibilities. I could not get such a long leave of absence and had to quit my job at The Mennen Company. We ordered a

Mary and Noel Olmstead were like second parents to us. They had no children of their own and adopted our family.

new Volkswagen Beetle for delivery in Hamburg and traveled by car to many countries in Europe, including a month behind the Iron Curtain—in the Soviet Union, Poland, and Czechoslovakia. It was the first summer in which foreign automobile travel was permitted in the Soviet Union. I describe the Soviet portion of this trip in some detail in a later chapter.

By the end of the four months, we had traveled 18,000 miles and taken 1,700 photographs. Besides Germany, Austria and Switzerland, we also traveled in Yugoslavia, Greece, Turkey, Italy, Spain, France, Belgium, and Liechtenstein.

Upon arrival at home we found that our dear friends, Mary and Noel Olmstead, were packing up to move to El Paso, Texas. I could not comprehend why anybody would want to live in the desert. That was before we visited them years later and I learned about our magnificent desert southwest. Until then I had thought of a desert to be endless sand dunes, much like the pictures I had seen of the Sahara.

After returning from our European trip in September, I took a job with the Warner–Lambert Pharmaceutical Company in Morris Plains, New Jersey. While I could have returned to Mennen, we were hoping to start a family soon and it seemed unfair to Mennen to rejoin them and then leave again after perhaps a year or so. Besides, Warner–Lambert was only three miles from our home in Denville, and the job they offered me was in the accounting department.

1961—The Busy Life of Homeowners

The year 1961 found us happy in our little house, doing all of the things that homeowners do—repairs, maintenance, painting, building a patio, and gardening. We loved being homeowners.

Mal was out of town a lot. For months at a time he came home only on weekends. Weekday evenings I kept busy with working overtime, sewing my own clothes, and with different projects around the house and yard. In the summer of 1959 we had built a concrete and flagstone patio in the back yard, and a walkway from the driveway to the front door. Now we made improvements on the house and the landscaping.

I was beginning to learn about gardening. The great puzzle was: which are the weeds and which are the potential flowers coming up from the seeds I had planted. Trial and error taught me after I had no flowers in some areas, and the weeds were doing well. In the clay soil which we had, it was always difficult to pull out anything. I finally came to the conclusion that, if it pulled out easily it had been a flower, and if it was extremely hard to pull out, it was a weed.

My Friend Olga

One Sunday in the summer we invited another Price Waterhouse man and his wife who lived in an apartment in Brooklyn, New York, to

spend the day with us at our home. The men enjoyed each other's company, and Olga and I "hit it off" from the moment they walked though the door. This day together started a lifelong friendship between the four of us. Mike (Masahisa) Saito was Japanese and Olga was from Argentina. What a combination they were! Olga and I often teased Mal by telling him that he was up against three foreign born

Olga Saito is one of those people who always has a smile on her face and is truly fun to be with.

citizens, and therefore was in the minority.

Olga was so much fun. She and I did crazy things together. When Mike spent several months in Japan on business, Olga would come and stay with me for weeks at a time. She did not work, and whenever Mal was away, Olga and I had a great time together. In the winter we went sledding whenever there was snow, and ice skating early in the morning before I went to work. We would always think up dif-

The kitchen of our Denville house. While small, it had room for a kitchen table where we ate all meals. There was no dining room.

ferent things to do. For me it was nice to not only have Olga's company, but also she would prepare dinner which was ready when I came home from work. Olga was a good cook and I loved her Argentine cooking.

One time she prepared the grated potatoes for me to make German potato pancakes after I got home from work. We had invited my brother for dinner. Peter was still a bachelor at that time. The three of us always had the best time together, and one of the funny incidents which happened that day still has us laughing now, forty years later:

The three of us were sitting around the table, chatting, laughing, and enjoying the potato pancakes. At one point there was one more pancake left and everybody pushed the plate to the next person, saying: "you eat it." The truth was, we all had eaten enough. Finally, I shoved the plate with the pancake in front of Peter, banged my fist on the table (in a humorous way), and said: "Come on, Peter, you finish off this last pancake." Peter was startled, and having been sitting on the edge of his chair, he slid down to the floor. In the process he accidentally hit the edge of the plate with his hand. The plate flipped, the pancake jumped off and made a perfect landing on top of Peter's head, who was sitting on the floor by then. It was the look of surprise and bewilderment on Peter's face that caused our hysterical laughter. His expression was absolutely priceless, as if he wondered where he was and how he had gotten there. It was not until several seconds later that Peter realized he was sitting on the floor, and joined into our laughter. He still did not know that he had a pancake on his head, which made Olga and me even more hysterical.

Over the years, the memory of the story we called "Peter and the pancake" became a never–fail source of laughter with Olga, Peter, and me.

Learning about Measurements

As a homeowner I had a lot to learn. I was handy with tools and could take care of minor repairs when Mal was traveling. I enjoyed putting up curtains and changing furniture arrangements. House plants became a hobby, painting and wallpapering my specialty.

Eventually, I also had to learn about a liquid measurement which did not make sense to me. We drank a lot of milk, so I had a milkman deliver milk to the door. One morning I left a note, asking for a pint of whipping cream which I needed for a certain recipe. The milkman left two little bottles of heavy cream. I knew that there were four of those little bottles to a quart and I just assumed that each of them contained a pint. Therefore, I complained about receiving two bottles when I wanted only one pint. Mal asked me what I had ordered. I told him one pint. He said that it was exactly what I received—two half–pint bottles. After discussing this back and forth, I was forced to accept an illogical fact for someone who is used to the logical metric system: While one gallon equals four quarts, one quart does not equal four pints, but rather only two. As a result, we had a lot of apricot whip to eat up, and Mal has not asked for any since that time.

7

Our Marriage

Mal and I were married in 1958, and now in 2004 we have been happily married for forty–six years. Sometimes young people ask us how long we have been married, and when we tell them they always look at us with surprise and somewhat in awe. What seems like a relatively short time to us, to today's "throw away" generation it represents a commitment which most young people must find difficult to make.

Marriage was a commitment which both of us took seriously. There was never any question that we each intended to "give and take" to make it work. We certainly had a good example. Mal's parents were just seven months shy of their seventieth anniversary when Father passed on at age ninety–two. Both Mal and I intend to make it to our seventieth!

When we look back on our marriage, probably the biggest factor in our success has been the willingness of each of us to give the other room to do their own thing, without the other also having to be there. Mal has always been deeply involved in aviation, and annually he spends ten days at the largest aviation event in the world—AirVenture at Oshkosh, Wisconsin. Yes, I like airplanes, but not to the same degree that Mal does. With my blessings I send him on his way to this event each July, and he does not insist that I come with him.

In turn, for many of the last twenty–three years I have taken an annual camping trip—without Mal—first in our 1981 Bronco in which I could sleep, and in recent years with a tent and a Jeep Cherokee. I love to get off by myself, camping and hiking in Utah, Arizona, Colorado or New Mexico, as well as anywhere along the way. Most of the time I am gone for four or five weeks, and I return totally refreshed and with my batteries charged up. Mal is not really welcomed on these trips. He does not enjoy camping, but he understands and respects my need for solitude, as well as my wish to explore this beautiful country by car rather than just flying over it.

Throughout the earlier years of our marriage we saw just about every corner of the United States, including Alaska, from the air. Our children grew up with an airplane in the family, and they were used to our "flying" vacations. It appealed to my gypsy nature to not have to spend a whole vacation in one spot. At the same time, flying trips contributed to my education in that I developed a good mental picture of the "lay of the land" of the whole country. I can look out of the window of an airliner and, taking into consideration the length of time en route until then, pinpoint exactly where we are. Almost always, the pilot passenger announcements confirmed my conclusion.

During our years of taking flying trips, I would often look longingly out of the window at the countryside below, and wish that I could be down there and explore. "Some day," I would say, "I am going to get into my car and drive all over this country. I want to feel the distances and the space; I want to touch the rocks and sleep among the trees, and feel the sand in my shoes." Eventually I made my dream come true.

Initially I was so taken with the magnificent desert southwest that I went there a number of years in a row, camping and hiking in all of the National Parks, and crossing the desert country with my four–wheel drive vehicle. After we moved to the Pacific Northwest, I included the Pacific Coast States and southwestern Canada in my annual explorations. At this time, being now age seventy, I am still looking forward to my annual camping trips, and I hope to do so for some years to come.

Mal's Parents

Mal's father was an electrical engineer with General Electric X–Ray Corporation, and a pioneer in x–ray development. At the beginning of World War II, at about age 35, he joined the Army as an officer in the medical corps. He was stationed first in St. Louis, and later in Savannah, where he was responsible for visiting Army hospitals in the United States to advise them on the proper installation and use of X–ray equipment. He traveled virtually all of the time from these two locations.

Fortunately, the family was able to join him in both St. Louis and Savannah, so they could stay together.

In 1945, when it became obvious that the war in Germany was about to end, Father was released from the Army in order to accept a special government

Mal's mother and father on the occasion of their 50th wedding anniversary. They are standing in front of our home in McLean, Virginia.

assignment as a civilian to investigate the progress Germany had made during the war in x–ray and medical equipment development. After this six–month assignment, he returned to General Electric to become Vice President of Engineering of the General Electric X–Ray Corporation.

Mal's mother graduated from the University of Chicago, Phi Beta Kappa, with a degree in sociology. She was the first in her family to attend a university other than a teachers college. It was an era in which the wife was expected to stay at home and raise the children. Up until World War II, it was not customary for a family to have two incomes. People lived on the husband's earnings.

Mother also took her responsibility to serve her community very seriously. In 1946 she received a Red Cross certificate "in recognition of meritorious personal service performed in behalf of the nation, her armed forces, and suffering humanity in the Second World War." In 1969 she received a certificate of appreciation for her years of service to the Red Cross Blood Program. Mother left deeply ingrained in Mal his responsibility to "give back to the community."

Mal's Childhood

Mal was born in September 1933 in Chicago. He has one sister, Linda, who is seven years younger. Perhaps a defining moment in Mal's childhood was his first flight in June 1940 from Chicago to Portland, Oregon where both sets of his grandparents lived. This was an era be-

Mal, age six, arriving in Portland after his 11–hour flight from Chicago. His grandmother took this picture. He has had a love affair with airplanes since then.

fore travel by airplane became common, and the airlines were anxious to convince a skeptical public that flying was safe. United Airlines offered to assign an off–duty stewardess to accompany Mal, then not yet age seven, on the trip from Chicago to Portland. It must have taken Mal's mother courage to send her then only child off with a stranger on an essentially new, and perceived as dangerous, form of transportation. The flight was a long one. It involved stops in Omaha, Denver, Salt Lake City, Boise, and Pendleton before finally reaching Portland, eleven hours later. Once the plane got to Portland, United Airlines had arranged to have the Portland Oregonian take pictures for publicity purposes. Mal spent the summer in Portland and returned in August. He traces his lifelong love of aviation to those flights.

During the war years, the family moved from Chicago to St. Louis, then to Savannah, and later back to St. Louis. During the time when Mal's father was in Germany immediately after the war ended there, the family moved to Oregon to stay with his grandparents. Finally in 1946, the family settled in Wauwatosa, Wisconsin—a suburb of Milwaukee— where General Electric had moved the X–Ray company after the war. By that time Mal was in eighth grade, and he stayed in Milwaukee throughout his high school years.

Mal's father was transferred back to General Electric's headquarters in Schenectady, New York in 1950 between Mal's junior and senior years in high school. Fortunately, Mal had enough credits so that he could graduate in midyear, and kind neighbors let him stay with them in order to finish high school with his friends. The Korean War had started by then, and immediately after graduation in January 1951 Mal started college. Had he not done so he would likely have been drafted for the Korean War. He graduated from Lehigh University in June 1954. While in college he also enrolled in an Air Force Reserve Officers Training Program (ROTC) which was integrated into the college curriculum. When he graduated from Lehigh he received a reserve officer's commission in the Air Force, and had an obligation to serve for two years. An accounting major, Mal immediately joined Price Waterhouse in New York City with the understanding that he would be called up shortly to serve his two–year obligation.

In December 1954 Mal was ordered to active duty at Presque Isle Air Force Base in northern Maine. This was a fighter interceptor base, but his assignment was not as a pilot, but rather as an auditor. Mal's eyes were not 20/20 uncorrected, and he could not fly for the military. However, once at Presque Isle, he found that there was a local flying club where he could learn to fly, which he promptly and enthusiastically did. His first flight was on January 8, 1955, and he has been flying ever since. Presque Isle is a cold place in the winter, and all of his instruction was in airplanes with skis, not wheels. Barely two months later he bought his first plane, a two–place Cessna 140, and on March 30 he received his private pilot's license. In August 1956, Mal obtained his instrument rating. He says the instrument rating is what separates the men from the boys in aviation. A month later he sold his Cessna 140 and bought a four–seat Cessna 170A, which was the plane he owned when we first met.

Mal's Career with Price Waterhouse

When Mal was released from the Air Force in December 1956, he returned to Price Waterhouse in New York. For the first six or seven years he worked as a junior accountant, largely on major Fortune 500 clients (IBM, International Latex, West Virginia Pulp and Paper), and traveled a great deal. It was a rigorous work schedule. When he was not traveling he commuted to New York, which took an hour and a half each way. He usually had to catch a train just after 7 a.m., and if he left the office at 5 p.m.—which he seldom did—he would be home by 7 p.m. Once dinner was over and the children put to bed, there was little time left before we had to go to bed, too. This was the routine that was expected of young accountants who wanted to get ahead, and we thought nothing of it. In retrospect, it was hard on me. The days were long and Mal was often gone on Saturdays as well, so that there was hardly ever a relief from little children for me, or a chance to go somewhere alone.

Financial and Accounting Guide for
Nonprofit Organizations

By Malvern J. Gross, Jr., C.P.A., Partner, Price Waterhouse & Co.

The 1st Edition, published in 1972, quickly became the definitive work in its field, establishing Mal's professional reputation.

When Mal became a "manager" he also started to serve smaller clients, including a number of nonprofit clients ranging from religious to large charitable organizations. Over time, Mal became an expert in nonprofit accounting. This prompted him to write a more than 540 page book, *Financial and Accounting Guide for Nonprofit Organizations*. It became the definitive work in his field, and is still in publication thirty plus years later, now in the sixth edition. While the book continues to include his name, other Price Waterhouse partners have long since taken over the necessary periodic updating of the book.

Mal became a partner in 1968. At the time there were two hundred other partners; today there are several thousand, and the Firm is many times larger. Mal had a distinguished career. As witnessed by his book, he was a pioneer in establishing sound accounting and reporting principles for the nonprofit sector at a time when it seemed to him that "anything goes." In the early 1960's he was also one of the first at Price Waterhouse to develop auditing techniques that utilized the then new room–size computers.

In the late seventies when the first Apple II desktop computers appeared on the market, Mal early on recognized their future significance. In those days you could not go down to a store and buy software. If you wanted one of these early computers to perform a task for you, it was necessary to first write a program in "BASIC" to do what you wanted. And Mal did. He wrote a flight planning program that was about 100,000 lines of code long, and eventually he sold close to a thousand copies to other pilots, through the Aircraft Owners and Pilots Association. It was rudimentary by today's standards, but he was one of the first—and I became one of the first "computer widows."

Mal also recognized early on that individual partners within the Firm needed to specialize in the accounting and business practices for specific industries. Up to that point most partners were "generalists." While this was not a popular idea, he was appointed National Director of Industry Specialization and took the first steps to reorient the Firm along industry lines. Today, fifteen years after his retirement, Price Waterhouse—now known as Pricewaterhouse Coopers—is largely organized along industry lines.

Mal with his Price Waterhouse hat

In order to pursue his first love—aviation—Mal elected to take early retirement at age fifty–five. On retiring he became the President of the National Aeronautic Association, the national aero club of the United States. In that capacity he represented United States sport aviation at the Fédération Aéronautique Internationale, the international sport aviation organization then headquartered in Paris. He retired from that organization in 1993 when we moved to Orcas Island and built our retirement home on a lovely piece of property which we had purchased ten years earlier and had named "Island in the Sky." Mal remains active today in aviation circles as a member of the Board of Directors of EAA, the largest sport aviation organization in the world.

Moves

I am a gypsy at heart. One of my real regrets of our marriage is that Mal's career did not call for frequent moves to other cities and different parts of the country. Mal started out in the New York office, and the only physical move during his thirty–eight year career was from New York to Washington, DC. We made up for it, though, in our many travels as described in more detail elsewhere in this book.

Our life together started in Morristown, New Jersey, in Jacob Ford Village. This was a complex of garden apartments, and we both happened to be living at opposite ends of the same building when we met. Mal had been sharing an apartment with another Price Waterhouse man. When we were married, Mal moved into my apartment after we had made other arrangements for Mom, and Peter had decided this was a good time to get his military service out of the way. Within a year we were bored and started thinking about buying a house. We sold Mal's Cessna 170 to raise the down payment for our first home.

Altogether we have owned five homes.

Denville, New Jersey

Denville was our first home. It was located about ten miles further from New York City than Morristown. Denville was on the rail route of the Erie, Lackawanna & Western Railroad, which was the commuter railroad into Hoboken on the New Jersey side of the Hudson River. Our house was a small one, nine years old at the time, and probably less than 1,000 square feet in size, but we remember it with all of the enthusiasm that a young couple brings to their first home. It was charming. Built on a concrete slab, it had hot water pipes in the floors to provide radiant heating. The house was situated on a hill and our property backed onto the Lackawanna Railroad right–of–way at the bottom, hence we had a patch of woods beyond our back yard instead of another house. We quickly got used to the sound of trains passing by. In choosing the location of this home, we had to consider the nearness of rail transportation to New York City for Mal. Living within walking distance of a railroad station avoided the

The patio and back yard of our Denville home. It was small but cozy, and for a young couple it was our castle.

need for a second car. I was still working for The Mennen Company at the time.

We lived in our cute Denville house for six years. Here we learned about gardening, lawn mowing, painting, building a patio, and all the little improvements which were so exciting to new home owners. I even built shutters for the windows—and what an improvement that was to an otherwise plain house!

Randy joined us in 1964 while living in Denville. Mom is proudly holding her first grandson.

Early in 1965, only a few months after our son Randy joined the family, we moved back to the Morristown area. We needed more space. While the Denville house was quite adequate for the two of us and an occasional guest, we now needed a separate room for the baby whose crib was wedged in between a wall and Mal's desk. In time, we also hoped to add another child to our family.

Randy was Mom's second grandchild. Peter's wife had a little daughter, Denise, the year before, and Mom was the happiest grandmother in the world. While she kept her little house in Florida, she had temporarily moved back to New Jersey before her granddaughter was born. She just could not stay so far away from her grandchildren.

Morristown, New Jersey

Our Morristown house was a new one which was already completed when we first looked at it. A split–level home, it had three bedrooms, an unfinished upstairs room, a family room and a basement, as well as an attic—six half levels in all. It was considerably more spacious than the Denville house, and best of all from Mal's perspective, it was located in a new housing development near the Morristown airport. By then we owned another airplane, and I had obtained my pilot's license the year before while I still had time to enjoy local flights in the evenings after work. This freedom changed once I had a baby to take care of.

In 1965 we moved into this new house in Morristown, New Jersey. It was a lovely home, with 4 bedrooms. Two years later Michele joined our family.

There was a large back yard which we had professionally landscaped, although we built the patio and did the stone work on the slope.

Mal and I both had lots of energy and enthusiasm, and over the next couple of years we completed the house and landscaped the back yard. I had learned how to wallpaper, and during the nine years we lived in this house, had wallpapered most rooms and repainted the whole house, inside and out. We were very happy living in Morristown, and ours was the type and size house that we would still enjoy living in today.

Our guest room was being kept busy. Mom had moved back to Florida, and she would come to visit us, as well as Peter's family, for weeks at a time. A couple of years later when Father retired and Mal's parents moved to the Eastern Shore in Maryland, they visited us more frequently than they had when they lived in Rochester, New York. I always loved having them. Mother and I got along so well, and I felt extremely lucky to have such a wonderful mother–in–law. Having been lovingly accepted into the family by both of Mal's parents contributed greatly to the success of our marriage. We got along splendidly, and I could not have asked for more wonderful in–laws. I grew especially close to Mother. She was my "Emily Post" and educated me in the customs and manners that were different in this country. Whenever I was unsure of the proper etiquette, I would ask Mother for help. She was my mother–in–law for forty–four years, and there had never been a cross word between us. My words are inadequate to pay tribute to her. She was a grand lady, and I loved her dearly.

At the time we moved into the Morristown house we did not have a great deal of furniture, and for the first few years the living and dining rooms remained sparsely furnished. We felt that it would be wise to spend the money on landscaping so that the shrubs and trees could start growing, and that furniture purchases could wait. A couple of large house plants were excellent "fillers" of vacant areas in the living and dining rooms until, little by little, we could purchase furniture. The decision to tend to the landscaping first paid off. Our back yard was magnificent, and we thoroughly enjoyed being outside. We stayed in this spacious house until 1974, at which time Mal transferred to the Washington, DC office of Price Waterhouse. Randy was then ten and Michele seven years old, so the children remember Morristown.

McLean, Virginia

McLean was like a "dream house" when we first saw it. It was about ten years old and had been beautifully redecorated within the previous

Randy (10) and Michele (7) standing at the front door of our McLean home shortly after we moved there in 1974.

We had a lovely back yard. Here are two views, one showing the rear of the house, while the other is taken from the dining room window. Note the tree house on the left and the stream in the distance.

two years. The house had a place in history, in a way. The first owner was Bill Moyers, the Press Secretary at the White House for President Johnson at the time. The "historical" part of the house was that President Johnson had eaten dinner in our dining room.

The setting was magnificent. We had a number of huge, old oak trees on the property, the massive trunk of one being centered in the dining room's picture window, only four feet away from the house—unbeliev-able, but I measured it. Behind the house was a little stream that tumbled over rocks and eventually emptied into the Potomac River about a mile away. There were five bedrooms upstairs. Each of the kids had a room, I had a sewing room which also served as a guest room, and Mal had a room for his office. In a family room adjacent to the kitchen was a built–in barbecue next to the fireplace, which saw a lot of use.

Our McLean home was perfect for our family at the time, with a big yard for the children to play in. There even was a tree house which had been built for the two boys of the previous owners. Needless to say, the tree house was a popular attraction for the children in the neighborhood.

Eleven years later, when Randy was in college and Michele was about to finish high school, we decided to simplify our life. The house was high maintenance, particularly the beautiful grounds. Soon after

This was our Goldsboro townhouse. It was quite narrow, but had 4,000 square feet of space on three floors. The Association took care of all external maintenance. It was perfert for our needs at that time. My Bronco is in the driveway.

we had moved to McLean, I became interested in bonsai trees and took lessons. After I owned a number of bonsais, I found that I was unable to spend the time that these little trees required because I had this big yard to take care of which took so much time. The bonsais suffered from neglect until we decided to move into a townhouse and thus eliminated the constant yard work. Chapter 9 discusses my bonsai hobby.

Bethesda, Maryland

Bethesda is located just across the Potomac River from McLean, where we found a luxurious, three–story, 4,000 square foot townhouse. I love to move, and I thoroughly enjoyed this six–mile move from McLean to Bethesda. Having had lots of moving experience from childhood days on, this move was the most fun one so far. We had closed on the townhouse more than two weeks before we needed to be out of the McLean house. With my Bronco I moved all household gear and whatever I could fit into the car—such as lamps, pictures, and our clothes—often making two or three trips a day. By the time the movers brought the furniture, the kitchen was organized and functional, and the clothes were in the closets.

We had a narrow back yard, but it was big enough to place tables for my bonsai trees. This was where I got serious with my hobby because I did not have other plants or a yard to contend with.

Like the McLean house, this location was close to Mal's office—fifteen minutes, even in rush hour. The best part of the townhouse was that the front yard and outside house maintenance were handled by a homeowners' association. This meant we could lock up the house and travel without having to be concerned about neighbors complaining about tall grass. There was no lawn to mow. We had Blue Rug Junipers planted to cover the postage–stamp–size front yard, and the tiny back yard became my bonsai trees' haven. Both children still had their own rooms to come home to, but soon they were out on their own.

I filled my empty nest with bonsai work, as well as other interests for which I had not had time before then. One of those was to start writing this book; another was traveling. Mal did a lot of work at the London office of Price Waterhouse, and I accompanied him on several of his trips. After touring London on foot, I took day trips by bus to the surrounding areas such as Stonehenge, Bath, and the Cotswolds. Together, we took a couple of week–long bus tours to Scotland and the north of England.

A year after we moved into the townhouse, we built a little house on property we had purchased on Orcas Island in 1983 so that we had a place to stay whenever we were visiting the island. We loved being on Orcas, and soon we took every opportunity to spend time at our little house there. Sometimes I would stay on for a week or ten days after Mal had gone back to work. The planning and design of our future retirement home on Orcas Island became my next hobby. I collected ideas

This is the driveway entrance to our Orcas home. Situated on 12 acres near the top of Buck Mountain, we named the property "Island In The Sky." At 1,250 feet we are often in or above the clouds, giving us an aerial view of this beautiful country.

and wrote notes about features I liked, either in our previous homes or in other people's houses. We loved the vaulted ceilings and open spaces of this townhouse, and incorporated those features in this first home we ever built from scratch.

For seven years we were happy in Bethesda where we lived until Mal retired—for the second time—and we moved to Orcas Island, Washington, in December 1992.

Orcas Island, Washington

Orcas Island—where we now live—is one of the San Juan Islands of Washington State, about eighty miles north of Seattle, right on the Canadian border. Once again, I enjoyed the move itself tremendously. The gypsy in me could not have been happier. My then eleven–year–old Bronco had to haul a trailer for the first time—three thousand miles across the country—carrying about fifty bonsai trees, their tables, soil mixes and rocks, in early fall 1992.

View of our main house, facing west. It is snuggled into the side of the mountain and has a magnificent view of the San Juan Islands, the entire Olypmic Range of mountains, as well as Vancouver Island, and the Gulf Islands. On a clear day we can literally see 100 miles in all directions. We also have a guest house attached to a two–car garage with bedroom, kitchen facilities, and living area.

A week before Christmas, my Bronco and I made another trip from Washington, DC to Orcas Island, and it turned out to be the most glorious trip ever. I saw nothing but snow from the moment I entered the Pennsylvania Turnpike to cross the Allegheny Mountains until I had crossed the last of the Cascades and approached the Seattle area five days later. The whole country had been a fairyland of white! Of all the long–distance driving I have done, this one had been my favorite trip by far. I loved every mile of it despite the possibility that I might spend Christmas by myself in a motel room somewhere. However, my faithful Bronco had four–wheel drive, new tires, and a heavy load—computers and tools—and thus no problems crossing any of the mountain ranges. The happy gypsy would do that trip all over again, anytime.

For a year we lived in the little guest house while we enjoyed the process of building our own home for the first time.

We have this incredible view from our living room. While not visible in this picture, the snow–covered Olympic Mountains can be seen to the left (south), and the mountains on Vancouver Island to the right (west and north).

The San Juan Islands are a group of volcanic islands lying between ten and twenty miles west of the mainland. There are no roads or bridges to the islands; in fact the ferry takes nearly an hour and a half to make the sixteen–mile trip to Orcas Island. There are only five or six ferries a day each way, and one has to plan carefully when going "off island." While these ferries are sizeable—several of them can carry almost two hundred cars—the San Juan Islands are a popular tourist destination in the summer, and the ferries often have overloads. Being on the overload means that one has to wait until the next ferry, which typically runs three hours later.

We are living on Buck Mountain, 1,250 feet above the water. It is difficult to describe the view. From our living room we can often see the entire range of the year–round snow–covered Olympic Mountains which are between fifty and one hundred miles away. At night we see the lights of Victoria in Canada and of Port Angeles on the Olympic Peninsula. On clear days we can see an island in Canada that is almost ninety miles away.

There is, of course, an airport on Orcas Island—otherwise Mal would never even have considered buying property here. While Mal decided to sell his beloved Cessna upon reaching age seventy, he still has his small single–seat airplane, a Mooney Mite, which he uses in good weather to keep up his flying.

Orcas Island is about the same size as Manhattan in New York, but has a population of less than five thousand people. Tourism and catering to the retired are the principal occupations of the residents. A high percentage of the population is retired.

The pace of life is much slower here on Orcas Island than it is on the mainland, and we happily gave up the rat race and adjusted to "island time." There are limited health care facilities on Orcas Island, and we hope that our health will permit us to stay here for many years to come.

8

Our Family

My Brother Peter

Peter immigrated in August 1956, and quickly adapted to life in America. A couple of months before Mom arrived in the United States in April 1957, Peter and I moved out of Aunt and Uncle's house and into an apartment in Morristown, New Jersey. We were happy when our little family was together once again and we had an apartment all to ourselves. It was not to be for long, though. Fate had other plans for us.

After I met Mal near the end of that year and we made marriage plans for 1958, both Mom and Peter had to find a new place to live. Peter, then nearly twenty years old, decided to join the Army to get his military service out of the way. He finished Basic and Advanced Infantry training with the Army Reserve Unit and was discharged in six months. At the time, military service was mandatory and Peter's service requirement was considered satisfied. Upon returning from Fort Dix, New Jersey, he found a room in a boarding house in Morristown, bought his first car—a used Mercury—and was now on his own for the first time in his life.

Peter in the Army—1958

Peter's three children: (from left) Denise, Eric, and Dana Marie, in October, 2003

Peter's three children and our two on the jungle gym in our back yard in Morristown, New Jersey

From top: Randy, Eric, Denise, Michele, and Dana Marie

As I relate elsewhere in this book, Peter had been offered a job by Bill Mennen at The Mennen Company even before he arrived in the United States. Once back from the Army, Peter stayed at Mennen for his entire career of thirty–seven years. Towards the end when the Mennen family sold the company to Colgate–Palmolive, he continued until his retirement in 1993.

Peter married Jean Coviello on September 9, 1962. They have three children—a daughter, Denise Marie; a son, Eric John; and another daughter, Dana Marie. They have been blessed with eight lovely grandchildren—three girls and five boys—and Peter is a happy and loving grandfather. He enjoys baby–sitting and being involved in their lives.

Peter and Jean have owned two homes over the years. Being a nature lover as our Mom had been, Peter loved working in the yard. He always created beautifully landscaped gardens, did a lot of rock work, built decks, and for his most recent house he had designed a picnic area in a grove of birch trees, complete with a pond and a bridge leading to the picnic grove. While he has worked hard, Peter counts his blessings for the things he has been able to accomplish in this great country, which could never have happened had we stayed in Berlin all of our lives.

Our Mom

When Mal and I got married, Mom also had to find another place to live because Mal and I were planning to live in my apartment. Bill Mennen once again played an important role in our family's future. He was on the Board of Directors of Morristown Memorial Hospital, and he had not only arranged for Mom to get a job at the hospital months earlier, but now to rent a part of a small caretaker's house on the hospital grounds that was then being used for storage. After a little more than a year in this country, Mom had her own "place" and a steady job, too.

It was while working at the hospital that Mom met Jim Finan, a jovial Irishman who was also working at the hospital. They married in July of 1959, and Mom was happy when they moved into an apartment in the neighboring town of Madison. Sometime in 1961, Mom and Jim went on a vacation trip to Daytona Beach, Florida, and Mom fell in love with Florida. Jim had at one time lived in the Daytona area. They decided to leave New Jersey and move to Daytona. In due course Mom

Mom and I at her home in Daytona Beach in the early 1960's

bought a trailer home which had a living room added onto it, and which stood on its own lot. While very modest and not in the best neighborhood, it was "her" house, something that she could not have dreamed of having in Berlin. Mom was so proud of having her own home. She decorated it beautifully, and enjoyed planting a flower garden.

Mom worked at a number of seasonal jobs in the Daytona Beach area, which were mostly food preparation work in restaurants. The heat bothered her greatly, and during the summers she made occasional trips back and forth to New Jersey. Her marriage with Jim was not working out, and in due course Mom was "single" again. True to her gypsy nature—I wonder from whom I inherited the love for change of environment—Mom closed up her trailer house and moved back to New Jersey for a time to be near her children, and to enjoy her first grandchildren. She never had trouble finding work wherever she went. One time she worked in a factory sewing sweaters. Piecework is hectic, but she enjoyed doing some sewing again for a change, and we received gifts of beautiful sweaters.

Mom's English was quite adequate by now. Early in 1964, Peter taught her how to drive. Mom earned her driver's license and soon bought a car.

Eventually Mom moved back to Florida for good. She took a job at the hospital in Daytona Beach, which she enjoyed. On one of our visits we talked her into selling the trailer home and helped her buy a house with proper air conditioning. She found a cute two–bedroom house in Holly Hill just north of Daytona Beach. It was less than two blocks from the Halifax River which is a part of the Intracostal Waterway, and a much nicer location. We enjoyed many happy vacations there when our children were young, and Mom was delighted to be able to offer us a vacation spot. Peter with his wife and three children also spent vacations at Mom's, so that she got to enjoy all of her grandchildren. We parents happily took advantage of the free baby–sitting services to take occasional evenings off for a movie, or to go out to eat without little ones tugging at our sleeves all of the time. Mom would be right in her element when she had children around her.

Having our own airplane, it was no problem for us to fly to Florida for a few days to have Thanksgiving or Christmas with Mom. We would appreciate a few days in warm weather at a time when New Jersey was wearing a winter coat, and Mom got to enjoy Randy and Michele. Most years we celebrated Christmas at our house in New Jersey, and Mom would join us there. Our guest bedroom was occupied often. With Peter's family living in New Jersey as well, it was easy for Mom to divide her time between us.

Mom lived in Florida until we brought her to Virginia at the end of 1975. For a couple of years we had noticed increasing signs of confu-

sion. Suspecting that something was wrong with Mom, we thought that she should no longer live alone. We wanted her to be near us so that we could visit frequently and keep an eye on her. After Christmas we made arrangements for her in a retirement home in nearby Alexan-

Mom's Florida home. We enjoyed many happy times visiting her here. Randy is standing near the front door.

dria, Virginia. Alzheimer's Disease had not been given a name at that time, and the doctors did not really know what was wrong with Mom, but told us she had some type of dementia. Luckily the retirement home had a nursing facility to take care of Mom as her illness progressed. Memory and language were the first facilities to leave Mom, and I missed being able to communicate with her.

Mom died in 1987 at the age of seventy–eight, after many years of deteriorating with Alzheimer's Disease. It had been an eleven–year ordeal, and I suffered greatly. It was hard on the whole family. What hurt me the most about her illness was the unfairness of it. Mom's whole life had been a struggle for survival. Born in 1909, she experienced World War I and its aftermath in Berlin, a runaway inflation and years of very hard times. Then came the Great Depression. She married in 1929 and my father, a typesetter at a publishing company, was out of work for nearly five years. Just before I was born in 1934, he found a job as a tobacco goods salesman. It wasn't great, but it was a job. They had to struggle. Peter was born in 1938. At about that time the economy started to pick up, but a couple of years later Mom found herself alone with two young children when World War II was in progress and Papa was drafted to serve in the military. Her struggle for our survival, her strength, adaptability, and her unselfish devotion, is described in *Memories of World War II and its Aftermath*. Peter and I would not have had a chance of surviving had it not been for our Mom's unselfish love for her children.

Mom had the gift for making the best of every situation, no matter how difficult, and for seeing only the positive side of it. She was always cheerful, and a happy person within herself. With her characteristic Berlin humor she mastered every obstacle in her life. She could turn enemies into friends, and win battles with her relentless humor and goodwill. Alzheimer's Disease, unfortunately, was one enemy against whom she was totally powerless.

Some of Mom's best years were after the hopelessness of World War II's aftermath eased up and things got better overall in Berlin in the early 1950's. I had a job and only Peter was still in school. Then came my good fortune in that I was invited to immigrate to the United States of America, and eventually Peter and Mom followed me. Mom did have about twenty good years here in the United States. When she was sixty–two years old and finally retired, her social security payments were meager. However, by that time Mal was doing well enough in his career so that we could subsidize Mom's income, and thus insure that she would have no financial worries. Finally, for the first time in her life she "had it made;" but then came the dreadful illness which prevented her from being able to enjoy a few years of carefree retirement. She had been most deserving of it. However, life can be quite unfair.

Adoption

In September of 1962, I left Warner–Lambert Pharmaceutical Company to take a two–month trip to Germany. Hoping to get started on a family soon after my return, I went to work for Manpower for several months. It was interesting to work for a number of different companies, and I thoroughly enjoyed the diversity. Each company I worked for offered me a permanent job. At the same time, I was on Warner–Lambert's list to be called in for temporary work in the Budget Department. Their workload had monthly peaks, and they used to rely on my help when I worked in Accounting where I was not always busy. In early spring of 1963 I went back to work for Warner–Lambert on a permanent basis, to be the secretary to the Director of Purchasing and Transportation.

In the fall of 1963, after five years of marriage, we started to check into adoption. To me, a family is not complete without children, and Mal agreed. After being approved by an adoption agency in New York City early in 1964, we were able to adopt an adorable, smiling baby boy whom we named Randolph Eric. He joined us the day after Thanksgiving. I remember that Thanksgiving Day to be the most special one ever. We had a particular reason to give thanks for receiving this most precious of gifts. Randy was three and a half months old when he joined our family.

In August of 1967, a beautiful baby sister, Michele Andrea, joined our

Randy with his perpetual smile

Randy welcomes his new sister

happy Randy–boy four weeks after her birth. Our family was now complete.

Our Son Randy

If we had been able to take our pick of a hundred little boys to adopt, I cannot imagine we could have picked one that would have had more of a perpetual smile on his face, or brought more radiance and happiness into our family. This charm and affability would turn out to be one of his major strengths throughout his life. Randy was always smiling, and I called him my "happy–boy."

What a change his presence made in our family! As is almost universal, a child changes the focus of the family in ways that are hard to describe, but which are quite real. Perhaps the best description is that it changed the focus from the two of us to include another human being into the circle of love and happiness, and in the process made us the richer for doing so. How we have silently thanked the unknown mother who chose to give Randy up for adoption that he might have a better life, and with this decision made our lives more complete.

Randy on the patio he "helped" build in Morristown.

Randy was an outgoing boy who made friends with ease, particularly among adults. In his early developmental years I spoke only German with him when we were alone. Whenever Mom visited, she and I would converse in German and Randy continued to pick it up. However, once he went to nursery school he stopped speaking German since no other kids spoke that language. He would later at home respond in English when I spoke to him in German or when Mom and I conversed, which demonstrated understanding, but he stopped even this by kindergarten. However, his early exposure to a different language would be helpful to him later when he became interested in learning foreign languages.

An excellent student, Randy was not terribly athletic and tended to avoid team sports, but he excelled with swimming lessons and still loves to swim today. He read voraciously, devouring books and magazines, and he loved watching television and listening to the radio. His love for music was seen early on, as he stood on his tippy toes to look down into our huge

Randy's third grade school picture

Fisher stereo in the living room and watched the records spin. Randy loved to sit with his father's big earphones listening to his early favorites. He was overjoyed when in second grade we got him his own Sony clock radio for Christmas, and the following year he received his own little record player. This love for music was something that Mal passed down to him, although their tastes in music were different.

Randy started school in the Morris County school system, but starting with the third grade we were able to switch him to a private school, the renowned Peck School in Morristown. Randy was back in public school when we moved to McLean, Virginia. He was then ten years old and started fifth grade. His high school years were a mix of private and public school, and he seemed to thrive best in a private school setting where classes were smaller and he had more attention.

During virtually all of his childhood we had an airplane, and most of our family vacations involved traveling in the plane, usually long distances. Consequently, both children grew up with flying and took flight as a more or less normal way to travel. These travels throughout North America showed them the vastness of the continent, something that appealed to me greatly in contrast to my childhood in Europe. Later in life, our children acknowledged that the many vacations we took as a family in Mal's airplane were eye–opening. These travels taught them that there were many different people and cultures in our nation, and dramatically different ways of living beyond the privileged suburban walls of their upbringing.

During junior high school, Randy had the choice to take either French or Spanish in the eighth grade. Even though his impulse was to take French, Mal insisted on Spanish, rationalizing that this was the second most prevalent language in the United States and on the North American continent. Randy followed Mal's direction, and ended up loving Spanish class. The following summer before he started high school, Randy was invited to join our family friends Olga and Mike Saito and their children at their vacation home in Spain for a month. My friend Olga, who was originally from Argentina, insisted that the only way to learn a language was to speak with the natives of the country. This opportunity allowed Randy to practice his Spanish by using it in conversation, which later proved an asset in his professional career, just as Mal had said it would. Randy admits his gratitude for this guidance. In addition, he says that this first trip to Europe was his best summer vacation.

Another fond memory for him was the trip several summers later when Mal took Randy to Mexico City, and to see the ruins of Chichen Itza on the Yucatan Peninsula. Randy loved being the translator for his father. Now it is clear to us that our love of travel and adventure has been passed on to our son, although his definition of vacations and his destinations are quite different than our own. He loves traveling to Europe and is attracted by the history and antiquity, as well as the different cultures in the various cities, and where he can indulge his love of languages.

While Randy did not have the love for aviation that Mal has as a pilot, he nevertheless—perhaps to please Mal—took flying lessons as a fifteen–year–old so that he could solo an airplane on his sixteenth birthday—the minimum legal age. Only after that first solo flight— which is quite an accomplishment for anyone regardless of age—did Dad take Randy to the motor vehicle licensing office to get his driver's license. Randy did not continue his flying lessons much beyond soloing. While Mal was inwardly disappointed, he was wise enough not to push. Flying is serious business, and if the heart is not in it, one should not be flying. Randy has commented repeatedly later on in life that in addition to being a thrilling experience to fly in the sky alone, this soloing experience showed him that if he wanted something badly enough, he certainly could do it.

Washington Post Caption: "McLean Man and His Son Set Speed Record for Small Plane in Flight from San Francisco."

One notable flight: Randy, then age twelve, accompanied Mal on his record–setting flight—San Francisco to Washington, DC—on January 1, 1977, and suddenly found his picture on the front page of the Metro Section of the Washington Post. Picked up by the wire services, the story was carried throughout the United States and abroad. Randy did not know about his picture being in the paper until his classmates commented on it and were impressed.

Randy's high school years started out somewhat tumultuously, but after he changed to Harker Preparatory School in Potomac, Maryland, he felt comfortable. A small and very structured private school, he thrived in this setting and found his academic self; his favorite and best subjects were American and European history, German, and English. The high points of his senior year were when his classmates voted him Most Likely to Succeed, while his charm and effervescent personality won him the seat of Class President. Filled with confidence he was ready for higher education. Mal and I had always emphasized that education was the key to success in life, and skills learned would always be an asset for him regardless.

Randy went to George Washington University and received his BA in Education and Human Development. Between his junior and senior year, he took a summer job on a children's unit in a Washington DC psychiatric hospital which changed his outlook. He no longer wanted to be a teacher but rather decided that he wanted to be a nurse. After researching his options, he told Mal that he would complete his education degree at George Washington University first and then he would like to get an accelerated BS degree in the nursing program at Catholic University. We agreed to help him with this additional quest for education as we always felt that an education is the most valuable gift one can bestow on a child.

Randy graduated in 1989 and took a job as a nurse on a surgical unit at Georgetown University Hospital. While working at the hospital, Randy took advantage of the generous benefit of free tuition and pursued an MS degree in Adult Health Nursing. By the time he graduated, he had clear visions for a new life and job in New York City. Randy loves big cities, and living in New York would also have the benefit of being near his sister and niece who lived on Long Island. Mal and I had moved to Washington State the year before so that Randy no longer had the close connection with us. Randy and I always had the best talks when he stopped by the house after school to have lunch with me and to do his laundry.

Randy moved to New York City and joined Memorial Sloan–Kettering Cancer Center, the best cancer center in the nation, if not the entire world. He accepted a job as a staff nurse, and proved his worth by rapidly climbing the ranks to reach the top position of Clinical Nurse Specialist at their breast center. As an expert in breast cancer, besides loving the clinical part of taking care of patients, Randy excelled at all that came with the job. He traveled nationwide to speak at conferences, published articles and textbook chapters on breast cancer and nursing, conducted his own nursing research, and repeatedly was recognized with accolades for all his work. For years he has managed the breast cancer Q&A board on the WebMD website. Additionally, using the skills from both his education and nursing degrees, he taught both nursing lecture and clinical courses in New York City for several years. Presently, his love for the clinical care of patients combined with his desire to advance himself has taken him on a new journey, and he is now pursuing a postgraduate degree as a Nurse Practitioner in Women's Health at Columbia University. Upon completion, his goal is to be a primary care provider for healthy women.

Randy's smile, humorous nature, and his compassion combined with his sharp intellect make him an excellent nurse. Years ago, we once asked him why he didn't go on to get his MD and become a physician, and he responded: "Doctors diagnose and prescribe treatments, and spend just minutes with patients. Nurses deal with all the responses that illness inflicts. They are the ones that spend the time with patients, and that's what I love to do." Randy strongly believes that an understanding and smart nurse is the key to a patient's recovery, and seeing him in action, I believe it.

Randy's life in New York City during his thirties was both a series of professional and personal successes. The exciting activity of city life has always appealed to him in contrast to the tranquility of the suburbs, and the city was certainly the

Randy, RN, in his lab coat at Memorial Hospital in New York City.

place for him in the 1990's. Like me, Randy loves to walk everywhere in the city, and he has taken me on walks to his favorite places, like along the Hudson River or across the Brooklyn Bridge. However, the 9/11 attack on the World Trade Center affected him deeply. Luckily he was at work uptown on the morning of the attacks, but his apartment is just twelve blocks north of the site. Again, he was lucky that his apartment was not damaged and he was physically safe; however, he lived in the aftermath of damage and carnage to his neighborhood for months. Though he initially rallied with his love of the city, as every New Yorker and American did, the sheen of living in New York City has paled for him. He mourns the loss of a city that he once loved. Randy said that this is not a unique feeling, but one shared by many New Yorkers as well.

He admitted to me that his own experience in no way compares to my experiences with war. However, given his emotions after the attacks, he says he cannot even fathom what I endured, even though he had read earlier drafts of my childhood years. My son has always been empathetic, but his years of work with cancer patients have given him a far greater understanding of human suffering.

Our Daughter Michele

Michele joined the family three years after Randy, and I was elated to have a little doll for whom I could sew pretty dresses and put ribbons in her hair. She was a beautiful baby who grew into a wonderful daughter.

A different personality than Randy, she had a mind of her own as a child, and was not hesitant to express herself. She loved being in charge, and in her early years played teacher with her dolls and stuffed animals, lining them up, each with paper and pencil while she "instructed" them.

Like Randy, Michele started nursery school at age three, where she further demonstrated her insistence of wanting to be in charge. Her ability for being a leader rather than a follower surfaced early. She was well–liked by her peers, though her teachers often found it challenging to deal with her temper when she did not get what she wanted. As every mother wants her child to be a model of good manners and behavior, I lived in constant fear that my "perfect" daughter would be kicked out of school because the teachers could not handle her.

Michele and I are having a good talk

Michele started Kindergarten at the Peck School in Morristown. Standing out in my memory is the pre–admittance testing by the headmaster of the school. Michele was given a few tasks to test her intelligence, one of which was to draw a stick man. No problem for my daughter, except that she decided to outfit her stick man with three arms. Kindly, the headmaster asked Michele how many arms a man has, and she correctly answered: "two." "Why did you draw three arms on your stick man?" was the headmaster's question. Michele's answer: "because I WANT three arms!" I was surprised when the headmaster accepted this and admitted her into the kindergarten of this fine and prominent old school.

Remembering how much I always liked water and not having a chance to learn how to swim until I was thirteen years old, I took Michele to YMCA Gym and Swim classes at age two, as I had done with Randy three years earlier. Michele also became a good swimmer.

As most of her friends did, Michele took ballet lessons and did very well. She was graceful and agile, and the teacher was impressed with her performance. I enjoyed going to the recitals and loved to watch her dance. She was good! As may be natural for doting mothers, I visualized a budding star ballet dancer.

Next were ice skating lessons, and while we did not come up with an Olympic skater, we had much fun. New Jersey winters provided some frozen ponds, and I got myself back into skates and took the children skating.

The children's early years meant a lot of driving and car pooling—I often drove more than one hundred miles a day—but I remember them as wonderful years with my children. I certainly wanted them to partici-

Michele, not yet three years old, about to dive into the community swimming pool.

Michele, age 6, playing school in her room

pate in any lessons for which they showed an interest. After we moved to Virginia, we honored Michele's request and bought a piano. Both Randy and Michele then took piano lessons for the next four or five years.

In the summer of 1974 we moved to McLean, Virginia, where Michele started second grade in public school. At that time, the trend in school administration was to have large classrooms with one hundred twenty kids, a teacher and one or two assistant teachers. It was chaos. This was a "permissive" era and the kids could do whatever they wanted. We were appalled at the lack of discipline caused primarily by the large class size which was called an "open classroom system." Michele did not prosper in this environment, and we became concerned. With her strong personality she needed an atmosphere where discipline was maintained and the class size was small enough to provide individual attention where needed. We moved Michele into Cloverlawn Academy, a very small private school where the average class size was only five to eight students. This turned out to be an excellent choice for these early years, and Michele prospered. She rejoined the public school system in seventh grade.

Her teenage years were typical for an adolescent girl growing up in suburban America. I struggled to understand her desire for brand names—this type of jeans, and that type of jacket. My childhood was completely different than my daughter's; we had been lucky to have a few noodles in our soup. Michele was just trying to be like all the other girls in school, which was developmentally normal, but hard for me to relate to. It was difficult for my children to understand how I grew up, and my stories somehow never seemed to penetrate; they found it impossible to relate to them from the context of their comfortable suburban home. However, years later, both have said my writings have explained to them the circumstances of my childhood far better than I could verbally. Perhaps this also comes with the wisdom of maturity, as my children are now adults out in the world.

Michele's high school years were her best academically, as she joined her brother at Harker. She was always popular in school, and was a leader among her peers. She demonstrated her smarts and graduated as salutatorian of her senior class. Her best subject was math. Much like her father, she had an innate comprehension of numbers and business. Later in life this understanding would prove beneficial when combined with her savvy, common sense, and take–charge approach. Harker was the best decision we made for both our children; the school was structured to bring out the success in the student, and this environment prepared each of them with confidence so that they could move on to the next step and to adulthood.

Michele went further away from home than her brother did. She chose Guilford College in North Carolina, but the lack of structure of the campus setting in that remote college town didn't work for her. Perhaps another school or one closer to home might have changed the outcome, but this particular college had been her decision. She realized that academic higher education was not for her at that time in her life. Instead she went to Katherine Gibbs, the premier secretarial school. Not only did Katherine Gibbs turn out women who were well trained technically, they also ingrained into their students a culture and sophistication that clearly separated a Katherine Gibbs graduate from all others. I vividly recall the white gloves that traditionally the girls were supposed to wear. However, even the Katherine Gibbs School admitted that hats and white gloves were out—for the time being.

Michele preparing to drive to Harker High School

In 1987, Michele married her high school sweetheart Richard Caswell. They had dated off and on all through high school, but became serious when she returned to Washington, DC. They were married in a lovely ceremony, and had a reception at the Washington Golf and Country Club. The marriage lasted less than a year. The realities of being married at such a young age—both were twenty—were a cold splash of water, and the marriage dissolved under that pressure.

Single and dating again, Michele was attracted to the lure of a man in a uniform; he was the polar opposite of her former husband—an athletic Marine with a gruff and imposing demeanor—and she ended up marrying Peter Moser two years later. She moved to Long Island where she had her first child. During her pregnancy, Peter was serving overseas in the Gulf War. Meagen was born in 1991, and today is a teenager who is both an excellent student and a popular girl. When Peter returned, with the glitter of the Marine Corps behind them, that marriage, too, faltered.

Michele then had a number of years struggling as a single parent before she married again, and for the last time. She has been married to John Siderius for seven years. He was everything that she wanted in a man—and he cooked! Michele was never attracted to cooking as a young girl, nor as a teen, although she is developing this skill, especially in the line of party foods. She has often asked me for recipes. One of those was how to bake pumpkin bread, which she now bakes every year during holiday time, and just like me, she gives the breads to friends and family.

Michele and Johnny have two sons, Johnny and Justin. Johnny is school–age and has the most charming disposition. He loves to play and be social, and he always smiles for the camera. Justin is a toddler and developing into himself; he watches his bigger brother avidly as he grows by leaps and bounds. He will be a big boy if his feet are any indicator. We are now blessed with three lovely grandchildren.

Sibling Bond

The bond between siblings is a strong one, and growing up together instills an unspoken communication and understanding of one another. Michele and Randy's was a special one, much like Peter's and mine, though of course, their environment while growing up was completely different. Siblings are lucky to be able to rely on one another, often for survival and support; and they learn from one another—regardless of the context of their upbringing. When very little, Michele loved to play with her big brother, and he in turn loved to share his toys with her. But she was far more outspoken as a child with a determinedness modeled most likely from Mal. She was very different than her brother. In her early years she idolized him and always wanted to be included in his games, but she somehow managed to take charge, and he invariably shared his world in his role as big brother to her. As she moved into her teen years, she surpassed her brother in the social realm of high school, as she was far more outgoing and socialized easier,

Michele and Johnny on their wedding day— July 4, 1997.

Michele's three children: (L to R) Justin (6 months), Meagen (age 12) , and Johnny (age 5).

though she relied on Randy as her confidant regarding her various teenage "dramas." Michele always appreciated her brother's sartorial flair, and she will still rely on his style advice if she has an occasion. In turn, he will rely on Michele for her common sense approach to life.

Randy had a major role in her learning to drive, and he loved this instructional relationship. However, as a teen himself, I am sure he had a motivation for her to learn to drive—so he didn't have to be her chauffeur to her many teen social events anymore. Michele's popularity in high school ensured her lots of fun, and she was always out.

As young adults, my children's paths took them each in completely different directions professionally and personally—Randy in the city and Michele in the suburbs—but their bond remains. As grown adults, this connection and friendship is even stronger. Randy frequently visits Michele from the city, and they talk to one another all the time while still relying on each other's strengths.

Michele has a fine business head on her shoulders, is well organized and extremely efficient in both her business and her home life. She balances the rearing of three children while managing the office for a plant service near her home where she lives with her family in Sayville, Long Island, New York. Like her father, she has a head for business and efficiency.

While I am still a gypsy at heart, Mal and I envy them the roots that the Siderius family has in their community. Perhaps attracted to a home much like she had known during childhood, Michele loves her roots in the suburbs and is content with the tranquility that it provides.

Johnny's sister, Janet, often visits, and Johnny and Janet have that sibling bond which is so special. Janet is married, has two little girls, and lives in a nearby town. The weekly meeting point is at Johnny's parents' house, less than half a mile from theirs. I always love being a part of these family gatherings when we are visiting.

Michele's life as a mother and wife is different than mine was, as both today's culture and necessity require her to work outside the home. However, my daughter gracefully meets the challenges. Perhaps modeled on some of our more idyllic family vacations, Michele's favorite pastime is camping with her family in upstate New York or Eastern Long Island. It seems that this is when my daughter is most content. She loves her family and enjoys relaxing in their presence.

Grandmother Gross

Grandmother Gross came to visit us in 1965 to celebrate her ninetieth birthday. Mal's father had talked his mother into this trip. He told her that he would visit her in Portland, Oregon for her birthday; however, if she came to the East Coast instead, she would be able to see not only him, but could also visit with the rest of the family, including her first great–grandchild, our son Randy. This made sense to the practical German woman that Grandma was, even though she was of the opinion that, had the good Lord wanted man to fly He would have given him wings. We teased Grandma mercilessly when she admitted that she liked the speed with which she got from Portland, Oregon to New York, and she seemed impressed with air travel. We all enjoyed her visit tremendously. She had a great sense of humor and Mal al-

Grandma Gross in 1964. She was a practical German lady, and I felt very much at home with her.

ways had fun teasing her. It turned out to be our last visit with Grandma. She passed away two years later.

Aunt Martha and Uncle Adolph

The role which Aunt Martha and Uncle Adolph played in my life in the United States has already been described in detail. In time, they became another set of happy grandparents to Peter's and to our children. Unfortunately, Uncle Adolph died suddenly in February of 1970.

Aunt Martha loved children and was always a willing baby–sitter. Randy and Michele spent many happy days with Aunt Martha and Uncle Adolph when they were quite young. Once she was a widow and we still lived in New Jersey, Aunt Martha would often spend a week or more with us, and while there, treat all of us to some of her wonderful cooking and delicious baked goods. The children remember Aunt Martha getting up early to bake fresh doughnuts for them before they went to school. I was not willing to even try and beat that.

Our dear Aunt Martha passed away after a third heart attack at the end of 1979. I had the pleasure of caring for her after her first heart attack which had happened while she was visiting us in Virginia in 1975. Aunt Martha had done so much for me by helping me immigrate to the United States, and by initially giving me a home. Now I was glad to be able to do

Aunt Martha and Michele

something meaningful for her when she was "stuck" with us in Virginia where she had no visitors because all of her friends lived in New Jersey.

Mary and Noel Olmstead

Our wonderful friends Mary and Noel were like another set of parents to Mal and me, and like grandparents to our children. Living in El Paso, Texas, "Aunt" Mary made sure that Randy had a complete outfit of cowboy clothes for his second birthday. We spent a number of happy vacations visiting Mary and Noel in El Paso, and touring western Texas and New Mexico, as well as Cuidad Juarez. An outstanding memory for Randy was when we were listening to "Uncle" Noel do the countdown for a missile shoot at White Sands Missile Range where he worked.

Noel would make homemade ice cream for all of us outside on his immaculate back yard terrace. Their home was on a slope of one of the mountains edging the city of El Paso. An evening of barbecue and eating homemade pistachio ice cream with that spectacular sweeping view was always a fun family experience.

Mary Olmstead, our Welcome Wagon hostess who introduced Mal and me to each other, eventually suffered from Alzheimer's Disease, but she mercifully died of pneumonia in 1984. Our dear friend Noel was spared the agony which this dreadful disease causes those who have to watch it progress. I was thankful for that. At the time, Mom was in a much more advanced stage than Mary had been. I had started to prepare Noel for this,

Randy, age 2, in his cowboy outfit given to him by Mary and Noel Olmstead. They adopted our family as theirs.

especially since he was against putting Mary into nursing care and tried to handle her by himself, which would have become impossible in the future.

Mal and I made many trips to El Paso to visit, and in later years to make sure that our very close friend Noel was properly taken care of as he aged. He lived to be nearly ninety–seven years old.

Bill Mennen

While not a member of our family, my unremitting gratitude goes to Bill Mennen who has been my guardian throughout the early years in the United States, as mentioned in the chapters dealing with those years.

Through his lovely wife, Audrey, we have stayed in touch and I have made a couple of visits to the Mennens at their retirement locations, most recently in January, 2001, in California. I was happy to see them to be in good health and enjoying life, and still traveling a great deal. At age ninety, Bill—with Audrey, of course—went on a second trip to the North Pole! A distinguished accomplishment for a great person.

Bill Mennen celebrated his ninetieth birthday on July 6, 2003, and I was lucky to be able to talk to him on the phone and to wish him well. I feel fortunate to have had his friendship throughout my life in the United States.

* * * * *

I have been very fortunate. When I made the fateful decision in 1954 to come to the United States, I was making a decision to travel into the unknown—to a country with a different language, different customs, and different values—and I thought I was giving up my own family to do so. As it turned out, my immediate family quickly followed me, I found my "true love," and together we raised two wonderful children who have each grown up to be responsible citizens and loving human beings. They in turn have blessed Mal and me with their love, and with three wonderful grandchildren.

Mal and I in the summer of 1991

Nevertheless, I cannot forget that none of this would have happened but for the generous offer of Aunt Martha in that she and Uncle Adolph provided sponsorship for my immigration. This unselfish act to a girl she hardly knew was the essential first step without which I would not be in the United States today.

9

My Little Trees

For the last thirty years, Japanese Bonsai has been my hobby. I have always been attracted to Oriental art because the simplicity of it appealed to me.

When we still lived in New Jersey, I was a guest at somebody's home one day where the shrubs in the garden had been styled by a

Japanese gardener, and I was enchanted. Never did it occur to me that I could learn this art.

Soon after we moved to McLean, Virginia in 1974 and became members of the Smithsonian Associates, Mal read in their Events Calendar that Bonsai classes were being offered. "Here is the opportunity you have been waiting for," he told me.

I signed up, and for the next ten weeks I spent an enjoyable evening a week at the Smithsonian's Arts and Industry Building in downtown Washington learning how to style, plant into pots, and take care of little trees. With the instructor's guidance, each participant created a beautiful, tiny bonsai tree out of a small juniper. Mine became the centerpiece on a kitchen counter where I could enjoy it—and would remember to water it every other day. To my great disappointment I had a dead tree four months later. Somewhere during class I must have missed the instructor's comments about junipers being outdoor plants, and that they will not survive indoors.

After a second set of lessons at the National Arboretum the following spring, I went to work at "styling" the huge junipers in our yard.

Potomac Bonsai Association

I joined the Potomac Bonsai Association and went to lectures, demonstrations, and workshops to learn more. The Club organized collecting trips—where a group of bonsai people receive permission to dig up small trees on somebody's wooded property—which is a good way of acquiring bonsai material. Between collecting and some purchases I ended up owning about a dozen trees within the first few years.

It was interesting to note that most of the club members were men, until I figured out why. Bonsai work is a very time–consuming hobby. Women, especially if they have young children to care for as I did, do not have the necessary time to also care for the little trees. During the hot summer months—and Washington, DC's summers are hot and long—some small trees need to be watered twice a day. I placed mine near the automatic sprinklers, but not all trees have the same water requirements. Japanese bonsai masters say that an apprentice spends five years learning how to water. A bonsai tree is a work of art which is never finished. It is necessary to constantly work on it and care for it.

A Japanese Maple—about thirty years old

I loved spending time at the Arboretum where the National Bonsai Collection, a bicentennial gift from Japan, as well as the American Bonsai Collection are housed in special pavilions. Sometimes our bonsai club staged bonsai shows for the general public, where club members exhibited some of their best trees. These shows were always extremely popular. People just loved looking at the delightful little trees.

Our McLean property, while only a little over an acre, had many shrubs and areas which needed weeding. In this climate of extremely high humidity everything grows fast, and I would spend all of my available time pruning shrubs and weeding. Once I finished at one end, it was necessary to start again at the other end. My bonsai trees were planted in the garden where they were left to take care of themselves. I never really had enough time to pursue my hobby while the children were at home and I had the large property to take care of.

Time for Bonsai

Just before our daughter left for college we bought a townhouse in Bethesda, Maryland. The front yard was postage–stamp–sized, and we

From nursery stock, this Juniper was shaped and trained since 1988. It is more than twenty years old.

had ground cover planted. The small back yard became my bonsai garden. I began to attend every workshop which our club made available. A workshop is usually given by a bonsai master, often nationally renowned, who will assist a limited number of participants (no more than twelve) with styling a plant from nursery stock which is suitable for bonsai, and with potting it up. I found that I always came away from a workshop with a good tree because I had an expert's help and advice. My bonsai collection grew.

With both children out of the house and no large yard to tend, I finally had the necessary time to work with my bonsais and to enjoy those enchanting little trees. In the meantime I had grown quite a few tiny trees from cuttings, added a number of azaleas, and owned many Japanese Zelkovas (gray–bark elm) which were left from a soil experiment I conducted under Clif Pottberg's guidance with a hundred, one–year–old trees. Clif Pottberg, my bonsai instructor, as well as his German mother and I had become good friends, and I continued to learn from Clif whenever I spent time at his nursery.

My "bonsai garden" in the tiny back yard of our townhouse in Bethesda, Maryland.

Orcas Island

When we moved to the Pacific Northwest, I brought nearly fifty trees three thousand miles across the country in a U–Haul trailer hitched to my Bronco. The reason for personally moving them was that they had to be watered during the five–day trip, and no moving company would take that responsibility. All of my trees survived the long trip.

Our house on Orcas Island has been built to accommodate my bonsai hobby. My little trees are displayed on specially designed benches on a deck where they are safe from the thriving deer population who would love to have access to the salad bar. We have installed an automatic watering system to take care of the trees when we are traveling, which we do often.

A greenhouse with a watering system accommodates house plants, as well as Elmar and Benji—our two indoor bonsais—when we travel, and shelters freshly repotted bonsai trees. Benji is a willow–leaf ficus which was started from a cutting in 1982. Elmar, a Chinese elm, came

One large section of our deck is dedicated to my bonsai trees to keep them safe from deer. An automatic watering system takes care of water requirements when we are traveling.

You can see the bathroom window (center) from which we enjoy a good view of the trees even in stormy weather. The greenhouse is conveniently located to the right. We are 1,250 feet up on the side of a mountain and get a lot of heavy winds on this deck. That is why the main roots of the trees must be wired into their pots.

Elmar—a Chinese Elm—joined the family in 1991, and we were told he was then over fifty years old. He is one of only two indoor trees.

View of my little trees from our bathroom windows. Elmar is seen in the bottom right of the picture.

to us in 1991 when he was more than fifty years old. He has a beauti-fully gnarled trunk and occupies a place of honor on a step of the spa tub in our bathroom where we can admire him daily. We have a great view of the bonsai trees out on the deck through the bathroom's two large corner windows, as well as the bedroom windows.

Repotting

One room of the house is dedicated to bonsai work at repotting time in the spring, and to year–round flower arranging which I also enjoy. Every two or three years each tree is taken out of its pot, bare rooted, the roots pruned, and the tree repotted into fresh bonsai soil, which is a special, well–draining mix. This is a major job and takes up about two months of my time. Each year I repot one third to one half of my trees, depending on time available and need of the trees.

I keep a detailed historical record on each tree from the begin-ning—either since it was a cutting or acquisition—which helps remind

In my bonsai workroom I am bare rooting a large Kingsville Boxwood which is forty–six years old.

me what I last did to which tree, and when. Photos often document the progress of certain trees over the years. These records are, effectively, the medical records for each of my trees.

Before starting to repot a tree, I style it while it is still solidly in its pot. Bonsai–styled little trees do grow out of shape quite quickly. Next I remove the tree from the pot, wash the pot and put in new wires. I might prepare a larger pot if the tree needs it. It is common practice to wire a tree into the pot to help hold it, especially in windy areas, since the pots are shallow for aesthetic reasons. Next I bare–root the tree, prune the roots if they are too profuse, place it into the pot, and secure the roots with anodized aluminum wire. It is imperative to spray the roots with water as soon as they have been bared, to keep them from drying out and before I fill the pot with soil mix.

Then the time consuming job begins. I have to work the soil between all the roots so that there are no air holes, or the tree will not survive. This is done with a wooden chopstick which will not scratch the roots. Lastly, the potted tree is set into a water pan to which Superthrive— a vitamin–hormone and root growth stimulant—has been added, and I allow the tree to soak from the bottom up until the soil is

Kingsville Boxwoods are perfect material for rock plantings. Here three small box-woods create the feeling of a hillside where one would like to run up the hill and lie down in the shade of a tree.

completely wet—about half an hour. Then I let the pot drain, before finally placing it in the greenhouse to protect it from strong sun or wind for a few days. The repotting process takes up to three hours, or longer for very large trees.

To protect the trees' roots from freezing in the winter, the pots are placed into deep bark mulch in the ground, in a fenced–in shelter underneath a part of the deck where the deer cannot get to them.

My Collection

My bonsai collection, at last count, was sixty–nine. It includes Japanese maples, elms, junipers, a high elevation cedar, Hinoki cypress, Japanese Zelkovas, a Japanese and an American hornbeam, euonymus, a Japanese black pine, and quite a few small and six large Kingsville boxwoods. None of the azaleas I brought from the East Coast have survived in this much drier climate and the twelve hundred fifty foot elevation. The maples are not happy here, but are surviving, though they look good only in early spring. Their leaves would like much higher humidity.

Over the years, each bonsai enthusiast develops a preference for a particular type of tree. My choice has become the Kingsville Boxwood—"The Little King of American Bonsai," as it is fondly called by bonsai lovers. This type of boxwood is quite a special one with many desirable characteristics, some of which are its tiny leaves of dark green color, and its growth pattern in that the smallest tree can look as though it were ancient. The Kingsville boxwood is especially slow growing, though tough and forgiving of under–and over–watering, and it is more resistant to diseases than most other trees. While it likes deeper pots, it does not mind being planted in rock crevices and it therefore makes it possible to create attractive rock plantings with multiple trees. Some of my favorite creations incorporate lava rocks.

Bonsai has been a most gratifying hobby for me given my love of nature, and of trees in particular.

An automatic sprinkler system is essential because the pots are so shallow

Two Kingsville Boxwoods—they are six and thirty–seven years old

PART III

ADVENTURES

10

1962
Berlin and the Cold War

My 1962 Trip to Berlin

In the fall of 1962, still childless, I left Warner–Lambert and went back to visit Germany for two months. After taking delivery of a new car at the Mercedes Benz factory near Stuttgart and a visit with relatives in the vicinity, I drove the car north towards Bremerhaven, stopping for more visits in the Rhineland. From Bremerhaven I shipped the car off to the United States before flying into Berlin. We decided I should not take the new car across East Germany, and I really did not need a car in Berlin. I spent the next six weeks visiting relatives and friends, and listening to their reactions about the latest Soviet harassment measure—the infamous Berlin Wall, which had been built a year earlier.

The Infamous Berlin Wall

On Sunday morning, August 13, 1961, Berliners had awakened to construction in progress. Under the protection of heavy tanks and armed police and soldiers, concrete barriers and barbed wire fences were being put into place to seal off the borders of the Soviet–controlled sector of Berlin and the Soviet occupation zone, i.e. East Germany. The monstrous construction project was continuously reinforced over the following years. It became known as the infamous Berlin Wall. This ugly wall was to stand for more than twenty–eight years and caused hundreds of deaths among those who tried to escape. It encircled, and there-

This picture captures The Wall being constructed. East Berlin is on the right side. West Berlin is on the left.

fore isolated, West Berlin, and cut it off from the eastern part of the city as well as from surrounding East Germany.

Berliners in both East and West Berlin went into shock. West Berliners who were visiting family or friends in East Berlin on that fateful weekend were not allowed to return home. East Berlin residents who worked in West Berlin were cut off from their jobs. Any human contacts between families and friends that had still existed in the divided city were now cut. The *S–Bahn* (city train) and subway through–traffic was interrupted. Anyone who tried to escape in the years to come was ruthlessly shot.

Direct telephone service had been cut during the Blockade in 1948, but phone calls had been possible afterwards by routing a call through West Germany and East Germany, back to the other part of Berlin. Now even this circuitous way was no longer possible.

The soldier is standing in East Berlin. The Wall is on the left, and anyone walking in the open area in the center would be shot. Note the buildings on the left are in West Berlin, and ahead and on the right is East Berlin. The Wall cuts right through the center of residential areas of Berlin.

On this visit to Berlin a year after the construction of The Wall, I found that people had still not recovered from the shock. If anything, they were more disheartened than ever. The Wall affected their everyday lives. People could not attend weddings, births, and funerals on the "other side." There were sad scenes, where a bride and groom would stand on one side of The Wall on their wedding day and the parents or grandparents on the other, straining to get a glimpse of the happy couple.

Aunt Lotte and Uncle Martin had lost the sales personnel in their butcher shop. Help was extremely hard to find in West Berlin. At that particular time there were more jobs available than there were people to fill them. This led to the importation of guest workers from Turkey which, years later, turned into a migration, and some areas of West Berlin became wholly Turkish.

The Wall is in the process of construction here. This picture gives a good view of the obstacles that someone would have to overcome when trying to escape.

The apartment building is right on the border, and it became part of The Wall. Note the bricked–up windows. The street is in the West. Apparently someone jumped from an upstairs window and either died from the fall, or was shot. This was a memorial to him.

I also found a number of Berliners who were quite disappointed, and even angry, that the Americans had watched this happen and had done nothing to stop The Wall from being built.

In addition to the countless heart–wrenching experiences which befell the battle–weary Berliners, there were many tragedies. The Museum at Checkpoint Charlie tells some of the stories of the many people who tried to escape under, over, and through the fortified "wall system." It tells of the lucky ones who made it, and of the many who died trying to reach precious freedom. The museum has numerous ingenious inventions on

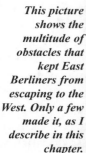

This picture shows the multitude of obstacles that kept East Berliners from escaping to the West. Only a few made it, as I describe in this chapter.

display with which people tried to escape, such as inconceivably small and hidden spaces in cars, homemade flying machines, underground tunnels, and many more.

My term "wall system" means the following: The wall or barbed wire fence was not just a wall of concrete, or posts between which barbed wire had been strung. The fifteen foot high reinforced wall with rolled barbed wire on top which was visible from the West Berlin side, was not all there was to it. On the East Berlin side there was the "death strip" which consisted of alternating barbed wire fences with strips of loose, raked sand to see footprints. There were mine fields, deep trenches, tank traps, and another reinforced barricade on the east side. In addition, there were spotlights every three hundred feet as well as watchtowers, each manned by two military men with binoculars. In some areas there were dog runs—each about half a mile long. Dog runs were fenced in strips of land in which trained vicious dogs were kept.

Not all of the above–mentioned reinforcements were in place in the beginning, so that a number of people did manage to escape during the very early days and months. Eventually, however, it became just about impossible to penetrate this barrier which in time had been reinforced to the highest degree.

A few words about the reason for building The Wall. At the end of World War II, Germany as well as Berlin, the capital city of the former Third Reich, were divided among the four Allies. While the three Western Allies jointly treated their sections of Germany and Berlin as de-

This section of The Wall was less than a mile from Uncle Martin's house. Note the wide barrier "death zone" area between The Wall and the barrier beyond which were dog runs. There were spotlights on posts (right side and center) that were lit all night long.

mocracies, the Soviets forced their respective shares into Communism. In the years following the war, quite a few people from both East Berlin and East Germany who were against Communism, fled to the West. As the years went by refugees arrived in West Berlin and West Germany by the thousands as the East German people became so dissatisfied with the Communist system that they preferred to leave all belongings behind in favor of freedom. Their numbers increased steadily and dramatically until by August 1961, refugees streamed into West Berlin by the *thousands each day*. The Wall was built by the Communist government to stop this mass migration.

The easiest escape route was from East Berlin into West Berlin. One just had to get on the subway or city train and get off in West Berlin. People who were escaping from East Germany had to come through Berlin because there was no passport check on the city trains. The hardest part for the refugees was that they had to leave everything behind in order not to arouse suspicion with cumbersome baggage. It was also necessary for all family members to leave, as anyone left behind would encounter the punishment of the Communist system. Still, to gain precious freedom people left everything they owned and came to live in refugee camps in the West where they received help with starting a new life. This help initially consisted of shelter, food, and clothing, and then jobs and aid in finding housing. Shortage of housing was, and still is, one of the biggest problems in Germany.

With the building of The Wall, the "door to freedom" had been shut mercilessly.

Escape from East Berlin

While I was visiting Berlin in the fall of 1962 and staying with Uncle Rudolf and Aunt Hilda, Mom's oldest sister, I had a most interesting experience. Two of my cousins (nephews of Uncle Rudolf) showed up at the door one day. The boys had just risked their lives by

The Wall was built to resist any effort to knock it down from West Berlin. This view taken on the East Berlin side shows how the concrete wall was reinforced, and tank barriers were placed to stop any type of vehicle trying to get out of East Berlin.

escaping from East Berlin two or three days before. The following is the detailed story of their escape as the older cousin, Horst, told it to me. I wrote down his words in a letter to Mal just days after it happened. The account paints a very vivid picture of life in Berlin then.

October 8, 1962

Horst is my cousin and we lived in the same apartment building in Berlin–Lichterfelde until we were bombed and the buildings destroyed in 1943. His family moved in with his mother's parents in Niederschöneweide which today is in East Berlin. Horst has a younger brother and a sister. His father was killed in the war.

When Horst had finished school, he became a stonemason. He took a job in West Berlin and worked and lived in an apartment there for four and a half years. Almost every night he went to East Berlin to see his mother and have supper with the family. After work on Friday, August 11, 1961 Horst went home for the weekend to attend his sister's wedding. That was the fateful weekend of August 13 when the borders were closed and a wall was built to separate East and West

Berlin. Horst could not return to his apartment or his job in West Berlin on Sunday night.

It was not so easy for him to just stay in East Berlin, either. The East German government gave him trouble because of his working and living in West Berlin, and they wanted to put him in jail. However, he told the police that he came as a refugee from West Berlin and would like to stay in the East now. They believed him, and he avoided jail, got a job, and earned a lot of money.

All of the time, however, he kept thinking about ways to escape. But as each day passed, The Wall kept getting reinforced and escape became more and more difficult. Most people also thought that The Wall could not possibly stay up very long. The Americans surely would do something about it!

In the meantime, Horst married a girl he had known for a long time. He was still thinking of escaping and was making all kinds of plans. When he told his wife about wanting to escape, he found out that she wanted to stay in East Berlin. So he stayed.

One day while playing soccer, Horst broke his leg and had to stay off his feet for many weeks. It altogether took about six months before his leg was in good enough shape to risk a possible escape, and by that time it was almost impossible to break through a barrier which was being constantly reinforced. Many young men were shot to death while trying. However, Horst was now more determined to leave than before, especially since his marriage was not working out. All kinds of ideas came to his mind. For a while he thought of having a tunnel built (his brother Jürgen and a friend also wanted to escape), but it is very expensive to build a tunnel and they could not raise the money.

Horst had a friend who lived on Harzer Strasse where the wall goes down the middle of the street. He thought of getting a rope out of the window (fourth floor) and sliding down on it into the West side of the street, but on checking it out he found there is one of the guard houses a little ways down the street and there would not be much of a chance to even get the rope out of the window without being discovered.

Another friend lived in a house which is a part of the border. The first four floors have all windows bricked up and no one lives there now. The friend lives on the fifth floor, is a Vopo (East Berlin Police) and often works night shifts. Horst planned to get friendly with his wife, also a Vopo, to have a chance to be in her apartment some night when her husband is gone, and then he wanted to knock her out (since she as Vopo would not have approved of his escape) and jump out of the window. However, it turned out to be impossible to communicate with West Berlin to have a net put up into which he could jump from the fifth floor. When he could not get a definite commitment as to time and date, this plan had to be dropped. Most of the mail between East and West Berlin gets read so that communications in a case like that have to be done very skillfully. Of course, no telephone connections have existed since the Blockade in 1948.

One day, Horst received orders that he was to report to the recruiting station to become a member of the East German army. That was the day. In the evening, he took his brother, Jürgen, and his friend out to have some drinks so they would relax and not be so scared, and perhaps try to chicken out at the last minute. He needed their help as well as they needed his. At that point he told them that they had to leave that night. They went home to their mother to say good–bye, but their sister and her husband were there and Horst did not want them to know about the planned escape under any circumstances. When his mother made sandwiches for the boys, Horst wrote with a knife on the butter of his sandwich that he wanted to see his mother alone. Horst and Jürgen went into the other room, but they were unable to tell their mother. Instead, they got out sweaters and jackets and put them on, and their mother knew what was going to happen. Horst says, she really pulled herself together and did not even cry when they kissed her good–bye. She never gave anything away, even though there was such a very small chance that the boys would make it across, and a big chance that they would be killed. Next they told their mother to whom she should give their clothes and other belongings since they could not take anything; and at 10 p.m. Horst, Jürgen, and their friend were on their way.

They had picked one of the most dangerous spots to get across, thinking that no one would expect anybody to risk it there. At the last moment, Jürgen and the friend, both only 19 years old, got scared and wanted to back out, but Horst needed them and talked them into it.

Horst carried the binoculars, Jürgen the wire cutters, and the friend a shovel which they might need. Their approach was a deserted airport in the southeast of Berlin. They crawled on their stomachs for almost three hours before they reached the first fence of barbed wire. It was very important not to be seen when approaching the border as the guards would know immediately what they were up to. Once before, Horst and Jürgen had started out elsewhere on a spur of the moment and were noticed already on the approach. Fortunately, they were able to act as though they were just out for a walk and got a little too close to the border by mistake.

Cutting the first fence was easy, said Horst. The barbed wire was an East German product which was quite soft, and easy to cut. They now had to watch out for the guards who patrol the section in between the first and the second fence, an area of about two hundred feet consisting of a strip of very loose raked sand (to show footprints) and ending with a ditch, inside which more guards would be walking. When crawling across the airfield, the boys noticed with the help of the binoculars that it usually took about twenty minutes before the guards returned. There are always two guards walking about half a mile before they turn around and come back. The whole border is lit up at night with floodlights which are about three hundred feet apart, and there are guard houses on observation towers from which they watch with binoculars.

The boys got through the loose sand all right. Here they needed the shovel to smooth it out again after they had been sinking in nearly up to their knees. They now had to hurry and get across before the guards returned. The moment when all three of them looked at each other and hesitated was when they had to jump into the ditch on the chance that the guards might just be walking in there. However, there was no question that they had to go on because they would be shot turning back, too. So they jumped into the ditch—and were lucky. Next they had to get through the second fence of barbed wire which actually consists of three fences of barbed wire held up by concrete posts with barbed wire rolls in between each fence. This time they found that the wire was made of good steel which was hard to cut. Horst told me this was the barbed wire that Krupp, a West German industry, sold to the East. The two younger boys were so scared and exhausted by then that Horst had to go first and cut the wire himself. Presently he was in this mess of barbed wire and his clothes were ripping when the two boys behind him started to giggle because his pants were torn. He could not understand how they could be so silly all of a sudden and disregard the need for total silence.

Now the worst part was to come—swimming through the Teltow Kanal in the icy water. Horst wanted the youngest to go first, so it was Jürgen's turn. Jürgen was scared, but there was no turning back. Horst told him exactly how to swim—about half way and then to the right. There was a bridge across the canal on the left and this bridge was Russian zone and had guards on it, so they actually had the East on two sides. On the other side of the canal was a factory and there was a freight ship in the water. Horst wanted them to end up on the right side of the ship so that they would have protection in case there was any shooting. When the friend was ready to go into the water, Horst noticed that he no longer had the shovel. He had left it behind somewhere, and Horst was mad because it would give them away if the guards found the shovel.

The boys had expected the swimming to be the worst part of the escape, and it turned out to be even worse than they had thought. The difficulty they had was in trying to swim

This is where my cousins swam across the Teltow Kanal. East Berlin is on the left and you can barely see some of the obstacles they came through. The factory they swam to is on the right. Horst brought me here several days after the boys escaped.

with all the clothes and heavy shoes. For a while they did not feel how cold the water really was, but they had trouble keeping above water. Because of the factory, the water was quite oily and smelly right there.

It took them ten minutes to swim across the canal. There was no shooting, and once they got out of the water they started to run as fast as they could, for nothing would keep the guards from shooting into West Berlin. In the frigid air of the night they started to feel the cold as they walked along in their wet clothes. They were extremely lucky that a truck passed them on the street. It was nearly 3 a.m. by then, and unlikely that they would find anyone in this deserted industrial area. The truck passed by them, then stopped and backed up, apparently realizing what had happened. The boys were so cold and exhausted that they needed help getting into the truck. The truck driver took them back to the nearby factory and the boys took off their wet clothes. Then the ambulance came and took them to the hospital where they were kept overnight.

It did not take long for newspaper reporters to show up, wanting stories, but Horst had them thrown out. The boys were not going to give details of their escape so as not to spoil a chance for others. In the morning they received clothes from the refugee camp, and the clothes they had worn the night before had already been washed and patched up as well as possible. Horst said they could not sleep all night wondering what would happen to their mother. She waited nineteen hours before they were able to get a message through to her that they had made it.

In the morning, the boys were picked up by people from the Marienfelde Refugee Camp where they had to go through all the formalities. It was like clearing into another country, said Horst. They also got jobs and had to wait to be flown to West Germany.

Horst said they had to write to their mother and act as though they did not plan an escape. They told her in the letter that they went out for a walk and discovered a chance to get across easily and that they are willing to try the West and don't know yet whether they made the right decision. The letter also had to state that their mother did not know the boys were planning to leave, otherwise they would put her into jail.

By now, East Berlin has put up an additional barbed–wire fence where the three boys came across, and they are talking about putting mine fields in between the fences.

The foregoing description is hard to imagine for someone living in the United States. Words do not adequately convey the emotions, fear and risks my two cousins took. Certainly I felt it to a large extent because only a few years earlier Berlin and the communist system had been a dominant part of Mom's, Peter's and my lives. The fact that these two cousins had "made it" when so many others had not, was really just a matter of chance.

Our very Close Call on the S–Bahn

The following is a letter I wrote to Mal about a week later which describes how close Horst and I subsequently came to disaster.

October 15, 1962

People here in Berlin are doing well except that they are very discouraged now because of The Wall, and they don't speak too favorably about Americans any more. I am sad to experience that, but then I don't live here and do not have to put up with the separation which The Wall causes.

Tante Hilda's living room looks like a refugee camp. Instead of going back to the camp, the two cousins from East Berlin stayed with us all week and were sleeping on the living room floor on air mattresses. Jürgen is still sad and does not want to go anywhere. Horst is interesting to talk to. We often go for a walk at night. It is quite informative to get all the first–hand information about conditions in East Berlin and East Germany.

I had the shock of my life this morning. The boys were flying to West Germany today. First we sent Jürgen off to Tempelhof Airport with his bag containing clothes they got in the camp, and both boys' plastic airline–type bags, bright green, with big white letters CARE U.S.A. written on them. They received these at the refugee camp here in Berlin when they first arrived, filled with toothpaste, towels, shaving stuff, and things they would need.

Horst needed to go to the refugee camp at Marienfelde and pick up their airline tickets. He told Jürgen he would meet him at Tempelhof. I wanted to see what the refugee camp looks like so I went with Horst. Luckily, Horst carried only a plain brown leather bag with his few belongings— and not the green one which said CARE U.S.A. on it.

Now something about the electric elevated, called S–Bahn. Remember the train run by the East Berlin government and which also goes through West Berlin? Normally once it gets to the first station in East Berlin , the East Police walks through and picks out some people who they think look like they purchased things in the West. Well, that train, unlike the streetcars, busses, and subway, is still run by the East and because the whole network of tracks goes also through West Berlin, they keep running the trains that way. Many of the trains run only to the border and then turn around and go back to keep them in the East, and the same here in the West, but there are still a lot of trains that travel between East and West Berlin. Army and police in East Berlin make sure that no West Berliners get off in East Berlin, and especially that no East Berliners are still in the train when it is ready to leave the last East station to return to the West.

Although in West Berlin, the S–Bahn runs almost empty, there are checkups on the people who do use the trains through East Berlin. Police will have them get out of the train, check their passports—you know those identification passports everybody here in Europe has to carry around

Jürgen (left) and Horst, each carrying their CARE U.S.A. bags. Jürgen went directly to Tempelhof while Horst and I went to the Refugee Camp to pick up their tickets, and then had our fateful S–Bahn "scare."

with him all the time—and they also check their luggage. If they find something they do not like, they'll either just delay the people, or never let them go again. Many people disappear this way because they get accused of this or the other thing. There are also times when the S–Bahn just won't stop at the last West Berlin station and that way they get people into the East who had intended to get off before then. West Berliners, of course, are afraid to ride the S–Bahn because of that.

The trains and track which are running in West Berlin are the property of the East. Horst says that as long as you are on the station platform, it probably is pretty safe. But on the train, or if you get kicked out on the other side and are on the tracks, you are officially on East Berlin property. In addition, some West Berliners are mean and angry, and sabotage these trains. They mine tracks, take door handles and arm rests off, or slice up seats. Well, if you sit in the train now and the East police rides on this train and goes through the cars to check—even while the train is in West Berlin they can check it because it is their train—and if there is an arm rest or door handle missing and they can accuse you of taking it off and then will take you with them and arrest you. How would you be able to prove that you are innocent?

Why would any West Berliner take a train through East Berlin? Because often it is very much shorter the way the city is divided. For example, Horst and I rode the S–Bahn trains all the time, but, of course, only in West Berlin. To go to the Swim Stadium we had to make a one hour S–Bahn and half an hour bus trip. If we could have traveled partly through East Berlin the trip would have been only a thirty minute S–Bahn ride, but partly through East Berlin, which we had to avoid.

This morning from the refugee camp at Marienfelde we took the S–Bahn to Tempelhof, the route being entirely in West Berlin. Even so, Horst said that if the people at the camp saw him ride this train as a refugee, they would all have heart attacks. He also told me never to ride the S–Bahn alone because it is not safe. People who are alone, especially in an empty car, which happens too often, can be kidnaped easily. While we waited for the train at Marienfelde, Horst told me that if he were seen here in Marienfelde by the East German police with that green bag which says CARE U.S.A. on it, this would be the end. We were glad that Horst had sent that ominous bag with his brother.

I started to feel uncomfortable and suggested that we should rather take a bus, but our train came into the station right then, and we got on. We changed at Papestraße three stops later, and crossed a big wooden emergency bridge to get to the other tracks for our connection. This bridge has never been rebuilt since the war, of course. East Berlin is responsible for keeping up the stations in West Berlin as it is their train and their station. In the nearly twenty years, this wooden bridge had deteriorated a lot, and my heel got caught in one of the boards which was coming apart from old age. Horst said that if the East police had seen it, they would probably accuse me of ruining their precious bridge with my high heels. We were mostly kidding at that point, and laughing about the Communist system's shortcomings.

We had one stop to go from there to the Tempelhof S–Bahn station. Suddenly we saw two East German police get on the same train. We thought at first that they were in another car and at the next stop, when they would come into our car, we will have gotten off. Were we surprised to see them at the other end of our car. There was not a soul in there besides us and the two policemen.

Horst and I were going from Marienfelde (arrow, lower center) to Tempelhof (right center), changing S–Bahn trains at Papestraße (left center). If we had been detained by the East German policemen on the train between Papestraße and Tempelhof, the train would have traveled only a few stops before it crossed back into East Berlin. Had that happened we might never have been heard from again.

Slowly they started to walk towards us, carefully looking over the train seats, all there, nothing missing, fire extinguisher still there. Then they looked us over. I had our camera with me, so we might have looked like tourists. That two–minute ride seemed never to end. We were sure they would ask us for our p a s s p o r t s, which is the normal procedure, and there would have been nothing wrong with it. The trouble was that Horst will not be issued a West German identification passport until he gets to West Germany, and at this time he had his and his brother's East Berlin Pass-

Three pictures of the S–Bahn trains and station. At the time of my "scare" very few West Berliners were so foolish as to ride these trains, even in West Berlin. Technically, once you are on an S–Bahn train you are subject to East Berlin laws, and can be arrested, and jailed.

ports in his possession, as well as their airline tickets to get out of Berlin. That and my American passport would have been a beautiful combination. All we could think was that we were lucky not to have the green bag with us. That CARE U.S.A. bag would have given us away.

For some reason we were not asked to show them our passports. We must have been hiding our fear pretty well and must have looked quite normal to them, despite the fact that we were holding our breaths. When the train finally stopped at Tempelhof, we got off and almost cried we were so relieved to get out of there. We had to really force ourselves not to start running away from the train and maybe look suspicious—we were still on East Berlin property while on the platform. The policemen went on into the next car to check it over.

And guess who will never ride the S–Bahn again? This was just too close a call, and Horst had a nerve anyway to ride that S–Bahn, being a refugee. I still shake when I think of it.

I'm glad the boys are gone, too. I saw them off at Tempelhof. It was their first flight on an airplane. The refugee camp is only a temporary shelter. It is too dangerous for East Germans to stay here in Berlin. Some day they just might forget to get off the subway at the last West stop and they'd be right back in East Berlin, which would be the end of them.

Also, you can't trust anybody, even in West Berlin. Somebody may be a spy from the East and talk to you and then drag you into East Berlin. One night when the boys and I were standing near The Wall, some man came up to us and talked to us. He tried to sound us out and asked whether we were planning to help someone escape, or why were we standing there, looking. We are still wondering who that man was. I tell you, Dear, there is nothing like a free country where you can trust people and leave doors unlocked. Even in West Berlin I am uneasy now. If you get sounded out by some spy and get kidnaped to East Berlin, you can't just take a train or subway back out of there.

Horst said that in East Germany almost everybody is in the army. They are not labeled army; they call them guards, police, border patrol, railroad police, but in reality they are all army. I'll explain everything better when I return. I have so much to tell you. This is the most interesting trip I ever had.

Perhaps these two writings—from more than forty years ago—help paint a vivid picture of why I so highly prize the freedom we have in this country.

After my return from Berlin, I kept up a correspondence with Horst for awhile. The boys had lived in a refugee camp in West Germany for a couple of months, found work and then an apartment. Their friend remained in Berlin where he had family. Jürgen missed his mother very much and eventually went back to East Berlin. He had not been sure about wanting to leave in the first place, but had done it more because his brother and friend needed his help.

Horst and I corresponded for perhaps a year. The last I heard from him was that he was moving, either within the city in which he lived or to another location. I do not remember, and I did not hear from him again.

The Cuban Missile Crisis

Meanwhile at home a major drama was unfolding which nearly started World War III—the Cuban Missile Crisis. I was oblivious of this. Mal pleaded with me on the phone to get out of Berlin, but I insisted on staying, not realizing how serious the situation was. The Berliners, still numb from the shock of The Wall dividing their city, their families, and their lives, did not react to this new danger which threatened the future of Berlin, and the world. Only years later did I realize how close the United States had come to war, and how vulnerable my beloved Berlin was—and myself personally.

Reproduced below is a summary of this crisis—"*The most dangerous moment of the Cold War*"— prepared and copyrighted by Nuclear Age Peace Foundation (*www.Nuclearfiles.org*). Reprinted with permission. I have included this summary because it helps paint a more complete picture of the time.

In October 1962, the United States and the Soviet Union came to the brink of nuclear war over the placement of Soviet missiles in Cuba. For 13 tense days, a fragile peace hung by only a thread as the U.S. instituted a naval blockade of Cuba to turn back Soviet ships. The crisis was ended when the Soviet Union agreed in a secret negotiation to remove its nuclear weapons from Cuba in exchange for a U.S. agreement to remove its nuclear weapons from Turkey six months later. The time lag was insisted upon by the U.S. so that it would not look to the world like the U.S. had engaged in a quid pro quo regarding the missiles in Cuba.

The crisis resulted in the creation of a Hotline Agreement between the U.S. and Soviet Union that would allow for instantaneous communications between the leaders of the two countries. The Cuban Missile Crisis stands today as a constant reminder of the immense danger that is ever present in the Nuclear Age. Subsequent meetings among key decision makers in the Cuban Missile Crisis have shown how many misperceptions there were during the tense period of the crisis, and how fortunate the world was to have escaped a dreadful nuclear holocaust between the two "superpower" states.

Former U.S. and Russian officials and military officers announced on 11 October 2002 that the world was much closer to a nuclear holocaust during the 1962 Cuban missile crisis than previously believed. A conference marking the 40th anniversary of the most dangerous moment of the Cold War heard the account of a U.S. naval officer whose destroyer dropped depth charges on a Soviet submarine carrying a nuclear weapon on 27 October 1962. According to declassified documents released at the conference by the National Security Archive of Washington, U.S. intelligence only photographed 33 of the 42 SS–4 medium–range ballistic missiles placed in Cuba, and never located the nuclear warheads.

On 27 October, an American U–2 spy plane was shot down over Cuba, and U.S. military Joint Chiefs of Staff recommended to President Kennedy that the United States proceed with an air strike and invasion plan. Later that day, when low–level reconnaissance pilots reported anti–aircraft fire from the ground in Cuba and photographs showed that some missiles had been placed on launchers, Kennedy told his advisers "time is running out." According to declassified documents, that day the crisis appeared to be spinning out of control.

The next day, Soviet Premier Nikita Khrushchev ordered the withdrawal of missiles secretly deployed in Cuba, pressed by U.S. photographic evidence and a naval blockade imposed on the island by President John F. Kennedy. Kennedy aide and historian Arthur Schlesinger stated, "This was not only the most dangerous moment of the Cold War, it was the most dangerous moment in human history. Never before had two contending powers possessed between them the technical capacity to blow up the world." Fortunately, Kennedy and Khrushchev were leaders of restraint and sobriety, otherwise we probably wouldn't be here today. President Kennedy's brother, Attorney General Robert Kennedy, later met with the Soviet ambassador in Washington, Anatoly Dobrynin, and offered a deal that included a pledge not to invade Cuba and the withdrawal of U.S. missiles from Turkey.

In the middle of the escalating tensions, the destroyer USS Beale was dropping depth charges on the Soviet submarine B–59, one of four at the quarantine line, each carrying nuclear–tipped torpedoes. According to National Security Archives director Thomas Blanton, the U.S. Navy "did not have a clue that the submarine had a nuclear weapon on board." The sub's signals intelligence officer Vadim Orlov said in an account issued by Blanton. "They exploded right next to the hull. It felt like you were sitting in a metal barrel, which somebody is constantly blasting with a sledgehammer." According to Orlov's account, the Soviet submarine's crew thought the war may have started and considered using their nuclear weapon, but decided instead to surface. Further declassified documents issued at the National Academy of Sciences' conference showed that by 27 October, Castro had ordered Cuban anti–aircraft gunners to fire on U.S. reconnaissance planes and expected an all–out U.S. air strike and invasion of Cuba within 24 to 72 hours. According to U.S.

Navy F–8 fighter pilot William Ecker, "We were shot at." Ecker and his 15 pilots flew 82 dangerous, low–level missions over the missile bases to take photographs that were presented by the United States at the United Nations.

* * * * *

This was a dangerous time, and I was oblivious to it at the time. I am not sure that many Americans today realize how close we really came to World War III. We had assembled a massive invasion force in Florida and were within hours of launching a pre–emptive attack. If the Russians had tried to break our blockade, or the Russian submarine mentioned above had tried to defend itself, history would have been quite different.

11

1989
Bulgaria

A final example of our exasperating encounters with Communism took place in 1989 on a trip to Bulgaria, twenty–seven years after my experiences described in the preceding chapter. The Iron Curtain was still in place, although there were signs that it was starting to crumble. I have included the following account as a reminder to future readers of what life under Communism was like toward the end of the twentieth century, more than forty years after the end of World War II.

In June of 1989, Mal took optional retirement from Price Waterhouse at age fifty–five, to become the President of the National Aeronautic Association, the national aero club of the United States. In that role he represented United States air sport organizations at the international sport aviation organization, the Fédération Aéronautique Internationale. The FAI—as it is referred to—oversees international sporting events much as the International Olympic Committee oversees other types of sporting events. In his new job we attended a number of international conferences which were held in a different country each year.

In September 1989, the FAI conference took place in Varna, Bulgaria, on the Black Sea. There were about 200 delegates from all over the world attending, and we were considered guests of the Peoples Republic of Bulgaria. Mal and I were rather looking forward to taking a trip to an East Bloc country, although from experience I have an inherent fear of doing so. I get nervous and feel sick to my stomach because I am so afraid of losing my freedom, having seen what Communism does to people.

In 1989 Bulgaria was still behind the "Iron Curtain" and was almost on a war footing with neighboring Turkey. We were in Istanbul and needed to get to Varna, only 200 miles north. The only way we could get there was by traveling on a train, first to Sofia and then changing to a train that went to Varna. Leaving Varna was almost as difficult because the airport in Sofia was closed (for four months) and we had to take a flight out of Bulgaria from a military field at Plovdiv.

We decided that it would be fun to spend a few days in Istanbul before traveling to Varna. Istanbul is also on the Black Sea and it looked like about 200 miles from there to Varna. But getting to Varna became more of a problem than we could ever have imagined.

Sofia Airport Closed

At the time of the conference at Varna which was held during the last week in September, the only airport at Bulgaria's capital, Sofia, was closed down completely for four months. The airport's only runway was being resurfaced. No foreign airlines were flying into Bulgaria at the time, and even the Bulgarians could not tell us how we could get to Varna. We received a different answer to each of the many inquiries we made before we left the United States. In the fashion so typical of the Communist system, no one seemed to know. It was most difficult to deal with this country. This was so familiar to me, having had first–hand experience with Communism's inefficiencies. Later at the conference, everybody had a story to tell of how they managed to get to Varna, and people were anxiously wondering how they would get back home. Here is our story:

Before leaving the United States, we had been told that there were buses and ships leaving from Istanbul, as well as trains, although trains would be a bit inconvenient since there was no direct connection to Varna from Istanbul. We were assured, however, that once we got to Istanbul we would have no problem making travel arrangements.

Not so. None of the travel agencies in Istanbul, including American Express, seemed to know how we could get to Varna. We found that Turkey was nearly at war with Bulgaria, so they were not really interested in helping us get to an enemy country. As far as we could tell, there were no buses, and certainly no ship. We even thought of hiring a private car and driver, but were told that no Turkish driver would be so crazy as to drive his car into Bulgaria.

In Istanbul, we met up with Lynn and Ray Johnson from Chicago who were also going to Varna, and with whom we had taken side trips in connection with other conferences. We thoroughly enjoyed seeing Istanbul together, but it was marred by anxiety about needing to find a way to get to Varna. We spent a good part of our time in Istanbul trying to get answers, but no one seemed to know.

Train Trip to Varna

At the last minute we ended up on a train from Istanbul to Varna via Sofia. Instead of 200 miles, we had traveled about 800 miles by the time we reached Varna. The route took us all the way to Sofia and then back east to Varna—two legs of a triangle. We spent twenty–six hours on the train—without anything to eat or drink. The dining car we had been told about did not exist. Lynn had a little roll and two chocolate mints in her airline bag. The four of us feasted on that. It was Ray's birthday dinner! Luckily, we did have a small bottle of mineral water, which we shared. After this unforgettable train trip I reacquired the almost forgotten habit of hoarding food. From then on, an occasional leftover roll or an apple disappeared into my handbag—provisions for hard times.

Every part of this train trip was an experience. Starting out at eight o'clock in the evening and expecting to travel throughout most of the night—nobody had been able to tell us how long a trip it would be—we had booked a sleeping compartment. Well, we could have taken turns sleeping if the rest of us were standing up during that time. The two opposite bench seats folded to meet in the center to make a bed which could have accommodated two people at best, but certainly not four. What to do with the other two people?

Even in the dark we noticed how dirty the train was. Picture a flashlight hanging down from the ceiling to light up a room—that was about all the light we had. Ray said that once the train moves, they'll probably turn up the lights. When the train moved out of the station, the tiny light on the ceiling dimmed, and that was that. Ray commented that the Orient Express left from that same Istanbul Station, and we began to wonder what we were in for. Eventually, we fell asleep in our seats.

At about one o'clock in the morning, we were awakened when the train stopped and we were told to get out. We wondered why, but then realized that we had arrived at the Turkish–Bulgarian border. It was freezing cold outside. Shivering without our jackets which were in our suitcases, we stood in line outside a building for forty minutes to have our passports and visas checked. Back on the train, we sat for more than two hours before we slowly moved into Bulgaria. The Communist system's legendary inefficiency had begun. Another check. This time, the Bulgarian official came into the train to check our passports. After studying Mal's passport, he turned to Mal and said in perfect English, and with a smile, which was a rare occurrence in a Communist country: "Happy Birthday." He had noticed Mal's birth date—the day after Ray's birthday. It was the only cheerful thing that happened to us on the whole train trip, other than laughing about our situation. Ray had commented earlier how nice it would be to have a cup of hot coffee. He and I now wanted that cup of coffee more and more. We had already found out that no food service of any kind existed.

Nobody had been able to tell us how long a train trip we had ahead of us, so we kept hoping. A map of Bulgaria had not been available anywhere, and we had no idea of where we were in relation to Sofia. We did not even know that we needed to change trains in Sofia. That was another ordeal. We had been told that we had purchased tickets to Varna. One of the many conductors who came through to check during

Lynn, Ray and Mal in the "sleeping" comparment on the train from Istanbul to Varna. The compartment seated six people. It took us 26 hours to travel what would have been about 200 miles if there had been direct transportation.

our long train ride told us that our tickets were only good to Sofia, and that we had to get off in Sofia, buy more tickets, and get on another train. With much trouble we did, and we nearly missed our connection from Sofia to Varna. At least a train to Varna did exist!

I had been happy at the prospect of traveling by train as I thought it would be wonderful to see some of the countryside. Although we traveled all over Bulgaria by train, we cannot say that we saw the country. The windows of the Bulgarian train were so dirty that it was literally impossible to see out. It seems that the Peoples Republic of Bulgaria forgot to include a window cleaning department in their master plan. From the faintest shadows we guessed that we were traveling through mountains. We never did find out for sure. The windows could not be opened. Later on in Varna we noticed that it was impossible to see through windows in restaurants, nor through windows anywhere we went. Next time I'll be armed with a bottle of Windex and a scrub brush—and emergency food rations, of course. Actually, long before the end of this trip we decided that there would never be a next time in Bulgaria or in any other Communist country.

Our arrival in Varna after ten o'clock that evening was another memorable experience. A number of cab drivers met the train, and one of them just grabbed some of our luggage started to run without saying a word. We ran after him, not knowing where he was going to. He led us to an ancient car that looked like it wouldn't make it halfway down the block. The trunk was not in working condition, having been jammed shut in an accident. The driver proceeded to pile three of the suitcases onto the roof of the car. There was no luggage rack and the bags kept sliding off. Finally, he motioned for us to help him hold that pyramid in place while he tied it up with string, which went through the inside of the car. Lynn and I looked at each other. Had we not been so dreadfully tired, we might have cried, or even laughed. Instead we stood there, somewhat detached, and stared in disbelief. We did not expect to ever see our things again, but we were beyond caring. Finally we piled into the car, and I held the remaining suitcase on my lap while others held the hand luggage for the approximately ten–mile drive. We were surprised that we actually arrived at the hotel with all our baggage.

Varna

Varna is a resort on the Black Sea. I don't know what we expected, but I guess endless sandy beaches and sunshine, somewhat like Florida. Instead, it was cold and hazy. The beaches were narrow and instead of sand there were pebbles. We would not have been able to spend time on the beach anyway. Aside from attending the conference, we spent all available time trying to solve the problem of how to get from Varna to Berlin, the next destination for Mal and me. We had been unable to book any of the Bulgarian part of the trip from the United States, but were told that we needed to do that once we were in Bulgaria.

Now, none of the two hundred delegates who had come to this meeting knew how to arrange travel out of Bulgaria at the end of the Conference. We got quite sick of hearing the words "it is impossible." They sent us from one place to another to get all kinds of permits. Finally, we took a taxi to the government travel bureau downtown. Tipping generously with dollars, we were able to get the taxi driver to stay with us and take us around to the different locations to gather the required permit slips. Eventually, we had enough permits to buy airline tickets from Sofia to Berlin. Except—the Sofia airport was closed. Nobody mentioned that little detail! Perhaps they did not know this in Varna—and how would we get to Sofia? On another train? Nobody knew the answer to that question. Still, we were happy to have gotten at least that far, even though we lost a lot of dollars. Everywhere we went, they

A typical sidewalk cafe scene in Varna

wanted us to pay in hard currency—dollars—but they never gave us any change. If the fee was thirty US dollars and we gave them forty, we never got the ten dollar difference back, always under the pretense that they did not have any change. It taught us to carry a lot of small bills on future trips.

At least we had tickets to East Berlin, though we did not know where the plane would fly from. Certainly not Sofia. By that time I did not even want to go to Berlin. All I wanted was to go home. Nobody can imagine how much I longed for the solitude of our desert southwest, and the spaciousness and freedom of the United States.

Evidence of a Dictatorship

Bulgaria is a beautiful country and the people are proud of it. As part of the conference, we had several bus trips to different areas and a chance to see the beautiful countryside which we had missed out on during our train trip. There was one day on which there were no meetings, and all of us were taken on an all–day excursion by bus. Miraculously, the buses, including their windows, were sparkling clean. The sights we were shown were not as impressive as the trip itself. Another unique experience, though shocking.

We started from the hotel in four buses, with police escorts. In addition, stationed on both sides of the road every 100 yards were two soldiers with guns, standing at attention. This was not just when we left the hotel, but actually throughout the city, and for about thirty miles out of Varna into the countryside. There had to have been more than one thousand such soldiers. It was the type of display you might expect if the convoy was carrying the President of the United States, or the Premier of Russia.

It was during morning rush hour when we left Varna, and again when we returned in the evening. All traffic had been stopped in the side streets to let our buses travel on the main avenue at high speed. There were no vehicles on the main street through which our caravan traveled, and all traffic lights were green. Once we had driven about thirty miles, the soldiers were no longer present but every vehicle in both directions pulled off the road to let us pass. Sometimes they had to pull into a shallow ditch to do this. Mal and I sat in the front seats of the first bus, and it was noticeable to us that this "ditching" was not done out of courtesy, but out of fear. We could tell by the way they pulled into the ditches after perhaps not having noticed the convoy of buses coming. Such a convoy could only have been an official government convoy, and these other drivers knew exactly what they were supposed to do. There were no sirens. I felt sad about human beings living in such fear. They stared at our buses with huge, sad eyes! I have seen this stare in people waiting at train crossings in East Germany, seeming to think "there goes a train to freedom—I wish I could be on it."

The Bulgarians are warm and hospitable people. We were entertained at several banquets and served the local food specialties. From our previous travels in East Bloc countries and the Soviet Union, we knew that the people are short on food and other necessities, but everything is available for the tourists and official guests. I felt guilty about leaving some of the food when we were served too much. They also arranged for Bulgarian folk dance groups in local costumes to perform for us. Those were special treats which we enjoyed.

Backstage, we noticed that grocery stores were poorly stocked and consumer goods stores had no selections. People bought not what they wanted, but what was available. This was not a surprise to us. We had experienced it in the Soviet Union and Czechoslovakia. For the tourists, lovely handmade souvenir items were available at quite reasonable prices. Those brought in hard currency.

The Bulgarians were extremely hospitable. Here a company performed typical folk dancing. This was the 82nd General Conference of the FAI, which was established in 1905 in Paris. The National Aeronautic Association was one of eight founding members. Mal served as President of the National Aeronautic Association from 1989 to 1993, and as such represented United States aviation at the FAI.

Many of the everyday things that are simple for us, and which we take for granted, were a problem. I wanted to buy some postage stamps at the hotel. The answer was "not today." I went back the next morning and was told "two o'clock." At two o'clock I was told "seven o'clock," and when that was not possible, I gave up. The next day, I found out from a lady in our group who went through the same ordeal that stamps were available at the hotel's gift shop. Why did they not tell me this at the reception desk? Because nobody knew what the other person was doing, and they didn't want to admit it. I thought it might have been a language problem, but we went through exactly the same thing with airline bookings, as well as other business details. The answer always was: "come back tomorrow" or "it is not possible." People who did one type of work really did not know what another person was doing.

Getting out of Bulgaria

How did we get out of Bulgaria? Well, everybody had that problem, though a number of people had arrived in rented cars or chartered mini-buses from nearby countries—but not Turkey. Those lucky ones were besieged by people trying to hitch rides with them. In fact, during the last couple of days of the conference, everyone was preoccupied with the problem: "How are we going to get out of here and get home?" It seemed that our hosts had not yet addressed the issue. Did they not know that the Sofia airport was closed? They seemed to have left it up to us to figure it out.

After much complaining to the "system" by participants of the conference, charter flights were arranged for to take us to Plovdiv, about eighty miles south of Sofia. Plovdiv is an air force base, extremely primitive by our standards, and not at all equipped to handle passenger air traffic. It turned out that Balkan Airlines was using Plovdiv during the time Sofia was closed. Foreign airlines refused to fly into Plovdiv. Too primitive. Fortunately, we were catching a Balkan Airlines flight to East Berlin.

It is impossible to describe the mess and confusion. I could write a whole chapter about our one–and–a–half hours at Plovdiv. Plovdiv's "airport terminal" was a quonset hut packed solidly with people. It was suffocatingly hot inside. There were no definitive lines. Anyone who had finally gotten to the counter and checked in, had to—and I am not kidding—crawl across baggage and waiting people to get out of the building. There were no signs telling us which flight we were checking in for. Hearing two businessmen speak the Berliners' German somewhere near us, I grappled my way over to them to inquire. They were returning to East Berlin, and I begged them to watch out for us and make sure that we get on the same flight with them. They were in a different area and I kept worrying that we would lose sight of them. Plovdiv was another experience which I hope will never repeat itself in my lifetime.

I am still amazed that we actually ended up on a flight to Berlin. There was no announcement on the plane telling us where we were headed and, although we had followed the two businessmen, I was relieved to see the city as we approached Schönefeld Airport. Arrival formalities in East Berlin were a snap compared with what we had been through to get there. Things were slow, but organized. God bless the Germans' sense for order! There was regular bus service between East and West Berlin airports. When we finally arrived at my Aunt and Uncle's house, I sat down on the steps and cried. I was absolutely exhausted, and so relieved to be back in the West. I vowed that I shall never again set foot into another Communist country. The following year, the International Conference was scheduled to be held in Hungary. I told Mal "without me"—but I ended up going because of what happened barely a month later—the collapse of the Iron Curtain.

12

Our Travels and Adventures

The Family Mistress

When I accepted Mal's marriage proposal, I was well aware that he had a mistress—his Cessna 170A airplane—and that flying would be a part of our life. As I relate in Chapter 5, he took me up in this airplane on our first date, flying over New York City and Long Island Sound on a beautiful, full–moon evening that could not have been more romantic.

Our honeymoon was a four–week trip in this plane around the United States, and to the Canadian Rockies. I started out married life knowing full well that an airplane would be an important part of our life together. It has been.

Realism, of course, requires adjustments when conditions dictate, and so Mal sold this airplane shortly after our marriage to get the down payment for our first home. In early 1963 Mal got airplane fever again, and we felt we could manage owning a small two–seat training plane, an Aeronca Champ. I think we paid all of eight hundred dollars for this plane, although we invested another five hundred dollars in an over-hauled sixty–five horsepower engine. I then started taking flying lessons, and on June 28, 1963—which happened to be our fifth wedding anniversary—I made my first solo flight.

My memories of "airplanes flying in the sky and dropping bombs on us," as well as "houses looking as small as match boxes" came back to me vividly during some of my flying lessons. A few months later, and partway to getting my pilot's license, we had a chance to buy a Luscombe 8A which had been lovingly reconditioned. It was also a

We flew in Mal's Cessna 170A on our honeymoon around the United States. One of our stops was in Corvallis, Oregon where we met Mal's two grandmothers and other relatives. Here we are at the Corvallis airport with the Cessna behind us. This plane flew at 120 mph, and carried fuel for five hours of flying. Within a year we sold the plane to raise funds for a down payment on a small house.

two–seat aircraft, and I earned my private pilot's license in it. I loved flying the Luscombe and had many hours of fun and good memories with it. In fact, I considered it to be *my* airplane. Frequently I would go to the airport after work and fly around for half an hour or longer, to look at the fall colors or whatever else was going on. Flying was a feeling of freedom for me, and I loved it.

Emergency Landing at La Guardia Airport

One of my memories is landing at La Guardia Airport one Saturday evening, something that few private pilots ever do. I had flown from Morristown, New Jersey to a private airport on Shelter Island, near the eastern end of Long Island, to attend a fly–in of women pilots, the Ninety–Nines. It was about one hundred and twenty miles from Morristown, and with a tailwind I made the trip in just an hour. By late afternoon when it came time to return to Morristown, the winds had increased, and I now had a headwind of close to forty miles per hour. Instead of returning home quickly, as I had come, I found that I was just crawling along. The Luscombe held only thirteen gallons of fuel, and as I got near New York

City, I became concerned that I would not have enough fuel to get back to Morristown, which was forty miles west of New York. To compound my anxiety, it was getting dusk and I had never flown or landed at night.

Well, I did the only sensible thing I could do. I was getting fairly close to La Guardia Airport, and I called them. The conversation went something like this:

N71497:   La Guardia Tower this is 71497 (my plane number).

Tower: 71497 Go ahead.

N71497:   La Guardia tower I am a sixty–five horsepower Luscombe airplane about five miles east of you— I am getting low on fuel and need to land—I don't think I can make Morristown because of headwinds.

Tower: Roger 497—Winds are two–nine zero at twenty–five knots—Plan straight–in for Runway 31.

N71497:   Tower, I am a new pilot and have never landed at night— I would like to overfly the airport to get oriented.

Tower: 497—Understand this is your first night landing— what is your altitude?—Turn on your landing light.

N71497:   I am at 2,000 feet but I do not have a landing light.

Tower: Roger 497 proceed directly to the airport and enter downwind for Runway 31

A few minutes pass.

Tower: 497 we see you over the field—you can turn downwind now—remember you will have a tailwind and will be going much faster—do you see the runway?

N71497:   Affirmative—do you want me to land on the first part of the runway?

Tower: 497 you can land anywhere on the runway—the airport
            is all yours.

Needless to say I was nervous, but I made a perfect landing in that I
gently rolled onto the big numbers at the beginning of the runway. The
wind was so strong that I came to a complete stop almost immediately.
My airplane was still on the big numbers.

Tower: That was a good landing 497—Now just taxi straight
            ahead and turn left at Taxiway Joliet.

I had to taxi slowly in this strong wind, and it seemed to take a long
time before I came to the first taxiway to get off the runway. The tower
then directed me to an area where I could park the plane. All of this
probably took about fifteen minutes, and I learned later that the tower
officials effectively closed the airport to everyone else while I landed.

*Starting the Luscombe. It has no electrical system and must be started by hand, as I
am doing here. This required two people—a pilot in the cockpit to handle the throttle,
and a person spinning the propeller. Both needed to know what they were doing.*

I am sure I was one of the most inexperienced pilots to have ever landed at La Guardia, but the tower personnel could not have been more considerate and helpful. They were obviously concerned about my safety and recognized that my decision to land was exactly the right decision on my part.

Once I got parked, I called Mal who drove to La Guardia. He then had the plane refueled, and flew it back to Morristown while I drove home. That was my one and only landing at La Guardia Airport.

Other Airplanes over the Years

Once our son Randy joined the family, a two–seat aircraft was one seat short of our needs, and by the time Michele came, it would have been two seats short. It was not long before Mal traded my beautiful Luscombe in on a used Cessna 172, a four–place aircraft. We had that airplane for nearly two years, but found that the maintenance costs were much higher than our budget permitted. We sold it in early 1969. By that time, because of family responsibilities, my flying had been reduced to the required number of take offs and landings to remain legal.

We were without a plane until 1972 when we bought a Cessna 182—also a four–place airplane—from our El Paso friends, Noel and Mary Olmstead. By that time Mal's career was well established, and we felt we could afford another airplane. The Cessna 182 was a faster and more powerful plane than the 172, and we kept it until 1975 when we bought an even more sophisticated aircraft, a Cessna T210. It was this plane in which Mal and Randy set the speed record for this category airplane between San Francisco and Washington, DC. It was a capable, high altitude flying plane (25,000 feet) that could handle most bad weather. Mal has prided himself on his professionalism in flying this plane under some fairly adverse weather conditions. I was no longer flying.

We kept that airplane for twenty–eight years, selling it in 2003 when Mal, then age seventy, felt it was time to reduce his high performance flying. Twenty–eight years is a long time and included most of the trips the family took; we all felt the loss when it was gone.

We owned this airplane for 28 years, and sold it in 2003. It is a high performance, six–passenger plane, flying at 200 mph, with a range of almost 1,000 miles. Its optimin altitutde was 25,000 feet, requiring us to wear oxygen masks. A mostly all–weather plane, it required Mal to maintain a high level of proficiency. N210MG was a member of the family, and we traveled to places that most people never have a chance to see. We miss Two Ten Mike Golf.

In 1995 Mal had purchased another plane, a 1955 Mooney "Mite." This is a one–seat aircraft and is a sport airplane if there ever was one. It has only a sixty–five horsepower engine, and barely room enough for Mal to sit in. It is a great good–weather–only airplane for local flying. Mal still has this plane, and he flies it with great enjoyment. In selling the Cessna T210 he has not given up flying, but he has given up flying IFR in bad weather. The Mite is the eighth airplane Mal has owned, and probably the last.

Flying Trips

Thanks to owning an airplane, our travels were unique in comparison to most of the population. Our children grew up flying all over the United States. For a number of years, Lake Powell in Utah was our favorite summer vacation spot. We would fly into a landing strip near Bullfrog Marina, rent a houseboat for a week or two at a time, and explore the canyons of that beautiful, one hundred eighty mile long lake. By road we made excursions into the back country to get to know the magnificent scenery of the State of Utah.

We took flying trips to many places which we would not have seen, or had a chance to get to know without an airplane. Twice we toured Alaska by air, and when returning from the second trip in 1976, we flew over a group of islands which enchanted me. These were the beautiful San Juan Islands of Washington State. It was love at first sight from the air. I had found "home." This new place which I felt was home, was investigated a number of years later and turned out to be Orcas Island where, seventeen years later, we built our retirement home.

In 1982 we even attempted to fly to Europe, but got only as far as central Greenland when mechanical problems forced us to return to the United States.

Camping Trips

Through our flying, having crossed the continental United States countless times in all directions, I have a comprehensive mental picture of this wonderful, spacious country. However, something was still missing. When I looked down from the plane and saw the distances, I longed to experience them. I wanted to feel the space rather than just seeing it.

In the summer of 1980 I bought an old Jeep Wagoneer. It was big enough for me to sleep in, and I took off on the first of what became annual camping trips, exploring in detail many favorite places in my beloved desert southwest. At the time we were living in Washington, DC, so that these were long distance trips involving four to six weeks. I always went without Mal or anyone else. Randy and Michele were teenagers and someone needed to stay home with them. Mal, of course, was working and could not have gotten away for that long a period of time even if he had wanted to; besides, camping was not his thing.

The Jeep was old and proved unreliable. For my 1981 trip, I bought a new Ford Bronco which provided even more room. I needed the four–wheel drive because I loved to go to remote places, such as The Maze in Canyonlands. There are many roads in Utah and Arizona labeled four–wheel drive only, which took me to scenery that rivaled what we could see from the air, but up close. I enjoyed the solitude, the opportunity to hike and explore, and do things at my own pace and direction. It was my way of recharging my batteries.

With few exceptions, these trips have become annual events and I am still taking them. I wore the Bronco out, and bought a Jeep Grand Cherokee a few years ago. With my advancing years, I am a little more cautious in where I go, but I still look forward to these annual camping trips. Living now in the Pacific Northwest, I have expanded my horizon to include Vancouver Island, the Canadian Rockies, the northern Rocky Mountains in the United States, some National Parks in California, and of course, our spectacular Cascade Mountains, as well as the Olympic Peninsula. Mal continues to respect my need for solitude.

Later in this book I detail my first raft trip—of eight—that I have made down the Colorado River and through the Grand Canyon. I hope this description helps you to see why I have been so enthusiastic about our great Southwest, and why I keep going back each year.

FAI Trips

As I indicated earlier, in June of 1989, Mal took optional retirement from Price Waterhouse at age fifty–five to become the President of the National Aeronautic Association, the national aero club of the United States. In that role he represented United States air sport organizations at the international sport aviation organization, the Fédération Aéronautique Internationale. The FAI—as it is referred to—oversees international sporting events much as the International Olympic Committee oversees other types of sporting events.

In his new job we attended a number of international conferences which were held in a different country each year. Between 1987 and 1995 Mal and I attended annual conferences of the FAI in Sydney, Varna in Bulgaria, Budapest, Berlin, Athens, Tel Aviv, Antalya in Turkey, and Johannesburg. In addition we made frequent trips to Paris where the FAI was then headquartered.

In many ways the FAI is a miniature United Nations, typically with delegations from fifty to sixty countries in attendance. There is simultaneous translation into four or five languages. Mal, as head of the

United States delegation, had many of the diplomatic problems that are common to the United Nations. Interestingly, he had excellent relations with his Russian counterpart, a retired army general and a "Hero of the U.S.S.R."—a title and honor equivalent to our Congressional Medal of Honor. Mal found that when the two of them agreed to a specific proposal, he could count on the Russian support. This was not always true in his relations with some of the heads of delegation from Western countries.

Mal retired from the National Aeronautic Association (the United States member of FAI) in 1993 because the stress of raising funds for a small nonprofit organization was starting to raise health issues. Both of us look back fondly on those few years, and particularly on the many international friends we made.

Visits to Berlin—1980 to Present

Over the years, I had done a pretty good job of keeping in touch with my relatives and friends in Germany by mail. However, once we moved to the Washington, DC area in 1974, I felt some loss as far as my German relatives who lived in the United States were concerned. Mom had Alzheimer's Disease, was in a nursing home, and just barely knew me. Peter, Aunt Martha, and my friend Evelyn were in New Jersey. Telephone rates for international calls were too high, and I did not just pick up the phone to make calls to Germany. For that reason I kept in touch by mail. Thanks to Mal also being an experienced typist, we always owned a good typewriter. In the following years I hardly ever had occasion to speak German.

Early in 1980, I took a three–week trip to Berlin and Stuttgart to visit my relatives. This was the first trip back since 1962. By that time, Aunt Martha had died after her third heart attack, and I had started to become interested in genealogy and wanted to get whatever information I could about Mom's side of the family from her sister Charlotte. On Papa's side, only Aunt Else was still alive of his Berlin relatives, and I wanted to verify some dates and get more information from her about that side of the family.

Grandma Stanneck had been born on a farm in an area which was given to Poland after World War II. Those of her brothers who were still alive lived in East Germany, and there was no chance of contacting them at that time, even if I had known where they lived. A few years earlier I had been able to get much of Grandma Stanneck's family information from Aunt Martha, who was Grandma's youngest sister. At the time she had been stuck at our house for three months while recovering from her first heart attack.

It was good to be in Berlin again. However the city had become strange to me after an eighteen–year absence. I found the population to be quite irritable and short tempered, which came across to me as being almost impolite. Perhaps I had forgotten how rude the Berliners appear to be. It had been such a long time since I heard the harsh sound of the way they speak, and I was not used to receiving an uncouth answer to a polite question. The hopelessness of the situation in West Berlin, of people being walled–in for so many years, and the hassle and red tape to get out of Berlin for a trip to anywhere, was evident in people's behavior.

Still, even while the Berliners were suffering from being shut off from the rest of the free world, their city had experienced a tremendous building boom. I was delighted to see facades of old buildings saved and restored, although they were painted in colors which I found somewhat too bright. When I thought about it, though, I had to realize that this is a country which gets little sunshine, and bright colors help greatly to dispel depression caused by gray skies. I vowed to send them some of Washington DC's eternal sunshine, and the heat and humidity to go with it!

The many contemporary box–like buildings, and even small skyscrapers, gave the city a different look and feel from the way I remembered it. The old streetcars were gone and the subway lines had been extended. The S–Bahn stations and the network of tracks for the city's electric elevated trains had been totally neglected, it being under East Berlin administration. Those trains were being boycotted by the West Berliners and were not running on regular schedules in West Berlin since The Wall had separated the city in 1961. Except for the different city scape, the city itself was bustling and alive, full of energy and enthusiasm, just as I remembered it. Surprised? No! As the Berliners would say: *Berlin bleibt doch Berlin!* (Berlin will always be Berlin!)

When I first arrived I had a difficult time with the language, but after a week I had learned a lot and became quite fluent again except for specialized subjects. A language develops constantly. The level of my knowledge of the German language was still at what it had been in 1954 when I left. For instance, a cousin who has an automobile repair business, taught me the German words for: clutch, drive shaft, automatic transmission, power brakes, power steering, and central lock system. Most people did not own cars when I was living in Berlin. I was therefore lacking the words for automobile parts.

Any special words connected with space travel, as well as the aviation language, were missing from my German vocabulary. I have handwritten pages of words and translations in my English–German dictionary.

It was wonderful to see my relatives and friends again. Everybody made me feel so welcome, and I fit in immediately. At times it seemed as if I had never left.

In the years to come I made regular trips to Berlin, and also to the Stuttgart area, where the Eckerleins live. Wolfgang Eckerlein is my father's first cousin, although he is closer to my age. Wolfgang and his wife, Gretel, own a home in a lovely small town in Swabia near the romantic Black Forest. It is beautiful, hilly wine–growing country. Over the years they have taken me and my family sightseeing in their area. On a visit to the United States in 1995, they spent two weeks with us on Orcas Island. We were proud to show them one of the most beautiful areas in the United States.

Family Trip to Berlin

In 1982, Mal and I took Randy and Michele to Berlin so that I could show them where I was born and raised. To impress on them where West Berlin is situated and how difficult it can be to get there, we flew into Frankfurt and took a train to Stuttgart to visit the Eckerleins. From there we took the train to Berlin which necessitated traveling through East Germany. This was an awesome experience for teenagers who had grown up in the United States. People who have not seen the Communist system in action have no idea of the anxiety and stress caused by traveling through the Soviet zone of occupation.

We boarded the train in Backnang for the approximately eight–hour trip to Berlin, a distance of only three hundred fifty miles. This alone tells a story of chronic delays, and those delays were all in East Germany. The train trip through West Germany was as normal as a trip anywhere else. However, Randy and Michele (ages eighteen and fifteen), did not expect the drastic change that took place upon entering East Germany. Here are some notes from my diary that I wrote at the time:

At stations (in West Germany), people always wave good–bye. Some cry. Interesting trip through the villages and cities. Everything looks so clean and tidy. It's evident that people take pride in their property.

At the border, Ludwigsburg/Probstzella, we are greeted by walls, fences, barbed wire, electric wires, guards, and dogs. Guards carry leather cases (walkie talkies?) and guns. Many have dogs. They watch the train carefully. The West German engine is detached and an East German one slammed on so hard that we nearly fall off the seats. The kids are stunned and have question marks in their eyes. I shake my head, meaning "don't ask questions now." They (the East German officials) get on the train. They check passports, look carefully at everybody's passport photo and compare it with our faces. They write down all information from each passport before giving transit visas. I am surprised that there is no luggage check. After the Peoples Police railroad officials leave (they always travel in twos to prevent one from defecting), Michele asks why they had been looking so carefully at everyone after checking the individual passports. Mal tells her to ask later.

Impressions of East Germany: Bleak. Damage to buildings from World War II bombing not repaired in most cases. Streets look deserted. Farmers' fields show skimpy growth and many weeds (lacking fertilizer and weed control). People stare at the train. At railroad crossings there are no cars, but many bicycles. Train stops once, at Halle—heavily guarded. Why a thirty–five minute stop? Nobody gets on or off, but people waiting for other trains stare. Can't forget their sad, sad eyes. Could feel what they were thinking—"there goes a train to freedom."

Between Potsdam and Wannsee, short stop before entering West Berlin. Walls, fences, and guards are left behind. No checking at all by West Berlin officials—and then the train stops at Berlin–Wannsee, the first station in West Berlin. I heave a sigh of relief. We get off at the Zoo Station, West Berlin's central railroad station, which is crowded.

There were several reasons why it took so long for the train trip through East Germany. The train can crawl along at only 25 to 35 miles an hour because the track is in disrepair. There is only a single track, the other having been removed by the Russians after the war almost forty years ago. This makes it necessary to pull onto a sidetrack and wait for any oncoming trains. Then there are unscheduled stops for seemingly no reason. It is not uncommon to stop somewhere other than at a station, and just sit there for 30 or 45 minutes.

Our kids were stunned into silence about the train trip. It took some time for the experience to sink in. On the return trip to Frankfurt, my diary reads:

Monday, August 16, 1982—The train was already at the Zoo Station when we got there, having arrived from Friedrichstraße, East Berlin's central railroad station. The compartment (for six) to which we had been assigned, was already occupied by a couple. They do not answer our greeting, and never speak a word for the next several hours.

Potsdam—two East German officials get on. Stone faced. Nobody dares to smile or talk. Silently we hand over our passports to be scrutinized and recorded, receive transit visas, and try to say "thank you" while holding our breath. Again complete, uncomfortable silence.

We pass East German villages and cities, ancient (pre–World War II) factories, and large, depressing–looking industrial areas; farmland, and even a Russian Army Post with countless tanks. Do not dare take pictures. The couple in our compartment does not trust us, and at this point we do not trust them.

Train stops at a couple of stations along the way, but is heavily guarded with machine guns and dogs. Vopos (East German Police/Army) walk alongside the train and check underneath each car by rolling mirrors under the cars. Their dogs wear muzzles. We stand by the open door between cars and watch. Nobody gets on or off, so why the lengthy stop? Michele asks what would happen if she just stepped off the train right now. Mal tells her: "they'll shoot." She is shocked and runs back inside to sit in our compartment.

Can't wait to get to the West. At the last border stop, between walls, electric fences and barbed wire, the East engine is replaced with a West engine. East German officials and guards get off at a deserted railroad station overgrown with weeds—and finally we chug into the free world. Sighs of relief. Faces light up, people start talking to each other, and even the train tracks are smoother. The silent couple becomes friendly and starts a conversation with us.

A couple of hours later, we pull into the monstrous railroad station of Frankfurt am Main.

This train trip demonstrated the fallacy of the Communist system. It was a good education for our children, and taught them to appreciate having the freedom to travel in our country.

Berlin 1989

After a trip to Bulgaria described in an earlier chapter, Mal and I traveled to Berlin at an historic time—the period immediately preceding the collapse of the Iron Curtain, and for Berlin, the Berlin Wall.

Mal had not been to Berlin since 1982, so we did a little bit of sightseeing. When we stood at The Wall by the Brandenburg Gate and looked into East Berlin, we never dreamed that very shortly the infamous Wall would come down. On television we watched the first train with East German refugees leave Prague, and arrive in the West. Mal said: "Something major is going to happen, soon." Exactly one month later it did happen.

After the Wall Fell

My next visit to Berlin was in 1990, and it was a most interesting one. The Berlin Wall had fallen the year before. Uncle Martin and Aunt Lotte lived within walking distance of The Wall and the south-eastern city limits, and while I was staying with them, I could easily observe what was going on at that time.

People from the former East Germany were coming to West Berlin daily by the thousands—to shop! Now this is a year after The Wall came down and they still shopped like mad. I was in the local Woolworth store and watched what people purchased. This told a sad story of decades of chronic shortages. They were buying consumer goods which we take for granted: kitchen utensils, pots and pans, dish pans, dish towels, socks, underwear, sheets and blankets, and similar items. The quantities they purchased were unbelievable, far more than they would currently need. They were buying and hoarding, fearing that supplies might not be available in the future. This was an understandable reaction to forty years of shortages which made them doubt that these goods would be available tomorrow. We had observed this type of buying frenzy in Moscow and other Russian cities when a particular necessary item had become available.

A special shuttle bus line had been put into service, to run from the Rudow subway station (the last station of Line 7 in Berlin) across the border into former East Germany. When one of the double–decker busses stopped, it filled up immediately, left, and the next one pulled into place. Continuously, all day long, people loaded with shopping bags boarded the busses.

By ten o'clock every morning the supermarkets were usually out of milk, eggs, butter, and other staples, as well as chocolate. One day late in the afternoon, we expected some of Uncle Martin's relatives from East Germany to stop by for a visit. They had a car, and it was loaded to where they could hardly sit in it.

When they arrived with their three children, everyone was hungry and Aunt Lotte and Uncle Martin fixed a huge platter heaped with sandwiches. They ate unbelievable quantities while we watched in amazement. When they could eat no more and there were some left-overs, the funniest thing happened. The youngest little boy, three years old, made a sweeping motion over the sandwich plate with his little arm, while he declared: "we'll take all this with us." The parents seemed embarrassed, but we thought it was so cute and funny—and sad as well. It instantly brought back memories of the bleak years right after the war when I was always hungry, and starvation was a constant companion. I felt for this little guy who obviously was worried that food might become scarce again.

Return to Straupitz

One day during my stay in Berlin in 1990, my cousin Klaus took me to the Spreewald in former East Germany to visit the little town of Straupitz, where we had lived for more than three years, from 1943 until late 1946. Many times over the years I had longed to see Straupitz again, it having been a tranquil part of my childhood and a respite from the air raids and destruction of Berlin.

Not too much had changed in the village. It is a bit larger than it used to be. I went to the house where my best friend from those times, Marga Konzack, had lived. There were two women and a man standing at the gate talking. I went up to them and asked if the Konzack family was still living in this house.

The man turned to me and said: "I am Manfred Konzack." I looked at him in surprise and exclaimed with excitement, "Marga's little brother—one brown eye and one blue eye!"

The man turned his face, looked at me in incredible surprise and I could see that he still had one brown eye and one blue eye! No one had uttered those words to him since childhood. I don't know whether he remembered me or not; he was several years younger, but he certainly knew I must have lived in Straupitz. It was an emotional moment for both of us.

Manfred gave me Marga's address. She lived in the nearby city of Lübben. Eventually we had a happy reunion, and we have kept in contact since then. Two lives had been lived in totally opposite circumstances, and it was challenging to compare notes. If Mom had not gotten Peter and me out of Straupitz when she did—on the last day the Russians had permitted families to return to Berlin from Straupitz— my life would have paralleled Marga's.

After Germany's reunification, two friends from childhood days came back into my life—my friend Marga (right) and an over1,000 year–old oak tree. Marga's husband, Werner, is in the center.

* * * * *

Over the years, some of my cousins, as well as aunts and uncles came to see the United States, and they stopped for visits with Peter and me, and met our families. It is always fun for us to show them where we settled and how we live. But no matter how often some of them travel in the United States, the space and vast distances in this country never cease to baffle them.

Other Travels

Moments before Mal asked me to marry him on that Valentines Day in 1958, he asked me what my plans for the future were. I told him that I was nearly finished paying off the furniture I had purchased for the apartment, and afterwards I planned to save up for some travels. Mal said we could travel together.

In the years to come, in addition to the trips discussed above, we did travel extensively, both in our plane and with the airlines. We have seen all of the United States, including Alaska and Hawaii, and have been to many countries in Europe, as well as to Russia (twice), Turkey, Egypt, South Africa, Australia, New Zealand and Antarctica. Health permitting, we are not finished yet.

Many of our trips have been unique. I will describe three of these travels in some detail in the next three chapters.

13

1960
A Pioneering Automobile Trip
Behind the Iron Curtain

This autobiography is also a book about a gypsy. So it is appropriate in these closing chapters to describe in some detail three trips that help express my love of travel and adventure, and perhaps in doing so, help to further paint a picture of the gypsy part of my life. This chapter is an account of an early adventure. It was written in October 1960, from diary notes I had made on a pioneering automobile trip behind the Iron Curtain, primarily to the Union of Soviet Socialist Republics.

Background—1960

Two years after we were married, Mal arranged to take four months off from Price Waterhouse to travel to Europe before we became encumbered with raising a family. We arranged for the purchase of a new Volkswagen Beetle for delivery in Hamburg, and in the following four months traveled 18,000 miles. We traveled on a shoestring budget, using a popular travel guide of the day—"Europe on $5 a Day." Early in our trip we visited the Soviet Union which, for the first time since World War II, had opened its borders to automobile tourists.

We were in the Soviet Union for three weeks, and drove about 4,000 miles. It was a critical time in the Cold War, and this trip offered us a unique experience. For four years the United States had been flying the U–2 spy plane over the Soviet Union at very high altitudes to monitor Soviet military buildup, using high definition cameras. The Russians knew we were making these flights, but their missiles could not get high enough to shoot down the U–2. That is, until Sunday May 1, 1960. On that day they were able to damage a U–2 piloted by Frances Gary Powers, disabling the aircraft and forcing Powers to parachute down. He was captured, and relations between President Eisenhower and Soviet Premier Krushchev deteriorated quickly.

It was against this backdrop that we left our hotel in Warsaw on June 17 for the 120–mile drive to the border crossing into the Soviet Union at Brest. Tensions were so high between the two countries that rumors were circulating in Warsaw that the Soviet border was closed to Americans. In fact it was not closed. We were welcomed, and had an exciting and pioneering trip. We met only one other foreign car in the three weeks we toured this country. Reproduced below is the account we wrote for a Price Waterhouse publication upon our return.

Behind the Iron Curtain by Automobile

The Soviet Frontier

June 17th was the day on which we made our really big plunge. Warsaw is 120 miles from the Soviet frontier, and it took just a little over two hours to drive that morning from our hotel. Polish formalities in clearing out of Poland were quite routine and not difficult.

Then came the Russian frontier—the procedures here were different. As we slowly drove across the border, we came to a pole gate blocking the road. A soldier with a Tommy gun stood at the side of the road. He apparently called his headquarters on a portable phone, but other than that made no motion to do anything. So we just sat and waited.

Perhaps ten minutes later, a Russian officer came walking down the road toward us and the other soldier perked up. This officer took our papers, looked them over once, and motioned for us to follow him in our car. The soldier raised the gate and at a snail's pace we followed this Russian officer.

Perhaps a hundred yards down the road and around a bend we came to a parking lot and several administrative buildings. He motioned for me to get out of the car and follow him, and then motioned for Mal to park near where several other soldiers were standing. Mal didn't understand why for the longest time, but finally when he got over to where the soldiers were it became obvious that they wanted him to park right over what appeared to be a type of mechanic's pit—the type you see in garages and with which they can get under your car.

This map shows the route we drove between Berlin, Warsaw and then across the U.S.S.R. to Moscow, and south to Yalta on the Black Sea. From Yalta we backtracked north to Kharkov, then turned west to Kiev, Lvov and entered Czechoslovakia at Uzhgorod. Altogether we drove 4,000 miles on this pioneering trip.

Once he got parked properly, a soldier went down under the car to make sure we were not bringing in anything that we weren't supposed to. In the meantime, another soldier with the help of a civilian who spoke a little English, asked Mal about the contents of our car. They did not make him take out our baggage to inspect the contents of the car other than looking closely at our camera and books. When they came to our book "Travel Guide to Russia" they looked it over carefully, but raised no objections. After that, Mal rejoined me inside a building where our papers were being inspected in minute detail.

Next they gave us our food and hotel coupons. We had had to pay for all our Russian accommodations—food, hotel, sightseeing—before leaving New York, and had been told that we would get coupons at the border. We also converted some dollars into Russian rubles for gasoline and miscellaneous purchases. After that we were released and were on our own.

Colorful billboards were everywhere, all of them political, extolling the vitues of the Communist system. This billboard was on a house wall in Brest, but we saw similar billboards everywhere along the highways we traveled.

The Trip Begins

Five kilometers from the frontier was the town of Brest, our first stop. We had meal coupons and were to have lunch in Brest. This coupon was only accepted at the designated Intourist restaurant, which took us some time to find since we did not have a map. Brest was a large town, particularly for a border town. After a good lunch we started on our long first leg, 350 kilometers, to Minsk.

Brest

The road was good—not excellent—but a good two–and–a–half to three–lane road, fairly straight, blacktop, and relatively little traffic. The road was uneven but not badly so. We found ourselves occasionally barreling down this road at 65–70 miles per hour, so you can see it was a good road. We quickly encountered one unique characteristic of Russian roads—the many large, colorful billboards on the side of the road—all propaganda of the U.S.S.R. (in Russian, of course). This same type of sign was in each of the towns and cities we drove through.

We arrived in Minsk after 9 p.m. and settled down in a comfortable hotel room after eating dinner. We changed time zones, losing an hour.

What was our first impression? It was of the thousands of Russian soldiers in Brest poised ready to put down any revolt that might occur in Warsaw. The town is behind a forest, and Polish peasants would never know from looking across the border that the Russian Army was ready to spring if there were an uprising in Warsaw. There were no other cars crossing the border in either direction, and it seemed unlikely that the presence of the troops was known. We were reminded of the Hungarian Uprising that had taken place in October 1956—less than four years earlier—where Russian tanks and soldiers brutally put down an uprising in Hungary. The Russians were taking no chances with Poland.

The road was well marked. Note the sign is in the cyrillic and western alphabets.

Minsk and Smolensk

The next day was typical of most of our days. We had breakfast at about eight, and then a local Intourist guide took us sightseeing for the morning in our car. Our tour was fairly uneventful and the guide did not seem overly informative except as to buildings, and overall progress of Minsk (a city of five hundred thousand). At noon, we again ate at the Intourist hotel and shortly thereafter started out for the next city on our route, Smolensk, again about 350 kilometers further east.

Sunday morning at a church in Smolensk. While mostly older people, everyone is free to attend, although subtle pressures discourage young people from doing so.

We did stop along the road to buy some strawberries from a boy (eight rubles a quart–eighty cents, U.S.). He was a young capitalist, about eight or nine years old. We tried to haggle him down in price but he would not budge.

We arrived in Smolensk late in the afternoon. After dinner we walked into a park where many people were walking because it was Saturday night, and we were stopped several times by people wanting to talk with us. Around eleven we collapsed into bed, exhausted. How were the people dressed? Just like us. If you were shown a picture of a street in a major Soviet city on our route, you would have had a hard time distinguishing it from a street in any western city. The dress was strictly western at least in the cities we visited. Of course, the store signs looked strange being in the Russian alphabet, but otherwise it would take an astute observer to know the picture was of a Russian city.

On our first Sunday we visited a Russian church. Yes, they do have churches in the U.S.S.R. and they are beautiful and reasonably well attended. However, the attendance is mostly by older people. We were told that younger people could go if they wanted to, but, in fact, few do. Another observation we made was that the stores were all open on Sunday, but closed on Monday. Why? Well, they say that people work hard and do not have time to go shopping during the week; it is only on Sundays that they can get away. Not illogical.

Our morning guide in Smolensk was more responsive than the one in Minsk. In fact we talked with him for almost an hour about difficult subjects, such as war, peace, spies (with the U–2 clearly the focus). Again, after lunch it was on to Moscow. We found that as we approached Moscow the number of cars increased, and many seemed similar to a car we had seen in Warsaw, which we were told was a copy of our 1942 Chevy.

Moscow

Our first impression of Moscow, as tourists, was perhaps typical in many ways of our overall impressions of the Rus-

The Ukraine Hotel where we stayed in Moscow. At the time it was very modern and impressive.

sian way of life—inefficient and bureaucratic. All tourists report to the "service bureau" of Intourist in the hotel to obtain a guide, or help in getting tickets. Unfortunately, this is just one big chaotic room with people pushing in and out trying to get service. Because we were now in Moscow there were many foreign tourists, and our uniqueness—being automobile tourists—was not apparent. We had to fight for service in the mob of tourists. We were lucky, however, for when we finally got a guide, she stayed with us, at our request, for the balance of the Russian visit and we did not have to go through this again.

Lana traveled with us in the Volkswagen and had her own meal and hotel coupons. We suspect they provided Lana to us as an easy way of keeping track of us since we were so mobile with a car. There was no charge for her services. This would not have been so, had we been traveling by air or train.

This raises the interesting observation that the tourist who purchases the first class or deluxe accommodations often does not get the best service. Take our case. We were traveling "motor class B" for a flat charge of $11.25 a day per person. The cheapest rate for air or rail tourists was around $18. The deluxe service was $30 a day for rail or air tourists; yet a deluxe tourist was only allowed a guide for three hours a day. We had a guide for our full four days in Moscow. Our hotel accommodations were excellent, and we often had a two or three room suite. So it is not necessarily what you pay that counts in the Communist countries, but how you travel.

Moscow had a number of cars and the traffic was moderately heavy. This had been in contrast to Minsk and Smolensk where the traffic had been light. Of course, it must be remembered that virtually all cars were government or state owned, rather than individually. Nonetheless, someone who had the money could buy one. A car was, however, very expensive. A small car cost about 40,000 rubles, and an average Russian worker earns about 900 rubles a month. So you can see that the number of purchasers is limited. Also, we understand that there is no install-

St. Basil's Cathedral on Red Square. In 1960 it was a museum displaying crown and other jewels of the Tsars.

ment buying of cars. At one point we were approached by an individual who wanted to buy the Volkswagen from us. That is, of course, against the law and quite possibly that individual was a government agent trying to trip us up. In any case, our Russian visa stamp in our passport indicated we came in with a car and we would not be let out of the country without the car.

Goods Available

Several things surprised us about the goods available for Russians to buy in Moscow. First, most basic goods available in Western

Night view from our hotel room

GUM department store at Red Square

Europe were also available in Moscow, including TV sets, shortwave radios, small appliances, and the like. Price wise they were expensive when compared to earnings per month—yet they were available. The quality appeared poor in many cases, but still adequate. From a tourist's standpoint there were few things that were bargains; we found three—books, phonograph records, and maps.

Of the three, maps were the most surprising. We found maps of every country in the world and in great detail.

Red Square. Notice the line of people to the very left, waiting to view Lenin and Stalin in the Mausoleum. After Stalin's atrocities became known, his remains were removed, leaving only Lenin's body for public viewing.

These map stores were jammed with Russians and the prices were low, even by their wage standards. We bought thirty full size world maps for a total cost of less than $5. In addition we bought a 200 page book of Russian road maps which cost us just a dollar. What surprised us was that these maps are available and they are priced quite low in an obvious effort to make them readily available to all.

As far as records were concerned, a large 12" long playing record (33 rpm) sold for only 7 rubles (70 cents). We bought the complete recording of Swan Lake for only $3. Books were equally cheap, but what surprised us was that there were many books published in Moscow in English, German, French and other languages. Furthermore we found a number of technical books that had only recently been published in the United States, and these books had already been translated into the Russian language. It would appear that few books published in the West go unnoticed.

At one point we wanted to look up a newspaper correspondent whose address and letter of introduction we had been given by friends in New York. We tried through Intourist to obtain his phone number. After three days of unsuccessfully trying to get his number, we decided the easiest thing was to make the visit unannounced, and so we drove to his address (which we did have). It turned out that although they have a telephone network, they do not have a telephone book as we know it. In fact, we were told that they have only ten typewritten copies of a book available to the public and then they are of only business phones.

Local Flying Club

One of the things we had been most interested in doing while in Moscow was learning something about the sport flying clubs in the Soviet Union. We had written from the U.S. in advance requesting an interview with the President of the local flying club. Although it took a number of phone calls by Lana, we did succeed in arranging an interview. It turned out that there are in fact a number of government spon-

A training aircraft used by the Central Aero Club

sored flying clubs in the Soviet Union. At the top of the flying club organization is the Central Aero Club of the U.S.S.R. which was the club located in Moscow. The primary purpose of the Central Aero Club appeared to be to train men and women to compete in international competition in all aspects of sport flying, parachuting, and gliding.

The so–called President of the Central Aero Club was, of course, a government employee, and judging from his office, a well paid and important official. He had two assistants with him, along with his interpreter. One of the assistants seemed to be making notes and was probably bilingual.

It was a two–way discussion, with the Russians asking a number of questions about U.S. sport aviation, as well as telling us about their program. After the thirty–minute discussion we were invited to observe a parachute meet that was in progress between the U.S.S.R., Czechoslovakia, and France. The meet itself was not particularly interesting, but the airfield was. In the course of the afternoon we got into several hangars and looked over some of the sport planes used by the U.S.S.R. These planes were quite similar in performance to the last plane we had owned (a Cessna 170) although they carry only two passengers. It had about the same size engine (one hundred fifty horsepower).

The U–2

The Soviets exploited the downing of the U–2. The wreckage was on display, and the line of people waiting to get into the exhibit was probably a couple of blocks long. We did not have to stand in this line, but were taken directly to the ex-

The wreckage of the U.S. U–2 spy plane which had been shot down only a month before. You are looking at the wings here. A Russian SAM missile exploded below the U–2 in a near miss. The concussion caused the plane to violently flip over, at which point the wings broke off. Gary Powers, the pilot, then bailed out and landed in the outskirts of Sverdlovsk. The wings "fluttered" down to the ground. Mal learned these details 44 years later from the son, Gary Powers Jr.

hibit. They wanted to be sure that we saw what our government had done. Interestingly, they make a distinction between the U.S. government and the American people. They didn't hold us responsible for our government's policies, and we were clearly welcomed in their country.

South to the Black Sea and Yalta

After four full and hectic days in Moscow, we started south. I am not sure how we managed to get our new guide, Lana, into the Volkswagen with all our luggage, but we did.

Leaving Moscow was an eye–opener. There was a road block where papers were checked. Ours were not looked at, but Lana's papers were examined in great detail, and many questions from the inspectors addressed to her, in Russian, of course. After we had cleared these formalities and were driving, we asked Lana about this and she explained that they need to keep track of people, and Russians need permits to leave Moscow. We then questioned her why this was so, pointing out that in the United States people can move around the country without having to show any papers. Her reaction: "That is chaos." Throughout our travels with Lana we never missed an opportunity to point out the differences in our two systems.

The drive south took us four days—we spent nights in the cities of Kursk, Kharkov, and Zaporozhe on the way down. These cities were interesting, although we had relatively little time to see them since we were driving long, hard days. Nevertheless, we saw many people, and everywhere the people were friendly to us.

The map on the opposite page is from a book of U.S.S.R. automobile maps which we bought in Moscow. You could not obtain individual automobile maps for a section of the country as we do in the U.S. About half the book are "strip" maps showing only the highway, and towns within about twenty–five kilometers of the main highway between major towns. The maps shown here are the first two of six strips that cover the highway from Moscow to Yalta on the Black Sea. Moscow is the city on the top left–hand strip. Each of these two strip maps covers about 220 kilometers from top to bottom.

There were few private cars in the U.S.S.R. in 1960, and getting fuel was a major problem. At the time there were only three gas stations in all of Moscow available to private autos, and even fewer along highways. In fact, every gas station outside of Moscow is depicted on these maps. On the left strip, there are none shown south of Moscow. On the right strip there is a gas station at the top (see arrow) and one at the bottom (see arrow), a distance of 221 kilometers between stations. It is about the same distance from Moscow to the first station (on the top of the right strip).

Most of the gas stations' pumps were the old–fashioned type not seen in the U.S. since the 1930's. The fuel pump had a ten–liter jar on top. On the side of the pump was a long handle that was used to hand–pump fuel into this jar. Once the jar was full, the fuel was allowed to flow by gravity through a hose into the car. Obviously you got charged for the number of "jars" used.

A couple of times the gas station was even more primitive and we had to transfer fuel from a 55–gallon barrel and filter it through a chamois skin to remove impurities. Later in the summer in Greece we had to have our fuel tank removed and sludge cleaned out because of the impurities we had picked up in the U.S.S.R.

МОСКВА — ХАРЬКОВ —

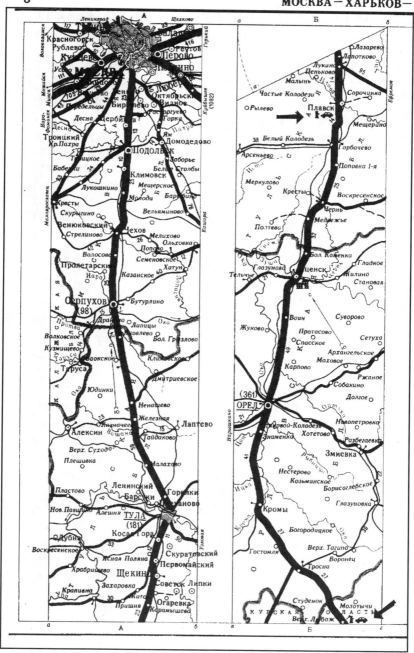

This flag plate was attached to our rear bumper. Until July 4th our flag had 49 stars. Several Russians were observant, and told us: "After July 4th: 50."

Our Volkswagen was quite conspicuous and drew crowds everywhere we went. On the back fender we had put a 3 1/2 x 5 inch plate on which the American flag had been enameled, clearly identifying us as Americans. There were several questions that every crowd was interested in: how many liters of fuel per 100 kilometers, and what did the car cost. Mal had Lana print out the answers to these questions in Russian on a little sign and we would answer the question before it came up by displaying it. Usually someone within the crowd—mostly students—would speak a little English and would engage in conversation with us.

Yalta was in many ways a disappointment because we had expected sandy beaches and a chance to relax in the sun. In fact, the beaches were primarily gravel and small rocks and were hard on bare feet. We celebrated our second anniversary by taking a three–hour cruise on the Black Sea.

Some of our time was spent in seeing Yalta and learning more about the Russian way of life. In that connection we interviewed a store manager in Yalta (a woman). What we were unable to learn was perhaps more significant than what we did learn. We found that the Russian people, including this store manager, did not really understand the overall structure of their system and could only describe their small part in it. For example, only one out of ten Russians we talked with had any idea of where the government gets its money from. Direct taxes are a small part of their salaries, simply because the government itself owns much of the means of production and can raise or lower prices to generate the income it needs. Few understand that the rent charged by the government for apartments is far less than the economic costs of building and maintaining the apartment. Policy dictates that rent be low, and it appeared that most people pay 5% or less of their salary in rent. It is difficult to compare costs in the Soviet Union with costs in the United States because of such distortions.

Bureaucracy

Everywhere we went we found evidence of government bureaucracy and inefficiency. Waiters in restaurants waited on you when they felt like it. Store sales people didn't get concerned if you waited a long time for service. Hotel clerks were indifferent to your needs, and Intourist guides didn't worry about you (Lana was the exception).

Many people think of the U.S.S.R. as being a Communist country. This is wrong. The Soviet Union is a socialistic dictatorship, and this distinction is important to remember. Under a Communist system, all workers would be paid on the basis of need, and there would be little or no incentive for a worker to exert himself. Under such a system, the individual usually has no choice as to what work he does, and everything is planned by the state. In the Soviet system workers, particularly youth, have some mobility. They can choose what occupation they want. If a Russian doesn't like his job, he can change. Of course, since the state sets wage levels, it can encourage people to take certain jobs without actually dictating to them. Certain jobs definitely pay more. The factory manager is paid more than the factory worker, and an engineer gets more than the accountant.

There are vestiges of our capitalistic incentives in the U.S.S.R. For example, a member of a collective farm receives his share of the farm output based on the number of units of work he has put in. If he has not worked he will receive little, but if he has worked long hours, six or seven days a week, his share would obviously be greater. We visited a farm in the Crimea, but this was a state farm. A state farm differs from a collective farm in that on a state farm the worker is paid a flat rate per hour of work without regard to the success of the crop. On a collective farm the worker gets a share of the crop, and if the crop is good he does well; otherwise his share is small.

Russians like their System

One of the things that we discovered to our surprise is that the Russian people like their system and just can't understand how we like ours. They look upon our capitalistic system (which they do not understand) as backward. At one point several young people told us after we had spent an evening in discussion with them, that they really felt sorry for us because we had to live under our system. This, we must confess, made quite an impression, for it was obvious that these young people really believed what they were saying. Perhaps some of the satellite countries may someday rebel against their system, but we would not expect this from Russia.

Kiev and West to the Czechoslovakian Border

We spent three full days in Yalta, and then drove north retracing our route to Zaporozhe and Kharkov. At Kharkov we turned west and drove to Kiev, taking three days in total from Yalta. The distances are great, and these were long, hard driving days. Kiev is the third largest city in the U.S.S.R., and is a modern, bustling city.

It was at Kiev that we got out to the airport and were able to see a little of Russian commercial aviation. We were stunned by the poor airport and runways which consisted of a large grass field, and only a short run–up section at one end of the runway which was paved. Yet they were flying four–engine planes and even jet prop planes (similar to our Lockheed Electra). If a plane were running up at one end of the runway, a big cloud of dust would fly up into the air, perhaps 300 feet. Landing aircraft would then have to fly right through this dust cloud in order to land. This must result in costly maintenance to the engines. We also noticed many commercial aircraft on the other side of the airport standing idle. It was obvious that the airline was not as conscious of the cost of letting airplanes stand idle as our airlines are. That is one of the basic problems of a socialistic system—no incentives.

Our drive west from Kiev was relatively uneventful, except for the time we accidentally took the wrong fork in the road. Lana, our Russian guide, missed it too, so it was truly an accident. We had only gone two miles when a military looking jeep passed us and then blocked the road. Out jumped a civilian who firmly advised us that we were on the wrong road and must turn back. We did as he told us. The funny thing was that he escorted us back, not just directed us. We were conspicuous with a foreign car and officials obviously knew where we were supposed to be. We were impressed with the efficiency of their system in getting us back on the correct route so promptly.

From Kiev we continued east to Lvov, and then Uzhgorod on the Czechoslovakian border. Lana stayed with us right to the border. She was a big help to us not only because she knew where to go and spoke the language, but she also gave us an opportunity to talk with someone in depth. She was with us for more than two weeks. We learned much from Lana about her country, and she enriched our experience. We were aware that her presence made it easier for the government to keep track of us, but that did not bother us.

Some Impressions

What were our impressions? It is difficult to come to any conclusion after only a month's visit to a country, and yet we feel that, relative to most tourists, we had an unusual opportunity. Superficial as our impressions may be, we do have some:

The best way to see the Soviet Union is by car. To fly into Moscow, spend a week looking at monuments and then fly out, would result in a most lopsided and false impression of the Soviet Union since the tourist's view would be directed largely to what the Soviet Union wants him to see—its monuments and big impressive buildings.

Although the Soviet Union may or may not be equal to the United States in its military and rocket power, it is very far from equaling the U.S. in consumer products. The standard of living is probably a quarter to a third at best that of the United States, and the inherent inefficiencies built into their system are such as to raise serious doubts in our minds as to whether they will ever be able to equal our then–existing standard of living. Everywhere, inefficiency was evident—and almost without exception it appears that this can be traced to lack of incentives.

There is a huge waste of manpower in the Soviet Union. We saw women working on road construction, crews moving rocks and gravel by hand. Everywhere we saw people doing things by hand, often old people, and doing things that in the U.S. we would not think of doing except by machinery.

There is a tremendous feeling of need for secrecy in the Soviet Union. We were not allowed to drive on any roads except the ones designated. All bridges, no matter how small, had armed soldiers guarding them. Our guide either did not know or was unwilling to tell us many of what seemed to us to be basic facts of how their system worked, and the people felt that it was desirable that this secrecy exists. The Soviet government does not tell the Russian people what is happening in the world, except if it meets their needs. For example, the Russian people were told that South Korea, not North Korea, was the aggressor in that South Korea had invaded North Korea for over a hundred miles before the North Koreans took up arms to defend themselves.

Along with this secrecy, the Russian people seem to have a national inferiority complex, which may account in part for their willingness to place so much emphasis on prestige projects (such as rockets to the moon). For this reason it seems unwise to us for the Untied States to try to compete with them on any single line of activity, for their government can put as much effort as it might want into any project regardless of how inefficient it might be. And the government does not have to justify their effort to the Russian people. Let's compete on an overall basis, but let's not try to match them, project for project.

The Russian people themselves are extremely hospitable to foreigners and are anxious to learn about the West. At the same time, they are anxious to show the foreigner their own accomplishments, of which they are proud.

Those then were our impressions. We have only this to add: We feel that it is extremely important to the United States that as many Americans as possible see the Soviet Union. We say this simply because we believe there is dangerous misinformation on each side regarding the other. Let there be no doubt, our impression still is that the Soviet Government wants to rule the world, but to judge our enemy solely from what we imagine he is like leads to further misconceptions. We say this also because we believe that the more foreigners the Russian people themselves see, the better the chances for development of international understanding.

Fall 1960

Final Observations

It has been forty plus years since we took this trip, and the pioneering nature of it can easily be overlooked in the current post–Cold War era. 1960 was the height of the Cold War, surpassed in tension between the two superpowers only by the Cuban Missile Crisis noted elsewhere in this book.

While it is hard to document, there were certainly less than fifty, and more likely less than twenty–five, foreign autos in the U.S.S.R. that summer. We saw only one other foreign automobile in our three weeks, and four thousand miles of driving in the Soviet Union. If there had been other cars, we would have seen them since foreign drivers were required to travel only on selected routes—and we traveled on most of these roads. Foreign cars were very conspicuous and we could not have missed seeing another car. There was almost no traffic on the roads.

We had no problems and our experience was both educational and exciting. However, after May 1st and the U–2 incident, we certainly were uneasy and could not know whether or not we were making a big mistake in traveling to Russia. While I had become a U.S. citizen, my new U.S. passport showed that I was born in Germany. It had only been six years since I left Berlin, and the memories of the Soviet system were quite fresh in my mind. Still, our sense of adventure prevailed.

We identified our biggest risk up front as a mechanical breakdown while behind the Iron Curtain. The Soviet tourist literature warned automobile tourists ahead of time that parts for foreign automobiles were not available, and while Russian mechanics would be glad to provide repair labor, they had no parts. Not said, but obvious, was that it would be impossible to have replacement parts shipped into Russia given the political situation. Our Volkswagen was brand new which decreased this risk, but even new cars can break down. Mal believes in being prepared, and so we went to the main Volkswagen headquarters in Wolfsburg and told them where we were going. They then prepared a list of parts that we should carry with us so that we would be 95% sure of having whatever parts could fail while in Russia. We then carried these parts with us not only in Russia (where they were not needed) but also on most of the balance of our European trip. We did use one of the parts in a rural part of Greece later in the summer.

There is still another indication of the uniqueness of this trip. Traveling with us while in Russia was Mal's college friend, and best man at our wedding, Bob Adler. Bob was single, living in Cleveland. I do not know how the CIA became aware of our trip, but Bob was discreetly contacted before we left, and asked for an itinerary. They knew the three of us were going, but not the details of where within Russia. The CIA made no requests of us, but when we returned, they wanted to see all of the pictures we had taken.

These were troubling times, yet in retrospect, we were adventurers who took advantage of our opportunities, and became wiser as a result.

14

The Colorado River and
the Grand Canyon

In September of 1974 Mal and I took our first river trip down the Colorado River through Marble Canyon and the Grand Canyon. The account that follows was written in October 1974. It vividly describes an experience which started my love affair not only with the Colorado River and the Grand Canyon, but also with camping and the desert southwest. It was a life–changing experience. This was the first of eight raft trips I took over the ensuing years.

Tuesday, September 24, 1974

A bus waited for us in front of the Empire House Motel in Page, Arizona. We met a bunch of strangers with whom we would feel like a big family during the next five days as we shared our adventure. One man was arriving late on a flight from Phoenix, so we had some time to spare. Our bus driver, Bill, who was also the boatman, took us to the Glen Canyon Dam which is only a few miles from Page. There we learned how the Colorado River's water flow is regulated. After enjoying a view of the dam and the bridge from the visitors center, we boarded our bus again. It was time to get our briefing on what to do and how to behave on our upcoming raft trip.

I do not remember everything Bill told us, but I do remember that he said something about scorpions and rattlesnakes. At that time I wondered whether it was still possible to cancel the trip. Bill did say that the rattlesnakes don't strike unless they get scared, but he did not say that about the scorpions. Apparently then, scorpions sting anytime they get a chance to. And it was the idea of those crawling things that gave me the creepy–crawlies. He suggested not to open and lay out our sleeping bags at night until we were ready to get into them because the scorpions like to crawl into warm sleeping bags. I was cringing! We were also asked to watch where we walk at all times, and not to walk around or move rocks after dark; to always wear our sneakers, and to shake them out before putting them on in the morning.

Do we really want to go through all this and camp out for four nights? Oh well, I guess somehow we will survive.

The forty–five minute ride to Lee's Ferry, our starting point, seemed to take forever. Finally we crossed Navajo Bridge and had our first look at the great Colorado, six miles downstream from Lee's Ferry. Lee's Ferry is the only access place to the river for vehicles for about three hundred river miles.

The bus drove right up to the beach. And there was the raft. This contraption—balloons of neoprene that could bend, twist, and wriggle through raging waters—was to be our home for the next five days. It did not look as big as we had imagined it to be. The cargo had already been loaded and seemed to take up most of the space. "Where are the people going to sit?" asked the man from Switzerland. I had to laugh out loud. "Did you expect upholstered lounge chairs?" I asked. This same individual, whom Mal and I later nicknamed "Hercules" because of his slight build, was to annoy us time and again on the trip.

We were shown where to sit and how to hold on to straps, ropes, gasoline cans, or whatever had ropes or handles— "Hold on? Hold on for what?"—"Hold on for dear life!" And we were to find out that these were not hollow words!

This morning at the hotel we had been given waterproof bags into which we put our clothes. At Lee's Ferry we re-

This is what we found when we got to Lee's ferry. The raft had already been loaded with the food, motors, fuel, and other miscellaneous supplies. Once we left Lee's Ferry we were committed. The only place a person could have gotten off and hiked out of the Grand Canyon was at Phantom Ranch, three days from here.

ceived ammo cans for things we wanted to get to during the day, such as cameras, sunglasses, lotion, or rain gear. A second waterproof bag contained a ground sheet, small foam pad, a down sleeping bag and bed sheet. All our gear was loaded onto the boat, covered with a tarp, and strapped down tightly with ropes. Only our ammo cans, while also strapped down, were accessible during the day.

Maybe I should say something about the cargo the raft carried. Most of Western River Expeditions' rafts which run through the Grand Canyon are motor powered. They are thirty–six feet long and sixteen feet wide. The forty horse-power outboard motor is in the center back and there is also a box–type of space for the boatman to stand in. In front of him on both sides are large boxes, each containing an extra motor, spare parts, tools, and throw ropes. The space between those two large boxes holds some of our gear as well as boxes with kitchen equipment, tents, stove, and the volley ball net and ball, all covered and strapped down. On either side of the large motor boxes and behind them are rows of gasoline cans, five gallons each. Then there is an aisle going cross-wise, and the center part of the thirty–six foot raft is loaded with food storage and freezer boxes. We had to be self–contained for the whole trip since we would be out of touch with civilization for five days.

The center space between the food boxes was filled with our personal gear, covered with a tarp and strapped down. Along the edges were strapped more gasoline cans and our ammo cans. Seating for eighteen passengers is on top of the padded food storage and freezer boxes, on top of the center loads, and, for the adventurous, on the center three front pontoons.

Within half an hour we were loaded and ready to start our adventure. In the meantime, our late passenger, Michael, had arrived, and we were on our way with a big "hurrah!"

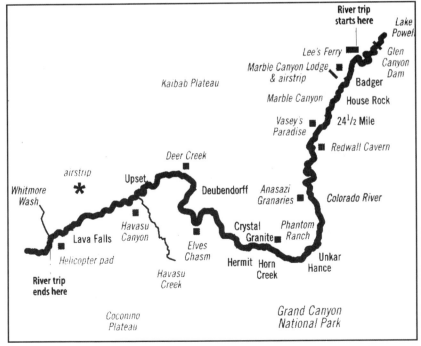

Map of our route through Marble and Grand Canyon, with names of major rapids

What calm water. We had been seeing pictures of huge waves in which the raft was mostly underwater. Mal and I were feeling a bit disappointed.

Less than an hour later there was a small, white sandy beach in the shade of Navajo Bridge over which we had crossed earlier by bus, and we stopped to have lunch. We could not believe all the goodies that came out of those food coolers. Not just plain sandwich materi-

Bill Kesterke, boatman and friend of thirty years.

als, but all the trimmings, too: pickles, olives, lettuce, onions, fresh fruit and two kinds of pie for dessert.

Almost immediately after we were on our way again, the motor stopped and we started to drift. Motor trouble already? We have not even come to our first big rapid yet. What were we going to do later on? At that time we found out that we carried two spare motors and dozens of spark plugs. Bill, our boatman, had to do some work on the motor here and a few of us thought we'd take the opportunity and dive off the raft for a quick swim. And, a quick one it was! The icy cold water was an unexpected shock, the water temperature now, at the end of September, being forty–three degrees. While we had been hot before, we had no trouble cooling off in a hurry.

We were told that the reason for the water being so cold is that at the time it is released from the bottom of Glen Canyon Dam it has not seen the sun for about two years. Because of the swift flow of the river it does not get a chance to warm up.

It was also explained to us that right now they were releasing water from the dam at the rate of twelve thousand cubic feet per second, which was about normal. Bill pointed out that a higher or lower water level makes quite a difference in getting rafts through the rapids. When the water level is low, there is more danger of hitting rocks in the rapids, and it is more difficult to get through.

Riding along on the Colorado River, walled in by the magnificent cliffs, was quite an experience. Nobody spoke. We were too busy admiring and enjoying. The long aisle of

Just above a rapid the water is very calm, but appearances can be deceiving. From this position one cannot tell that there is a major rapid just ahead.

Marble Canyon has been cleanly cut into the plateau by the River grinding for ten million years with rocks and pebbles. It almost seemed like the canyon walls had been polished by machines.

During the sixty–mile passage through Marble Canyon, the Colorado drops some four hundred feet. We were riding down a staircase of rapids, step by foaming step, into the earth.

"Rapid!" somebody yelled, and our hands automatically tightened around ropes and straps. That's Badger Rapid coming up" yelled Bill. "You'd better hold on tight!" We could just barely hear him over the noise of the motor and the roar of the raging water.

Badger Creek Rapid was our first big one with a fifteen foot drop and a rapid rating of five on a scale of ten. Coming up to it, all we could really see ahead of us was a bit of choppy water. Just above the rapid, the air was totally calm. We were silent and the roar of the water sounded threatening. Slowly drifting closer, we noticed that the river seemed to have disappeared below the rapid. Guess they really mean fifteen feet.

We had been told to hold on tight, and a moment later we received icy cold showers as our raft rode up and down the huge waves like a roller coaster.

"We made it!" somebody exclaimed, and I think there was a quiet sigh of relief to be heard out of everyone. We noticed that Bill was counting his "sheep," and some of us looked around to make sure everybody was still with us.

Moments later, our raft was gliding along on smooth water as if nothing had happened.

John Wesley Powell in 1869 had written: "And now the scenery is on a grand scale. The walls of the canyon, about 2,500 ft. high, are of marble, of many beautiful colors, and often polished below the waves. Each bend of the river ahead seems to be the journey's end."

To break the silence and awe, we hoped for another rapid soon. We did not have to wait long for it, and the next, and the next. From then on we were never dry again.

At House Rock Rapid, Bill had those sitting on the left side where Mal and I were sitting move to the other side, and he would allow only three people to sit on the pontoons up front. We were going to pass by some big rocks which were particularly dangerous. After another scary roller coaster ride on the turbulent river, there was a space on

This is typical of most of our campsites. Here we are starting to set up our kitchen. Most of us are finding a good place for our sleeping bags, and changing into dry clothing.

the front tubes and I took the opportunity to sit where I had wanted to sit right from the start. Mal stayed on the side. He said he wanted to be sure that the children end up with at least one parent!

The fun of riding on one of the tubes way up front is that one can see ahead, get splashed more than anyone else, and have a better roller coaster ride. However, one also has to hold on much tighter when the front third of the raft bends up to almost an eighty–degree angle. One of the items on the list of things to bring was a pair of gloves, and those were not to keep one's hands warm. The gloves were needed to protect our hands from rope burns when holding on for dear life!

Our first camp was set up at South Canyon, mile thirty–one, just above another rapid, so we had a cold shower to look forward to first thing in the morning.

By the way, all river miles count from Lee's Ferry, it being mile zero. This means we had traveled thirty–one miles on the Colorado River today.

We left our raft and found ourselves a "bedroom" on the fairly small beach. There were big rocks on which to hang up our wet clothes and it was quite a treat to be dry and warm. We had been shivering since mid–afternoon when the sun was no longer high enough to reach us at the bottom of the canyon. Since then we had been mostly in the shade, and had constantly been doused with forty–three degree water.

The campfire was a warm and welcome treat, and so was the delicious steak dinner.

It was fun sitting around the cozy campfire, talking, and getting better acquainted with our new friends.

It got dark early way down in the canyon and it could not have been later than eight–thirty when most of us headed for our "rooms." What a scenic hotel! Each room had four picture windows and a ceiling studded with stars. Who wanted to sleep instead of enjoying the splendor? Forgotten were rattlesnakes and scorpions as possible sleeping bag companions.

The evening campfire was especially appreciated this first night. It not only warmed us up but gave us a chance to get to know other members of the expedition.

Later, a glow lighted the crests of the cliffs above us. "What on earth is happening now?" A moment later we realized that it was moonlight bathing the high world above us before it penetrated our depth. Soon the almost full moon came up over the canyon and changed the dark monsters surrounding us into a fairyland.

I was fighting sleep so that I would not miss anything that was going on in the sky. Suddenly the stars were hidden by clouds. There was lightning flashing in the east. Oh dear, where are we going to go if it pours? I must have then dozed off for a while as it seemed only minutes later when the starry sky was as clear as it could be. Oh, I wish I knew something about astronomy! Then I fell asleep.

Wednesday, September 25—our Second Day
Mile 31 to 99

I awoke as the first sign of dawn was visible over the cliffs above, and I watched it get lighter and lighter. Someone seemed to be playing around with the floodlights on this stage, and each different set of lights changed the scene of fairyland. Oh, could we stay here? This has to be the most beautiful campsite in the world!

Noises from the "kitchen" called me from my dream world back to reality. It really was time to go and help a bit.

What a breakfast! Eggs, hashed brown potatoes and sausage. We are sure to gain ten pounds on this trip.

Loading and unloading the boat was a group effort. We would form a line and pass bags or boxes along from one person to the next. Soon everything was stashed away and it was time to leave. Would we find another campsite as beautiful as this one?

Soon we were on our way for our first full day on the grand Colorado River. Our first rapid for the day was immediately ahead. What a splash! With this we all had our morning showers, and we even had our teeth brushed with silt—or more accurately—we had our mouths rinsed out.

Just a little later we stopped and admired a large cavern at river level which John Wesley Powell had named "Redwall Cavern." He had estimated that it could seat 50,000 people. It was a huge cavern although I doubt that it could hold anywhere near that number.

We found remains of Bert Loper's boat. An old Colorado River runner, he had drowned in 24 1/2 mile Rapid in 1949 at age 79. We also found exploration tunnels which had been drilled for a proposed Marble Canyon Dam, where the government tested the rock for a possible dam site. They left behind all kinds of debris. At another point there had been a survey in 1889 to see if possibly a railroad could be built for a shortcut to the West Coast. The idea was abandoned—the president of the railroad company drowned in one of the rapids.

Redwall Cavern, which Powell estimated would hold 50,000 people

Wednesday was a long and exciting day. We traveled sixty–eight miles on the river and ran many of the major rapids. In late morning we left Marble Canyon and entered the Grand Canyon. Just about lunchtime we came to the point where the Little Colorado River joins the Colorado River. That was also the end of the clear water. Whenever it rains up on the plateau, the Little Colorado carries mud and rocks which wash down from the Painted Desert and side canyons. For the rest of the trip, the Colorado River was a mud stream. We were told that some weeks the river will be clear all the way, but this was not one of those times. Normally, Bill stops at a good place to swim in the Little Colorado, but he did not think we would be interested in a "mud bath." No, we weren't. Besides, who wanted a bath that badly? We have been wet ever since we ran the first rapid this morning.

We stopped for lunch and climbed up into a side canyon to look at a piece of wreckage from one of the two airliners which collided in 1956, killing all 128 people. Somehow the tragedy of humans did not make much of an impression. It seems only a tiny speck of a happening in the huge drama of destruction and creation of nature.

Several times so far on this trip we were amazed how fast Bill could change spark plugs. He could do that in a few seconds, and often it made the difference of being able to enter a rapid in a controlled manner, or drifting into it aimlessly, which would be a lot more dangerous.

At one point a spark plug change did not help. We had to change motors, and even that was accomplished within a few

To "hold on for dear life" became much more than a casual expression on this trip. Here you get a good view of how the raft flexes. Those sitting on the front part of the pontoons get the most violent ride as the pontoons can suddenly bend almost 90 degrees, and as quickly snap back to the horizontal. If you loose your grip you will be thrown into the water, and then could easily slam into one of the rocks that create the rapids. This could be fatal. In addition, the very cold water causes hypothermia in less than ten minutes.

minutes. How peaceful it was to drift along without the sound of the motor! Some of us thought that we ought to just forget about motors and enjoy the silence of this beautiful wilderness. But then another rapid would come along and we were glad for the help of the motor; Bill was able to then steer us safely around the boulders.

The afternoon brought more breathtaking scenery and many exciting rapids, which were also breathtaking, in the real sense of the word. We were beginning to wonder whether we really wanted that much excitement. So, the pictures we had seen in the sales brochure were real! We found out that they were not telling a lie.

A place way up on the front of the left pontoon had become my regular spot. There I enjoyed the wildest rides, often alone, when nobody else wanted to be a front rider. It was a good thing that I had heeded the advice and brought a pair of canvas gardening gloves or I would have had no skin left on my hands.

"Here comes Hance," our captain yelled. "This is a tough one—better hold on tight!"

Suddenly I realized what was going to happen. "Oh, no!" screamed someone next to me as we stared in disbelief into an abyss of turbulent water. Then the front end of our raft dipped sickeningly into the deep hole. We were committed. There was no turning back. A giant fang of water loomed over us. A moment later, the front of the raft tilted upward at a crazy angle while we heard the back of the raft crash down into the hole with the eerie sound of a giant belly flop in a dive. For a second we teetered on the crest of a twenty–foot wave, then zoomed downward with roller coaster speed into the swirling vortex.

"Hang on!" yelled Bill, as he tried to steer us clear of some huge boulders blocking our path through the raging waters. For a few seconds, Bill's expert piloting kept us properly in the middle of the wild rapids. A moment later we seemed helplessly in their grasp when the motor stopped. We climbed the next huge wall of water sideways, and roller coastered down backwards. But despite water cascading all

This picture was taken on my third trip. Bill is letting me handle the motor.

over us and churning rapids tossing our raft like a dancing cork, we bobbed our way safely through Hance.

"Inge, are you still there?" I heard my husband yell.

"No, I drowned in this one," I shouted back.

"Keep your mouth shut then so you won't swallow so much water" was my husband's advice.

"Well then, don't ask unnecessary questions—if I'm planning to drown, I'll let you know ahead of time."

Then the white thrashing water was behind us and we were floating serenely on the Colorado River in the Grand Canyon—while Bill changed the spark plugs once again.

That was Hance, our wildest one so far—a thirty foot drop—rated nine on a scale of ten, as far as difficulty is concerned. From then on we became aware of "drops" and "ratings." Whenever we heard the roar of a rapid, shouts of "what's the rating of this one?" were heard. Usually somebody still had the waterproof river map handy and looked it up quickly.

There was Unkar Creek Rapid, a twenty–five foot drop—rated seven; Nevills Rapid, a fifteen foot drop—rated six.

When approaching a rapid, the river would suddenly be calm, almost without a ripple, up to where it goes over the falls. Beyond the rapid, when viewed before entering it, the river seems to have disappeared from the surface of the earth. However, just as the boat enters the rapid, we could see the furious waters way down below, beating the river into foam.

At Sockdolager, ten foot drop—rated nine—we found out that John Wesley Powell's description of it as "the knockout punch of the world" was quite accurate: "At Sockdolager Rapids some of the canyon's biggest waves roll in a roaring cadence between the walls of schist without missing a beat." Powell wrote that this was the wildest place he had ever seen and he could not portage because of the sheer canyon walls. The waves were frightful beyond anything we had met. In running through Sockdolager, I lost my grip on one hand as I was thrown up and down, and during one of the "dives" the cargo shifted. We ended up with more space in the back and less in front. We also felt as if we were going to be knocked out or off each time we momentarily floated on top of a giant wave and then zoomed, with express train speed, down into an abyss of thrashing water.

I had become quite aware of how tightly one can hold when one's life depends on it. The most important thing was not to lose that death grip on whatever one is holding on to. We were told that occasionally somebody does fall off the raft, but so far they were always able to retrieve the person again. ("Retrieve" sounds like they mean alive or dead). Everybody is wearing life jackets at all times.

Theoretically, it is possible to survive a rapid by floating through it if a life jacket is worn. However, the great danger, and the most likely thing to happen, is that the person would sustain serious injury or even death by being slammed against rocks or canyon walls. Bill's instructions on what to do if you fall off were: "Float on your back, keep your feet in front of you pointing downstream, so you can push yourself off of rocks and walls. Try to stay clear of whirlpools and rocks, if possible, and 'float' through the rapid in that manner. The raft will then be able to pick you up (you hope!)—and whatever you do, don't panic! Try most of all not to get near the motor of the boat, or else, hamburger."

Well, I could just picture myself, remaining calm and relaxed while I experienced the trauma of being tossed off the raft, the shock of the icy water, fight to avoid the motor for fear of being chopped into hamburger; while at the same time enjoying a ride on my back up and down twenty–foot churning and crashing waves, remembering to hold my feet in front of me and carefully steering around boulders and whirlpools. And I would even find time to yell: "Take a picture of me, Mal!"

How in this turbulent, muddy, thrashing water would I even know which is front or back, right side up or down, when in most big rapids the whole boat seems to be under water. I do like to swim, but no thank you. I prefer to HOLD ON TIGHT!

Grapevine Rapid was next, an eighteen foot drop—rated eight. Hance, Sockdolager and Grapevine rank among the angriest and most dangerous.

We approached Phantom Ranch. Phantom Ranch is an oasis and a tiny speck of civilization down at the bottom of the Grand Canyon, known to tourists as a destination and overnight stop for the mule trips from the South Rim. There are rustic cabins, a tiny store, water, and even a telephone. River trips often stop and, time permitting, let the people hike the half–mile from the river to Phantom Ranch, to buy a soda pop, make a phone call, or just look the place over, having heard so much about it. "Anybody who has 'had it' can get off and take the mule trip up to the Rim," Bill announced. However, nobody had had it.

We passed under the Kaibab Trail Suspension Bridge and then under Bright Angel Suspension Bridge. Being late in the summer, the sun was getting low behind the rim of the canyon and each bit of sunshine was greeted with cheers by our freezing and wet little crowd. Some of us were getting quite chilled and hoped we would stop and camp soon. But we still had the most exciting rapids ahead of us: Horn Creek Rapid—ten foot drop—rated nine; Granite—seventeen foot drop—rated nine plus.

Then we ran the most fun one of them all, Hermit—a smooth fifteen foot drop—rated nine plus. We counted nine gigantic roller coaster like waves. Sitting on the front of one of the pontoons again, it was scary to look and then dip into a seemingly bottomless pit in the water, then immediately climb up to the top of a wave as high as a house, teeter there momentarily, and dive into the next abyss. Repeating this several times with icy, muddy water cascading all over us, we began to wonder why we had paid money to be so wet and so cold. Needless to say, after each roller coaster ride many of us looked around to make sure the other half was still there. "Mal, did you take a picture of this one?" Meanwhile, Bill counted his sheep and sighed with relief when nobody was missing.

The last rapid of the day was Crystal—a seventeen foot drop—rated nine and a half to ten plus! Crystal is one of the largest and, next to Lava Falls, the most treacherous. Until 1966 it was just a ripple in the great river when after six inches of rain, a flash flood came

This narrow part of the Grand Canyon is called the Granite Gorge. Its narrowness has created some of the Canyon's biggest and most fearful rapids.

tearing down one of the side canyons, carrying enough boulders and debris to partially block the river and create this monstrous rapid. With each rainstorm up on the plateau, rapids change slightly. Crystal is so dangerous and tricky to run that the boatmen stop on each trip, hike down to carefully look it over and plot their course through it.

After Crystal, Tuna Creek Rapid lay ahead of us but we stopped at a beautiful beach before we reached it. We set up camp in a hurry, and oh, that campfire felt good. Everyone was most anxious to change into dry clothes.

Bill is not only a good captain and a good cook, but he is also able to get organized immediately, have hot coffee ready in no time at all, and dinner soon afterwards. I don't know how he does it. We are exhausted and he and his crew, consisting of Larry as second boatman and Geri, Bill's wife, had done all the work during the day. All we had done was sit there, holding on tight, enjoying the wild rides and magnificent scenery. Maybe that is why we were so tired. We were tired from holding on for dear life. And boy, did we ever hold onto those ropes!

It usually got dark around six–thirty, and after sitting around the campfire for a while after dinner, most of us would be in bed by eight–thirty or nine o'clock. This had been an exhausting day because we went through so many of the major rapids. It was also one of the most spectacular ones for scenery, as we had traveled through the deepest and narrowest part of the Grand Canyon, the Granite Gorge.

Changing spark plugs and motors was an important skill. Here Bill, and his helper, Larry, are changing a motor. They had three motors, and we needed all of them.

Still, it was hard to give in to sleep. Would the sky put on another show tonight? I wish I could stay awake. On this second night, we were beginning to get used to our hard, sandy beds. The foam mattress which was supplied with our rented sleeping gear, was too short. If you wanted it under your back, you could not have it under your head, too. It bothered me more than I thought not to have a pillow, so I finally bunched up my sheet and used it for a pillow. Who needed a bed sheet in a sleeping bag anyway. Sometime during the night I woke up and opened my eyes to another moonlit panorama. The dark canyon walls looked like giant ghosts in the eerie light of the moon. And why are the stars so much brighter and more numerous than they are back home?

Thursday, September 26—our Third Day
Mile 99 to 137

We usually awoke when the first rays of sun lit up the upper part of the canyon walls. Another unforgettable sight. Bill would have the coffee ready and be preparing breakfast. He was always the first one up even before Larry and Geri. Before 7 a.m. we'd have the greatest breakfast. Well, doesn't everybody have pork chops with their french toast, and marshmallows in their hot chocolate at home? Besides that, Bill seems to always cook for 30 people instead of 16. Most of us had two pork chops and there were still some left over for lunch. Mal was getting spoiled. He said that from now on he expects more elaborate breakfasts in the mornings.

Again we formed a line to load the raft and then were on our way, ready (or were we?) to get many more cold showers than we wanted. I had been sitting on the pontoons up front most of the day yesterday, and since we were supposed to change seats to give others a chance for the "best ride in the house," Mal and I decided that we would sit on one of the coolers in front. I got on the raft as soon as I could and chose our seats—I thought. But no! When I had taken my seat, Hercules plopped himself right next to me, and he did not take the hint when Mal came and looked for his seat. Mal then had no choice but to sit on the side again.

The seats on the front refrigerator boxes were really excellent. One does not get quite as wet as when sitting on the pontoons, and one also has a better view of what's ahead. Hercules was not only a constant talker, but also a picture snapper. He spread himself out over most of the available seating space and just crowded me off. I ended up with only a tiny little edge, having to sit sideways and having to hold onto the ropes across the tarp and the gasoline cans behind me.

We stopped at a waterfall and swimming hole beneath the waterfall. After being splashed with the muddy Colorado River water, the clean waterfall could not be passed up, even though at first I did not want to get all wet again if I didn't have to. This is hard to understand now, but we were just so freezing cold all the time that we began to wonder why we had paid money for this. We may survive all the rapids without drowning, but we were surely going to catch pneumonia and die afterwards. Well, we were wet anyway, so why not take off the shirt and shorts and dive in? We always wore our swim suits underneath. The water in the swimming hole was delightful, much warmer than the river. It was also fun to swim into the little cave behind the waterfall.

Time to continue with our journey. Most of us were so happy to have had a good swim in clean water, that we did not want to get a muddy shower right away. The seats on the front pontoons were not popular at this time and I was able to get away from Hercules that way. I certainly did not want to pass up the chance of the more adventurous ride in front, muddy water or not. I was really mad when Hercules decided to sit right behind me on the pontoon and crowd me again! There were not enough ropes for two to hold on and still be far enough away from the freezers so they wouldn't hit us in the back in the wild rapids. Yesterday in Powell's "knockout blow" (Sockdolager Rapid), our cargo had shifted forward a few inches and that space was missed now.

Just before lunchtime we stopped and climbed up into a side canyon to Elves Chasm, where fern dotted walls surround a beautiful waterfall that falls from pool to pool on six terraces. Two other rafts of Western River Expeditions, who were traveling together, had stopped there and we were commenting to each other that we hoped we would not have lunch with them. We really felt that we did not want those strangers to intrude in our family. And here only three days ago we all were strangers.

Bill was the quiet type and he must have felt the same way. When we returned to our raft we traveled only a short distance and had lunch by ourselves. Pork chops and leftover chicken from last night, along with sandwiches, lettuce, pickles, onions and fresh fruit. Pie for dessert. My goodness, how much food did we bring? Was this a luxury liner on a cruise, or just a plain raft trip?

Time and again we were amazed at the speed with which Bill could change spark plugs. We must have used three dozen of them on this trip. Each time the whole motor got submerged in a rapid it would not start again. Often, approaching the next rapid, Bill had to change the spark plugs in a frantic hurry to still have enough time to maneuver the raft to enter the rapid at the right spot.

Rapids are caused by huge boulders and rubble washed in from side canyons during rainstorms, and from rock slides.

Rapid ahead! I am on the right front pontoon (you can't see me) which is my favorite position. The black rock is Vishnu Shist, the oldest exposed rock on earth.

The debris is often partially exposed, and the water has to tumble over it. The river, calm at the top of the waterfall, is beaten into foam below. It is dangerous to just drift into a rapid any old place. The raft could be sliced up on boulders and ripped apart. How, then, could it be so much fun to ride the rapids? We all enjoyed the ride tremendously, although sometimes my arms could hardly hold my weight when I was being tossed up into the air.

Along the river we met three small rafts carrying two people each. We waved and the men smiled and waved back, however, their wives looked sort of scared to me. In any case, they were not smiling. They must have been skilled river runners to survive those rapids. We noticed, though, that in between rapids they were busy bailing out the water. Maybe that was why the women were not smiling. Having to bail water after each rapid is a common problem with the dough-nut shaped rafts which most river companies use. Western River Expeditions has a patent on their J–Rig pontoon rafts, and these are self–bailing.

"Swim time," Larry called as he got ready to throw the lines out to tie down our raft. This time it was Deer Creek Falls and we were anxious to clean up under the shower of the waterfall. It was hard to get underneath and behind this 110 foot high waterfall. We had to walk backwards to keep the spray from hurting our eyes. But we had a lot of fun and most of all, we enjoyed the feeling of being clean once again.

A short distance and another rapid later, we found a beach on which to spend the night. And what a beautiful beach it was with a cave–type overhang under which we set up the kitchen. Bill thought it might rain during the night (it didn't), and since we arrived at this campsite ahead of the other rafts, we had our choice of the best site. After unloading, we found our bedrooms and then everybody was anxious to change into dry clothes.

It was only about 3:30 p.m. and it had been a fairly easy day for our crew. We played some games, explored a cave part way up the mountain, and Larry baked a birthday cake on the campfire for Mal and John. Mal had turned forty–one on the 24th. Larry even put icing on it and it was a delicious cake. We were really roughing it!

Hercules had chosen his place to sleep right next to ours—too close to us—and he had aggravated me so much all day that I got furious and we packed up and moved elsewhere with our gear.

Then the other two Western River rafts came by and somebody had the bright

At beautiful Deer Creek Falls, water cascades 110 feet into a pool.

idea of bombarding them with a couple dozen eggs. Boy, did they get it!

After dinner, Geri and Larry got into a fight (Geri is Bill's wife). It started with Larry squirting whipped cream on Geri with the spray can. It ended up by Larry getting hit with a load of leftover coleslaw and Geri getting pancake syrup poured all over her.

Sitting around the campfire was always the most enjoyable part of the evening. And, we were warm, too.

The beauty of the canyon with the constant changes in different light—in shade, in moonlight, sunshine, shadows—was almost too much to take in such large doses. I could have just sat there and cried. But then there were so many things to do and see and I didn't want to take the time to sit and cry. I could do that later. And I did!

Friday, September 27—our Fourth Day
Mile 138 to 179

The other two rafts had camped on a beach next to ours. About the time we were leaving we got a bit worried, wondering whether they, by any chance, might have a few dozen eggs to spare. We started out keeping way over to the other side of the river, but the canyon is not that wide and our "friends" were good shots. We were indeed bombarded with raw eggs. What a mess! And then we had to stop and pour buckets of water over ourselves to get those sticky eggs off. Oh, was the water cold! Hope the fish liked their egg breakfast.

The water was cold and the sun was not yet high enough to shine over the canyon walls. We were not really ready for the next rapid, but here it came, and it was a wet one. And so it went all day. We could hardly wait for Lava Falls, which was to come the next morning, our last morning on the river. Lava Falls is the biggest rapid in Grand Canyon, with a thirty–seven foot drop, and the highest rating, a ten plus.

Just before lunch we stopped at beautiful Havasu Canyon for a couple of hours of swimming and enjoying the sunshine and nature's artwork. Havasu Canyon is easily acces-

We did a lot of hiking which I really enjoyed. Here at Havasu Canyon we are climbing up one of the many terraces with small pools that flowed from one into the other.

sible because the granite cliffs are terraced. It was interesting to see where the turquoise water of Havasu Creek joins the muddy water of the Colorado. We walked about half a mile into the canyon to a beautiful set of travertine terraces. Each terrace was a separate little lake, spilling into the one below it. We enjoyed swimming and climbing from one little lake into another. Then there was time to sit and warm up in the sun.

Later on, the two other rafts arrived and we were glad that Bill took us elsewhere to have our lunch. We stopped at a beach just at the top of a set of rapids, and after lunch waited for the other two rafts to run through the rapids while we took pictures. We were happy to have this chance since obviously we could not take pictures of ourselves going through rapids. Whenever we went through rapids, even an underwater camera would not have helped because we needed both hands to hang on.

In the afternoon there were only a few minor rapids to run, and we got bored, which was a good excuse to have a water fight. We poured buckets of ice cold river water over each other, as if we had not been cold and wet enough!

Then in one of the rapids we lost the services of our second motor. This confirmed that we really did need all three of them. But this third motor did not behave too well. Bill said that by the end of the season (and ours was the last trip of the season), these poor motors have taken a severe beating and are much in need of an overhaul. Bill had to work hard to keep this last motor running.

"What happens if this thing quits in a major rapid, like Lava Falls?" asked Hercules. Bill did not answer. He did not want to talk about this possibility. As with Crystal Rapid, every boatman has a healthy respect for Lava Falls.

I especially enjoyed the places where the canyon was narrow and where the sheer rock goes straight down into the water, more so than the parts where there are small beaches and trees. "Presently, we drifted into a V–shaped cleft of stark, black schist walls which slanted upward from an unknown depth of earth. It had the feel of a fortress, an inescapable prison of black rock, and we seemed to be at the bottom of the crack of doom," wrote Powell.

Bill informed us that this black rock is called Vishnu Schist, and it is the oldest exposed rock on earth. In some places the rock wall was worn so smooth from the water's action that the river water reflected in it like in a mirror.

Our last night of camping out. It was windy and we felt it was bad enough to be wet and cold, the last thing we needed was to have sand blown all over us. It was hard to set up camp with sand blowing into everything. And then I found myself sitting on a rock in a sandstorm—daydreaming. I suddenly realized that this was our last night in this magnificent canyon and a deep sadness gripped me. I had to come back to this place. Mal had to shake me to get me back to reality.

Dinner was ready, but I could not eat.

There was always one tent in camp and that was the john, or affectionately called "the growler" because of the growling sound this chemical toilet made when being flushed. That night while we sat around the campfire playing games, somebody yelled: "the john blew down." Sure enough, the john tent had collapsed. Oh well, Larry and Bill put it back up. At least the good laugh we had lightened up our somber moods. It would have been even funnier had somebody been sitting on the toilet at the time.

Saturday, September 28
The End of the Most Wonderful Trip

I did not sleep well—I did not want to miss anything that might be going on in the sky. Also, I dreaded having to leave this beautiful canyon. I thought about how much I would enjoy being a crew member on these raft trips, spending a whole summer on the river and camping out all the time. But dawn came and Bill was busy preparing our last huge breakfast. The bacon smelled good. We had our bedroom fairly close to the kitchen this time, it being a small camp. The bats were returning from their nightly insect hunt.

A sort–of sad crowd gathered for breakfast, partly excited about upcoming Lava Falls and partly hoping that some miracle would happen and that we would not have to leave the canyon. Eggs for breakfast? Did we still have eggs after what we did with them yesterday? The fried potatoes were delicious, too. "There is too much food left over," said Bill, "so eat more." "We'll have it for lunch" somebody answered. "We will just have to stay for lunch then." Most of us were also talking about taking another river trip next summer.

We had camped close to Lava Falls, and had hiked down to look at it the night before. It looked awesome. After breakfast our personal belongings were packed into plastic bags and taken up to the top of a hill where the helicopter would land and lift us out of the canyon. We would be walking back up to this hill after running Lava Falls. Then for the last time, we climbed onto the raft, put on our life jackets, draped ourselves as gracefully as possible onto the pontoons, coolers, or wherever we could, and psychologically prepared ourselves for a deluge of a shower. Another cold morning. Who wants to get wet? Nobody. But who wants this trip to never end? Everybody.

Vulcan's Anvil, a huge chunk of lava sitting like a tower in the channel of the river, indicates that Lava Falls is one mile away. To ensure good luck and a safe run through Lava Falls, all boatmen go through the ritual of stopping at Vulcan's Anvil, kissing the rock, and depositing a penny for good luck.

We reached Lava Falls, 180 miles from Lee's Ferry, our starting point. Here, a million years ago, a river of lava poured into the great gorge, damming the Colorado River. Over the years, the river has gnawed away the lava dam and fallen boulders have created the river's most feared rapids.

Then there were excited and scared sounding shouts: "Here comes Lava"—"Get ready for Lava Falls"—Here it is"— "Quickly, make your will"— "Can we still get off?"— "Hold on, just HOLD ON!!"—Then the thundering water drowned out our shouts. It also killed the sound of our motor. It had stopped! Fortunately by then we had passed the most dangerous point, the "hole." It was a whirlpool which, if the raft had been caught in it, would have been extremely difficult to get out of even with the motor working. And without a motor? It could have been disaster.

Now drifting, we climbed a huge wall of water sideways and slammed down backwards, being tossed all over the place by masses of raging water. This was a time to realize how helpless man is against the power of nature.

But we did not think at that time. We were too busy holding on for dear life, and enjoying our wild game of survival against nature's fury.

Bill was working frantically. He changed the spark plugs in a few seconds. Still the motor would not start. Besides that, one motor mount had broken and the motor was trying to lay down on the job.

Our plans were to beach the raft just below Lava Falls and hike up the hill back to where our gear was and where the helicopter would pick us up.

Without the control of the motor, we drifted past that beach. Next came sheer cliffs on both sides. We were still drifting and Bill and Larry were struggling with the disabled motor. Another rapid—a minor one—and turning like a carousel we drifted down and past it. There was no way to get back to where the helicopter was to land. Perhaps this was the answer to our prayers, granting our wish to stay in the Grand Canyon!

A beach on the right—we drifted past—almost—and the motor started. What a job it was to go upstream just a few feet to reach that beach. The current of the river was much too strong for the outboard motor, and struggling terribly, we reached the beach. However, it was across the river from where we needed to be, and a couple of miles downstream. Oh, never mind the helicopter, and forget about our clothes. How about we just go on for a few more days? We surely have enough food.

Reluctantly, we went ashore, built a campfire and huddled around it, waiting. Secretly I was hoping that the helicopter would not find us. Nobody wanted to part from this magnificent scenery and from our new friends with whom we shared this unforgettable experience.

We had had only one icy bath this morning when we went through Lava Falls, but we were so chilled that we nearly crawled into the campfire. Alas, the helicopter found us, took a look at the beach to find a suitable place to land, and then went back to fetch our gear before returning to rescue us, a few at a time.

The pilot found us and was able to land on the beach. Bill and Larry, his helper, are walking toward the helicopter. It carried four passengers and had to make a number of trips to get us all out of the Grand Canyon.

What a spectacular sight it was when we were slowly lifted out of the canyon, while waving frantic good–byes to our group and to "our river."

The helicopter took us to a small airstrip on the North Rim called TUWEEP INTERNATIONAL AIRPORT—NORTH CONCOURSE. A six–passenger Cessna made a low pass to chase the cows off the landing strip before landing. Soon we were on our way back to Page, where we had left our airplane and others had left their cars. Other planes flew people to Las Vegas to catch their respective flights home.

The hardest part of writing about this trip is to find words to describe the beauty of the canyon, the solitude, the silence, the colors, and the power of the river. Words are most inadequate to describe the feeling of being overwhelmed by nature's splendor. Nature has certainly created a masterpiece in the Grand Canyon.

It was too much to take and comprehend in such a short time. We hoped to capture some of this magnificent scenery in pictures, but the pictures are not able to do it justice.

We can only remember what we saw, and how we felt.

That lonely, lost, beautiful world at the bottom of the Grand Canyon has cast its spell.

* * * * *

Subsequent Trips

The trip described above was but the first of eight river trips I took down the Colorado through Grand Canyon. Mal was with me on this first trip, but the next six, each of which were seven–day trips, I took without him. While he had enjoyed our river trip, it was not with the same intensity that I felt. I was the one on whom the Grand Canyon had cast its spell. And, with our children growing up, it was easier for one of us to get away for a trip than for both of us, so Mal became the baby–sitter.

I started a friendship with Bill, the boatman on this first trip, and his wife, Geri, which continues to this day. They ran the river trips as a husband and wife boatman team for a number of years for Western River Expeditions, but eventually the strenuous nature of this work— and several hundred trips—resulted in medical problems for Bill and they had to stop.

Tragedy

In 1996, Geri and I arranged for Western River to run a charter trip through the Grand Canyon, and we invited friends to join us on what became my eighth trip down the River. Mal joined me on this trip. Geri and I requested Western River to assign Bill Skinner, their most experienced boatman, as captain. I had traveled with Bill Skinner on one of my other trips, and Geri and I were delighted when he agreed to run our trip. It was fortunate indeed that Bill was our boatman. That trip ended in disaster for Geri!

It occurred while running Crystal Rapid, rated ten. Geri was sitting on one of the food boxes facing the front of the raft—as in the picture below. In front of her was a passenger sitting upright on the pontoon, holding onto ropes in front and in back of him—one hand in front and the other in the rear as instructed. You will recall I mention in my account above that in a major rapid, the front pontoons can bend up to ninety degrees to the main section of the raft, and that it is imperative that the persons sitting on the pontoons hold on for "dear life." Going through Crystal, Geri saw where the passenger sitting directly in front of her lost his forward hand grip in the violence of the rapid. Being a former boat crew, she instantly and instinctively placed her right foot on his back to help brace him and keep him from flinging backward. At that moment the pontoons suddenly bent to a perpendicular position. Geri was sitting on the main section of the raft, and the bend in the pontoons was between her and the passenger. She absorbed a crushing compression blow to her leg and knee. The pain was excruciating. She momentarily let her grip go and was instantly flung into the rapid.

Geri was in the water for about four minutes before both the raft and she were flung free of Crystal Rapid, and we got her back on board. Four minutes may not sound like a long time, but she would not have lasted much longer in that icy water before hypothermia set in.

Once they got her back onto the raft, we had to travel ten miles to Bass Camp, which Bill Skinner deemed suitable for a helicopter landing. He had quickly determined that Geri's injuries were severe and

This picture shows how easy it would be for someone sitting on the boxes at the right to instinctively put their foot out to brace the person sitting on the pontoon. If the pontoon then suddenly bends to a vertical position, it would be disaster, as it was with Geri.

that she needed to be flown out of the Canyon and taken to a hospital. There was little we could do other than getting her warm, immobilizing her knee, and trying to get help. It took almost three hours, using an aviation radio, before we were able to contact an overflying aircraft, and another hour after that before the Park Service got an emergency helicopter to us. Geri was evacuated first to Flagstaff, and then to an orthopedic hospital in Phoenix, 130 miles from Flagstaff.

We are thankful that Geri survived. Her knee cap was damaged, as well as a number of bones in her leg. She has had four operations that we know of, and her leg will never be back to normal. But she was lucky. She is still here, in part because Bill Skinner was so highly skilled and got her out of the water before hypothermia set in.

The rest of my eighth (and last) river trip was heavy with gloom.

I mention this terrible experience because it speaks volumes about the risks. Geri and Bill had made hundreds of trips, and were professionals. Yet, in a flash of a moment, tragedy struck.

This does not mean my love for the Grand Canyon or the Colorado River is any less. It is not, and I visit the Grand Canyon on every trip I make to the area. I also visit the River, albeit, by hiking to the bottom rather than rafting. I have hiked down from both the North and the South rims and have many wonderful memories.

The River and the Canyon still keep me under their spell.

The Antarctic
In the Footsteps of Shackleton and Scott

Ship's GPS—737 nautical miles from the South Pole

In February 2003 we traveled from New Zealand to the Ross Sea area of the Antarctic aboard the Russian polar research vessel, Akademik Shokalskiy. Our destination was the winter huts of Shackleton and Scott, and several other early Antarctic explorers. Scott and Shackleton were bitter rivals. It was from his "hut" on Ross Island that Shackleton started his attempt in 1909 to be the first to reach the South Pole, but had to turn back less than a hundred miles from his destination. If he had not done so he would not have lived to tell about it. Several years later, Scott left from his hut in 1911 and reached the Pole only to find that Amundsen of Norway had beaten him to the Pole by just three weeks. Scott and his team perished on the return trip to Ross Island.

Each year about fourteen thousand people visit the Antarctic Peninsula from South America, but only a few hundred visit Ross Island and

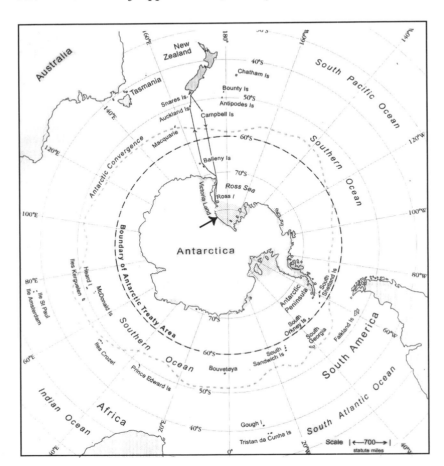

A map of Antarctica shows our route from New Zealand. Note the shaded area south and east of Ross Island, our destination (see arrow). This is the Ross Ice shelf, fed by glaciers from Antarctica to the south. The ice shelf itself rises over 100 feet above the sea, and 800 feet below. It is about 500 miles wide by 500 miles deep.

the winter huts of the early Antarctic explorers. There are good reasons. The northern tip of the Antarctic Peninsula is only about 750 miles from South America. Ross Island and McMurdo Sound are 2,200 miles from New Zealand, and only 850 statute miles from the Pole. Weather and ice conditions are also more severe that much further south. This means there are only two months a year in which the trip could possibly be made to Ross Island because of the colder temperatures and sea ice. Even during this two–month period it is far from certain that a ship can get through the ice, as I describe vividly below.

Antarctica is governed by a treaty in which a number of nations have responsibility for overseeing portions of this most remote continent. The Ross Sea area is overseen by New Zealand and they have very strict limits on tourism, including a requirement that a member of the Department of Conservation of the New Zealand government must accompany all tourists to ensure that the environment is not harmed.

The Akademik Shokalskiy is one of only two ships that regularly attempts to make this trip each year. The ship is chartered by a small family–owned company, Heritage Expeditions, located in Christchurch, New Zealand and they have been making this trip for ten years. It carries only forty–five tourists. The only way a private citizen can get to that part of the world is by ship—and only in January and February when it is summer in the Antarctic. This limits the number of tourists to a very few. In fact, in January, as related in the diary below, the Akademik Shokalskiy could not get further south than 74 degrees South latitude because of pack ice, several hundred miles short of Ross Island and the Shackleton and Scott huts.

We were more lucky in February. We got to both of these huts, but the ice stopped us from visiting the huts of several other explorers at Cape Adare and Possession Islands. We were also scheduled to visit the United States Research Station at McMurdo on the southern tip of Ross Island but could not get the last seven kilometers into McMurdo Sound, again because of ice. Two United States Coast Guard icebreakers were unable to keep the shipping lane open into McMurdo. The sea ice froze almost as quickly as a channel was opened. We stopped near an oil tanker that was waiting to get into McMurdo to unload desperately needed fuel. The tanker never made it, and eventually they had to lay portable oil lines five miles over the ice in order to off–load the oil. The pack ice was severe, and winter was upon us in mid–February.

Later we had our own scare when the Akademik Shokalskiy became trapped in the pack ice for almost five hours.

This was a very rigorous trip. As described in my diary entries that follow, we had to go through some of the most turbulent seas in the world, with the ship rolling first thirty degrees to the right, then immediately thirty degrees to the left, and then back again, all in less than eight seconds. The trip to Cape Adare, the northernmost point of that part of Antarctica, took seven days from New Zealand, and then two more from there south to Ross Island. This was summer. We wonder what it must be like in winter.

I paid a heavy price for the violence of the Southern Ocean. After returning home, I saw the doctor about my shoulders, the left one being the worst. In May, I had to have shoulder surgery to reattach several tendons that were torn off my rotator cuff. While I have long had problems with my shoulders, there can be little doubt that the violence of this trip was the final straw. The surgery was successful, but my surgeon said I had been lucky because the damage was almost beyond repair. He also said it will be a year before I am back to normal. Then in January 2004 I found out that I will need surgery within a year on the other shoulder.

The following are the diary entries I made during this expedition. The entries are a little disjointed, but for the most part they were my actual words written at the time. I hope that this account and the beautiful pictures we took convey some of the excitement of this most extraordinary trip.

Friday, January 31, 2003—Day before Boarding
Hotel Kelvin, Invercargill, New Zealand

Awoke to howling, whistling wind—is this a sign of things to come? After breakfast received a message from the Expedition Leader telling

us that our ship had just returned from the January trip. They could not get to McMurdo Sound. Unusual ice conditions caused by an iceberg the size of the state of Delaware—which calved off the Ross Ice Shelf a year or so ago—prevented the pack ice from drifting north and melting. The iceberg turned sideways and blocked the exit of the pack ice. There were also gale force winds. The ship tried for three days to find an open channel but could

Bluff is the southernmost port town in New Zealand. Notice the distance to the equator (5,133 km), and the South Pole (4,810 km).

not. In fact, it nearly got stuck in the ice and the safety of the ship itself was threatened. They only got to 74 degrees South. Ross Island is at 77:30 degrees South.

Well, at least our Expedition was not canceled, but I do hope we can get to McMurdo Sound!

We still had the car until afternoon, so we drove to the port of Bluff to see our home for the next twenty–five days, the Akademik Shokalskiy. While it

Akademik Shokalskiy the day before we boarded for our 25–day adventure. 230 feet long, it has a Russian crew. It cruises at 10–12 knots.

is a sunny day, the wind is very strong and at the harbor it was nearly impossible to walk into the wind.

In the evening, our group assembled for the first time at the hotel, and then visited a museum which had an extensive series of exhibits dealing with the Sub–Antarctic islands including the Campbell and Auckland Islands which we will visit. It was impressive—done by mostly just one man over a ten–year period who had extensively traveled the Southern Ocean. Afterwards the group had dinner together at the hotel.

Saturday February 1—Day of Departure

Not a good night's sleep—room was hot and I was restless. Very stormy outside. Apprehensive.

Breakfast at 6 a.m.; board bus at 7 a.m.

Aboard the Akademik Shokalskiy—a pleasant surprise to find the room, No 421, so spacious: three built–in closets (one with shelves), lots of drawers everywhere. There is a desk, sofa and chair, and a window that can open.

Got partially unpacked by the time we left and headed for Stewart Island in the lee of which we plan to have lunch. Ship is rolling and pitching more than enough for me. We have troubles staying upright. Get slammed against walls. Good thing I'm wearing a sea sickness patch. Stopped unpacking and sat outside in fresh air. Took a nap and felt better afterwards.

Out at sea. I didn't feel well despite the patch and the "astronaut" pills, but I did go to lunch. Lecture about shipboard life and regulations. Later, during the afternoon we had a lifeboat dress rehearsal in case of an emergency. We didn't need to put on warm clothes, hats and shoes plus gloves, as in a real emergency, but we were asked to put on our life vests and assemble at the station by lifeboat A; then were asked to board the enclosed lifeboat and the lifeboat pilot started and ran the engine of the boat.

Very rough sea, and it is difficult to do anything without being thrown against the opposite wall. I got bruised many times.

I did not feel well at all, but went to dinner to try and eat something. Ian, the chef, came to ask what I would like to eat. When I said potatoes, he personally brought me a plate with potatoes and veggies.

The night was one to remember! Mal gets claustrophobic in the top bunk so I had planned to sleep there. However, the space above the upper bunk was too low for me to get into without help. I couldn't bend my knee or put weight on it since the knee surgery had been only nine weeks

Our lifeboat was a sealed, enclosed vessel with a built–in engine. There were two lifeboats. It would have been very crowded. It is doubtful that we could have survived given the remoteness and harsh Antarctic conditions.

ago. So, not wanting to wake up Mal when I needed to get down during the night, he offered to sleep on the floor with the mattress from the upper bunk. Neither of us could sleep. The ship was rolling severely from side to side, for hours.

Then Mal and I changed beds. Being a camper, I insisted that I could sleep on the floor. It was a challenge and possible only with wedging a chair between the bunk and the mattress to

I caught Mal with the camera after he had taken a fall. You can see the three closets to the right. A small desk with several drawers is on this side of the cabinets. The bunk bed is to the left. The toilet and shower are to the left on this side of the bunk, and I'm hanging onto a short sofa–like seat.

keep from rolling off. During catnaps, I traveled all over the floor, including under the bed. It was impossible to stay on the mattress. This went on all night, and finally around five in the morning I fell asleep.

Sunday February 2—At Sea

At sea—pitching and rolling. There was no way we could take a shower without fear that we would be thrown against something sharp, like the shower faucets.

Mal had fallen into the shower faucet arrangement during the night which accidentally turned the shower on, and he had gotten soaked. Good thing we had another pair of pajamas with us.

There are no places for holding onto on the side of the cabin where the closets and desk are. This means that with the violent rolling of the ship we are thrown against the opposite wall. The ladder for the upper bunk makes the best hand hold, and the only good one in the room. Most of the time we are slammed against a door frame, into the bathroom, or onto the bed. This is hard on my hands, wrists, shoulders and I have bruises all over my body. The back of my head hit the upper bunk last night and it still hurts when I lie down.

This morning, the breakfast room was nearly empty, as people are seasick. Mal had a scary experience, which potentially could have caused a very serious injury. He was sitting on a chair at the desk, and the chair suddenly slid backwards and skidded across the room, then hit the bathroom threshold and tipped over. Mal landed on the bathroom floor on his back; the bathroom is not a large room but fortunately, Mal's head did not hit anything.

Mal complained about the upper bunk being too difficult to deal with, and Karen (staff) assigned him a vacant cabin with a lower bunk that he can use at night for sleeping.

At one point two of the three desk drawers slid out and spilled the contents all over the floor.

It is very energy consuming to travel on board the ship. The lecture room is two floors below in a small and stuffy room, and I didn't last long during one of the afternoon lectures. Dining room is below our level and we always huff and puff when we are safely back. It is not a long walk, but even the shortest one turns into an ordeal when we have to hang on tightly because of the ship's violent rolling.

I don't feel sick, but not well either. Had to take astronaut pills. Very dry mouth from everything. Note: "Astronaut Pills" (promethazine 250 mg) are a medication given to astronauts to prevent sickness from floating in weightless conditions, which is why I gave them this name.

The crew is talking about being almost out of the "roaring forties" as the gigantic swells of the Southern Ocean are called. We thought "good," until we heard that then we will get into the "furious fifties," and after that there will be the "screaming sixties." In the seventy degrees South range we will be in ice.

It is almost impossible to walk anywhere without holding on for dear life. All day long we are lurching from wall to wall. If I need something out of the cabinet, Mal stands behind me and braces me. I would time opening the door to when the ship is rolling away from us, then quickly open the cabinet door, grab what I want, and slam it shut before the ship starts rolling in the opposite direction. If I am too slow, the contents of all shelves would cascade onto the floor.

We found out at lunch that many people are sick, even those who had taken many cruises. It made me feel better because I knew that I was subject to seasickness and had gotten effective medications. This helped with my stomach, but not with the bruises my body is covered with. Trying to get to sleep at night was an ordeal. No matter how hard I tried, I was literally rolled from side to side by a force greater than myself. Everyone else was talking about the same experience. These are the seas where even the sailors get sick. I cannot help but think about the early explorers and their much smaller vessels, and especially Sir Ernest Shackleton's epic journey in a lifeboat.

Since this was a day of cruising, we had several lectures to prepare us for Campbell Island where New Zealand has a research station. Sleepless night because of stormy seas until we stopped at Campbell Island at three in the morning.

Monday, February 3—Campbell Island

Was it nice to wake up and be able to take a shower without being thrown around! We were to be in the lecture hall by 7:00 a.m. for a briefing on our trip to Campbell Island by rubber raft. This lecture had been canceled yesterday because so many people were sick.

After breakfast we packed our lunches for the day trip to Campbell Island. Another lecture was given by Botanist David Given. Campbell Island is part of New Zealand, but no one lives on the Island. It does have a small scientific research station although we did not see anyone while we were on Campbell. Scientists had wondered why the mountains were green when supposedly nothing grew on Campbell Island. Dr. David Given was one of the research team who spent several months on Campbell Island and discovered the green on the mountains was moss, lichen, and stunted shrubs, as well as alpine flowers. There were also mega herbs. The growing season is short, and the herbs and flowers grow very large during the long daylight hours of summer. We saw the huge daises which David had told us about.

When we first arrived on Campbell Island in the Naiad (Zodiac), the reception committee consisted of David taking

A female sea lion welcomed us when we stepped ashore at Campbell Island.

pictures of us scrambling out of the boat. Next to him was a sea lion watching our arrival with much interest. Within minutes we noticed many sea lions in the water in the dock area. Some were fighting.

The Island consists of granite and shist. Many volcanic columns can be seen. Wind and exposure control the climate on Campbell Island. The constant strong winds create windswept forests (bush) and many different ferns. Because of the very short summers, the plants need to use this time to reproduce.

David also told us about a four hundred year old Sitka Spruce, dwarfed, of course, which is labeled to be the loneliest tree in the world. We saw some areas where moss slides had occurred. Like an avalanche, a moss or tree slide erases all life from a section of mountain.

After our arrival, we admired the sea lions, then started our eight kilometer hike on a boardwalk to a certain place in the mountains. It was wonderful just to walk somewhat normally without lurching from wall to wall. Keeping balance was a slight problem after two and a half days at sea. Our hike went uphill, though gently, gaining six hundred fifty feet in

Our hike on Campbell Island takes us through an impenetrable rata forest. A path has been cut through the trees.

Campbell Island is home to 99% of all Southern Royal Albatrosses, estimated at 9,000 pairs. They spend 95% of their lives at sea, flying 90% of the time they are over water. Based on satellite tracking, they travel from 200–500 miles a day and do not hesitate to fly 1,000 plus miles for food. They routinely circumnavigate the entire Antarctic continent, flying a route that takes them to South America, Africa, Australia and then back to Campbell Island. It has been estimated that a 50–year–old Albatross has traveled a minimum of 3.8 million miles. Hard to believe, but since returning Mal has done research, and these figures are well documented.

elevation. The boardwalk had been installed to protect the plants underneath the boardwalk from tourists trampling them, and the path becoming too muddy to walk on. Campbell Island has extremely high rainfall.

The weather changed constantly—sunshine, lots of wind, driving rain, hail. We had been told to wear our GoreTex suits and warm clothes. The temperature was around fifty degrees but the wind made it feel much colder. At one point where we had climbed another hill, we saw something snow white and I thought it was rubbish. Upon getting closer, I saw a head and then realized it was an Albatross siting on a nest. The next moment I spotted them all over the mountainside to the south. What a sight! We could approach these large birds to take photos — close up—and they were not scared. They just ignored us.

At the end of the boardwalk, I was surprised to find that our group was allowed to hike up the mountain just anywhere. There was no trail. I worried about trampling down the fragile vegetation, but perhaps the high rainfall lets it grow back fast. There were stretches of dense bush with dwarfed windswept trees, as well as shrubs, ferns, mosses, and wildflowers. Deep pink and plum colored daisies grow into little trees. Many kinds of tiny alpine flowers were everywhere, as were the tussocks of dried grass. There were Albatrosses nesting everywhere.

Most of us took a hike up the mountain to overlook the harbor our ship was in, as well as the rest of Campbell Island to the South. It was a lovely day to enjoy this spectacular view.

A little over five hundred people a year are allowed to visit Campbell Island, but only with a representative from the New Zealand Department of Conservation.

Next we ate our packed lunches, and then headed back to the station. The Naiad boatman saw us and came over with two Naiads in tow, even though there was no pickup scheduled until 3 p.m. It was then 2 p.m. As we had done this morning, we washed and brushed our shoes, rinsed them in chemicals, and sat in the day lounge reliving the day's adventure.

The Albatross was the topic of the day. What a great bird with a wing span of ten to twelve feet. Seeing them in flight is awesome.

Now after dinner we leave the protected cove of Campbell Island and head out into the Southern Ocean. The captain said it would roll, and sure enough, I can write no more.

Earlier we had all decided to take showers before it became impossible. Five days to Antarctica and in rough seas! Will we make it without broken bones?

It was difficult to sleep and not only because of the severe rolling, but because objects were banging around in the closet and on the floor, including the waste basket in the bathroom. It was 4 a.m. before I got to sleep. It helps that Mal is in another room. The sea was wild and I was sure we hit a few icebergs during the night. Actually they were big waves. There are no icebergs, yet.

Tuesday February 4—At Sea

It is such a challenge just to get out of bed. I considered staying in. How can we get dressed while being thrown from wall to wall?

Just getting the clothes out of the closet is an ordeal because everything else falls out. Nothing stays on the table. What happened to the stabilizers this ship is supposed to have? Someone said the stabilizers are not working—how else could we roll twenty–five to thirty degrees? I am really afraid now of broken bones. Bed is the safest place.

Then I hit on an idea! How do I dress when I am camping? In bed! Whenever the ship rolled to starboard, I opened the closet and got one or two things out, then threw them on the bed. Most of the time I'd tumble after. When I had everything I needed, I would get into bed and get dressed. With the five available pillows, I lined two walls in my bunk to protect myself from being knocked against the walls and hitting my head.

This morning's lecture on Campbell Island Recap was canceled because the sea was too rough. Sat in the lounge and had coffee. Then I went back to bed and slept for two hours. Much needed! Afterwards I felt great. Seasickness (queasiness in the stomach) is very rare now for me, but I'm so drowsy that I keep dozing off in lectures. So does everyone else, though. Somebody said the room is too small for the number of people.

Before lunch the captain changed course, so it would be smoother while they placed two research buoys in the sea for a University research project. Stayed on the smoother course for lunch, and only a few cups and plates slid off the tables.

At 3 p.m. we attend an introductory lecture and slides on "The Antarctic—An Environment of Extremes." Extremes are: coldest, driest, windiest, highest place on earth!

Short nap. Then the next program: Part one of a seven–part series entitled "Last Place on Earth," a documentary comparing contrasts of Scott's and Amundsen's expeditions to the South Pole.

It is very difficult to write these notes every day. The ship is rolling so violently. At the end of the journey we will all be well trained in acrobatics! Every part of the body is getting a workout—or at least a big bruise.

Wednesday February 5—At Sea

We are not even quite halfway between Bluff and Cape Adare on the Antarctic northern coast. What a huge ocean!

Slept well for a change and feel more rested. At about 12:30 a.m. there was a very noisy crash and I thought we had hit an iceberg. When I awakened, I still heard things slide and rattle. Then there was silence so scary that I thought the engines were stopped. The captain had slowed the ship down. When nothing further happened, I read for a while before going back to sleep. Refreshed in the morning.

Unbelievably big sea. Shower and dressing were a big chore and a challenge. Banged up my right elbow, and with the shoulder and knee already being "out," it is my whole right side now that is gone.

Dr. Fiona gave me a pain medication (non–narcotic) to help with the Ibuprofen, and I put the Ace bandage on my elbow. I did not bring along enough Ace bandages. Between Mal and me we could have used a dozen.

At 10:30, we had the Campbell Island Recap which had been canceled yesterday.

During the Recap, everyone talked about their impressions of Campbell Island. Rodney and David had built the boardwalk a number of years ago. It rains so much that it would have been too muddy to walk to where we went. With the boardwalk, we could stop and look at plants and trees without sinking into mud.

Everyone was impressed with seeing the Albatrosses nesting on the hillside at our destination, and with how tame they were.

Afterwards we had a fitting for the Antarctic jackets we need to wear when we get there. They are wind proof and have a heavy lining. Why then did we bring so many clothes?

Later, instead of going to the "Sea Bird By–Catch" lecture, I got some needed sleep. I find it difficult to sit through two lectures in the afternoon. Too exhausted from walking around on board.

Thursday, February 6—At Sea

What a huge ocean, the Southern Ocean. We have seen nothing but water for several days since we left Campbell Island. This morning

This iceberg just appeared in our window and it is the first time we have been so close to one. I couldn't help thinking about the Titanic, since the part underwater is seven or eight times as massive as what we are looking at.

there is much excitement. At 63 degrees South we saw two icebergs. What a sight! With the sunshine on it there were green hues of color. The first iceberg had been passed at four o'clock this morning, we were told. We are still 600 miles north of the pack ice.

All day long we sighted scattered icebergs, but they were a distance away. The best photos we got were early in the morning.

Lectures and films throughout the day. The sea is quite a bit calmer and it is easier to get around. Our days will be busier from now on.

Just a couple of minutes ago (at 65:30 degrees South), an iceberg appeared in our window—quite close to the ship—and we ran out to take pictures. 7 p.m.—good time of the day—the iceberg was a beautiful shade of blue. I'm surprised how close the ship went. At midnight we passed the Antarctic Circle, and an announcement (a brief one) was made by Rodney. He had told us that we will celebrate the crossing of the Antarctic Circle tomorrow morning. Ship pitched quite a bit during the night, but I slept well and was tired still when I got up.

Here we are approaching Cape Adare. We had hoped to visit Borchgrevink's hut built in 1899. He was the first to winter over in Antarctica. Sea ice prevented our landing.

We turned and followed the coast south but found both pack ice and icebergs that had broken off the Ross Ice Shelf.

The flat–top icebergs rise about 100 feet above the water. Here we are working our way through the pack ice trying to get south into the Ross Sea.

Friday, February 7—At Sea

Awoke to a very rough sea—ship is pitching now. In our cabin, pitching is easier to deal with than rolling because things do not tumble out of the closets when opened.

We crossed the Antarctic Circle last night about midnight, however, in the interest of safety, the customary celebration had to be postponed for the time being.

A dreary, stormy day and again, the safest place to be is in bed, as suggested by Rodney.

About 5 p.m.—we were being battered by monstrous waves. Then a mega–monster of a wave came along and damaged the ship. A hatch cover blew away and there was damage to the ship's bow, after which we slowed down to 4 kts all evening and for most of the night. We are rolling again. The pitching had been easier to live with.

GPS at 5:40 p.m.—69:17 South—170:44 East. It never gets dark now.

Saturday, February 8
Plowing Through Ice

This is the day we will see the continent of Antarctica!

6 a.m.—occasional iceberg. By 9 a.m. we are seeing land ahead (Cape Adare), and numer-

ous icebergs which are totally flat on top. Those had calved off of glaciers and the Ross Ice Shelf more recently than the much older and more interestingly shaped ones, or, as one passenger put it: "icebergs with character," which we had seen farther north.

I am on the top deck, above the bridge. It is cold and we are working our way through the pack ice. Icebergs that are flat on the top have broken off the Ross Ice Shelf.

We are ready and dressed (which is a tremendous effort) to go ashore, but Cape Adare is blocked by pack ice (sea ice). The decision is made to try on the return trip, and head south instead while the channel is reasonably open. All bundled up—it is a cold eighteen degrees despite the lovely sunshine. We stand outside and are entertained by the now numerous ice floes and the penguins with their antics. The sea ice is getting more dense and our ship gets banged by ice as it tries to pick its way through it, keeping our two ice pilots busy.

While not as flat on the top, this iceberg had broken off the Ross Ice Shelf several years ago.

Our Russian crew makes repairs, (welding and painting), after yesterday's monstrous waves hit us and damaged the bow.

We get within a mile of the Possession Islands, our next destination, but the pack ice is nearly solid. At 4 p.m. we turn and try for the Ross Sea.

9:55 p.m. and bright sunshine. We are cruising south in

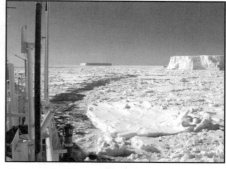

You are looking at the path we have made going through the pack ice. It will only be a few minutes before this channel freezes over.

the Ross Sea at eleven and a half nautical miles per hour. The sea is smooth with only scattered ice floes. We are headed towards "C–19," the iceberg the size of the State of Delaware, which calved off the Ross Ice Shelf. We hope to slip past it on its west side. Later, the sea ice is getting more dense and our ship is pretending it is an icebreaker. We hear the grinding and bumping of the ice on the ship. There is much floe ice in the channel and very slowly we pick our way through it, mostly having to shove sizeable floes aside. We glide past huge icebergs which are flat on top and have obviously broken off from the Ross Ice Shelf some time ago. From our window I see part of the Transantarctic Mountain Range in the distance to the southwest, and also the belt of sea ice.

Sunday, February 9—The Ross Sea

Overcast day, but bright. The sea is smooth and I nearly forget how difficult it was to get around when the ship was pitching and rolling.

At 9 a.m. we see an American supply ship a couple of miles ahead of us. To the east, there is still the seemingly never–ending iceberg C–19 in the distance, about fifteen miles away. I see it with the binoculars.

Intended to stop at Franklin Island, but sea ice prohibits. At 7 p.m. we turn around and head north to Drygalski Ice Tongue, to reach it in early a.m., or if unable, to Inexpressible Island and Terra Nova Bay. There is an Italian research base there and they said they would be happy to have us stop and visit. Plans after that are to attempt to get to McMurdo Sound and Ross Island later in the week—ice permitting. Last month's trip could not go there at all because of sea ice. Hope we can, but need to be sure of our ability to get back out of the ice.

At this point I feel some disappointment about spending so much time at sea and not being able to get off and see the huts of the early explorers. However, the ice can come in and go out at any time. At 9 p.m. we watched it freeze all around our ship when we were momentarily stopped to deal with getting a stubborn ice floe out of the way.

Monday, February 10—Cape Royds

At midnight we were icebreaking, trying to go north and into Terra Nova Bay. Learn this morning that there are 25 miles of solid sea ice all along the coast—very unusual for this time of the year, they tell us. We have given up on trying to get to Terra Nova Bay.

It is sunny and twenty–eight degrees. We are heading south again to make an attempt to land at Cape Royds (Shackleton's Hut) or Cape Evans (Scott's Hut), on Ross Island. The top of 12,450 foot Mt. Erebus glistens in the sunshine above a band of haze. Spectacular!

The penguins are fun to watch. There are groups of them on ice floes. When the ship gets close, they start running, then dive into the water if it is not frozen; or they just stand there, face the ship and squawk. It is quite unlikely that they have ever seen a human being, or a ship before.

10:30 a.m. Approaching Ross Island, we see Mt. Erebus, Mt. Terror, as well as the dark, cone–shaped Mt. Bird. The sea is smooth as glass with only occasional ice floes. Some have penguins on them. Whales are seen in the water. Whole stretches of water are open—then suddenly covered with ice floes.

It is now 3 p.m. and we have seen the massive shape of Mt. Erebus since this morning. Mt. Erebus is still an active volcano and one of only three in the world that has a bubbling lake of lava inside. We are trying for Cape Royds or Cape Evans on the west side of Ross Island.

Finally, at 7 p.m. our ship gets to Cape Royds. While a solid sheet of ice stretched half a mile out from the shore, there was an ice channel wide enough to allow the ship to get to this ice sheet. The ice was thick and safe enough for us to walk on. After dinner and a briefing, we donned our life preservers (in case the ice broke). It was 9:30 p.m. and sunny, thanks to the 24–hour daylight.

Shackleton's Hut

We got off the ship for the first time in a week, and many of us staggered with our sea legs. The snow which covered the pack ice was deeper than expected. Single file, following three leaders, we walked ten minutes on the ice, which had small tidal cracks in two places, before we set foot onto Ross Island, Antarctica! Terra Firma consists of lava rocks and gravel, compliments of Mt. Erebus which towers over the Island.

We walked up a bare hill and then down into a snow–covered bowl–shaped little valley. There stood Shackleton's hut. It was an awesome

The ship has been rammed into the ice about half a mile from shore. Here we hike across the frozen sea to visit Shackleton's Hut.

sight—and that is an understatement! It was exactly as it was left ninety–five years ago. Only the roof had been replaced and secured with crossed cables to protect it from the fierce winds. Nothing deteriorates in this extremely dry climate. Outside were the stables and some dog houses, as well as many, many crates which were still holding canned foods. All around the hut were cans and jars containing foods, some of which had rusted open and we could see dried beans and peas in them.

Our feet were cleaned with brushes before we were allowed to enter. Inside the hut there were mostly shelves with cans and jars, utensils, a cookstove. Everywhere stood cots on which lay reindeer furs, socks and mittens hung on clothes lines, and sledges were stored in the rafters above. There was also a darkroom for the photographer.

What an experience to have seen this! We climbed some nearby hills and enjoyed a flock of Adelie penguins which have a rookery here. The sun was not setting, but just hovering on the horizon. It was close to midnight when we got back to the ship. We were spending the night in our ice channel and going to try for Cape Evans, six miles south, in the morning.

This was our first view of Shackleton's Hut. Except for a new roof, this is exactly as he left it almost 100 years ago. Note the boxes and other supplies stacked up outside. You can see the sea beyond the pack ice we walked across.

What an exciting day we've had! It made up for all the hardships of getting here. By hardships I am talking about my bruised and battered body (head, shoulders, elbows, hips, and knees), having been slammed against walls and furniture on the violently rolling ship.

Tuesday, February 11—Scott's Hut

Cape Evans is six miles away. We cannot get there by ship. The Ross Sea is solidly frozen from here on south. To our delight, it is announced that we would travel to Cape Evans on the ice in two of the Naiads towed by the two Argo vehicles. It would be a forty–five minute trip. Half of our group would leave at 9 a.m. and the other half after lunch. We were in the morning group.

Getting dressed for an outing is always serious business. It is colder than before, nine degrees, as we are now at just about the farthest south we would get on this trip—77 degrees 36 minutes South. There is a light breeze and we would be riding, which creates additional wind. With our ship being jammed in the ice channel, we enjoyed not having

Shackleton's Hut was built in January 1908, and he spent that winter here. Shackleton with his expedition departed November 3, 1908 for the Pole, leaving a skeleton crew at the Hut. When he returned he was met by the relief ship Nimrod at Discovery Hut near McMurdo Station, about 20 miles south of here.

to fight to stay upright as we struggled into all the layers of warm clothing. It was sunny outside and snowing tiny little snowflakes.

We are ready in time to watch as our Naiads, which had been fitted with sled–type runners, are lifted off the ship and hooked up to the two Argos. What a unique mode of transportation. Two groups of thirteen each, we got to sit comfortably on the soft tubes of the Naiads and enjoy the magnificent scenery. The thought occurred to us that there was no land underneath the ice, but rather water. However, the anticipation of seeing Polar Explorer Robert Falcon Scott's Hut at Cape Evans eradicated the thought of danger. That is, until we got to a sizeable tidal crack, about halfway to Scott's Hut.

The crew had checked out the route during the night to make sure the ice holds all along the way, and were prepared. I had wondered why we carried a ladder in each boat. And we had been instructed to wear our life preservers. The ladders were placed across the tidal crack side–by–side, a distance away from where several sea lions were sunning themselves on the ice.

It was not a comforting thought to look into a blue crevasse and see water, and then have to balance, with our wobbly sea legs, and walk across the spokes of two ladders, one foot on each. I felt brave and walked across right after one of the guides was on the other side, ready to give people a hand. It was not as bad as I feared. After all, I had practiced balancing all day long for ten solid days!

After we were safely on the other side, they adjusted the ladders and drove the Argos with the Naiads across. We were on

Top: Two ladders span a tidal crack over which we walked very carefully.
Bottom: Our Naiad which was fastened to wooden sledge–type runners is towed across the tidal crack by an Argo.

our way, though the snow was too deep in places for the small wheels of the Argos, which are very low, eight–wheeled vehicles. We got stuck a couple of times and this seemed to be a sign of things to come. Each time we got stuck we had to get off our boat sled, help the crew detach the Argo, push it out of the snow, then help push the Naiad into place and hook it up to the Argo.

Shortly after 10 a.m., we spot Scott's Hut on a hill in the distance. We are excited. It is a dream come true. We are at Cape Evans and see the Hut in the snow. This is summer—what would it be like in winter, and in a blizzard? We cannot imagine, and our discomforts of rough seas and length of travel to get here pale in comparison to theirs nearly a century ago.

Scott's Hut is much larger than Shackleton's. In addition to the men he needed to attempt the trip to the South Pole, Scott's party also included a scientific research team.

Being inside the Hut is awesome. We see the bunks they slept in and their reindeer sleeping bags; socks, shoes, gloves, and shirts which

Scott's hut is much larger than Shackleton's. He was involved in Antarctic research and had a larger team. Scott made it to the Pole only to find that the Norwegian, Amundsen, had beat him by only three weeks. Scott and his men perished on the return trip.

the men wore so long ago. Then there are chairs, table, dishes and utensils; canned foods and everything they would need had it been necessary to survive another winter.

Outside are stables for their ponies, sledges and spare parts. There is also an almost 100–year old basket of penguin eggs and a stack of seal blubber slabs, which is oozing fat and smells awful, although it is not rotten.

As was Shackleton's, this Hut is in a bowl–shaped area for maximum protection from weather.

The return trip to the Akademik Shokalskiy was a longer one—we got stuck in the snow with our vehicle eight times. However, the sun was shining through the haze; Mt. Erebus showed itself, as well as Mt. Discovery. We had lots of time to admire the incomparable scenery, and we also got exercise by getting in and out of the Naiads.

Mal is standing beside Scott's chair at the dining table. One of the more famous pictures to survive from the Scott expedition is one showing Scott and his men at dinner, taken from this same place. Mal was emotionally overwhelmed. As with Shackleton's Hut, everything is exactly as they left it. Scott died on the way back from the Pole.

This corner of Scott's Hut was a well–equipped lab for the scientists in his expedition. It is amazing that everything is so well–preserved.

I am on a hill behind Scott's Hut. Note the amount of snow and ice, and desolation.

My Penguin Story

In the afternoon, while the other group was on the trip to Scott's Hut, we walked across the ice again to the penguin rookery near Shackleton's Hut. We were told to stay on the Shackleton Hut side of some orange markers so as not to interfere with the penguins' activities.

After about an hour of wandering up and down the hilly volcanic terrain, my attention was drawn to a group of penguins who were squabbling more noisily than normal. A fight, was my first thought, but it was definitely a verbal fight, if it were that. Penguins are boisterous talkers.

Looking in the opposite direction, I saw two groups of penguins heading towards the rookery across the ice from the open water, which was about three quarters of a mile away. The speed with which they waddled was amazing. A number of them would, now and then, slide along on the ice on their bellies and use their flippers as oars, which was faster than walking on their awkward short legs.

Giving my attention back to the group on the hill, I witnessed the last–minute excited–sounding squawking before one penguin left and started on a journey towards the arriving penguin groups. All that noise had apparently been the decision making process of who should go out and meet the arrivals.

The penguin in the center is bowing to each arriving penguin. They have come from the sea. The sea and Mt. Bird can be seen in the background.

The chosen envoy walked down the hill and started across the ice at his fastest possible speed. Meanwhile, the two arriving groups were strung out across the ice, proceeding at whatever speed their accumulating fatigue permitted. Way in the distance were more groups arriving. The envoy walked to a certain point, then stopped and waited. Fascinated, I wondered what would happen next.

The arrivals were quite strung out now. As the first one got close to the waiting penguin, the envoy bowed, greeted the arrival, and let him pass. So it went with each one of the arriving penguins. I captured a part of the "greeting ceremony" in a picture (previous page). You can see the black back of the envoy as he bows. There were also words exchanged during the greetings, in "penguinese," and I wondered what they were saying. It sounded much more peaceful than the earlier discussions up on the hill.

Well, our envoy stayed out there on the ice for more than an hour, greeting every last one of the arrivals. I was intrigued with their sociable behavior and thought they acted very much like human beings.

* * *

We are spending the night in our ice channel here at Cape Royds and will try for McMurdo Station, only eight miles south, tomorrow. We are grateful for another calm night.

Wednesday, February 12—Ross Island

Another glorious morning. Scattered low clouds and majestic Mt. Erebus sticking out way above them.

We leave our ice channel at Cape Royds and sail north past Mt. Erebus and Mt. Bird, anchor at Cape Bird which is located on the northernmost end of Ross Island. The Naiads take us to the beach for a "wet landing," meaning we wear our Wellingtons because we have to wade through water to get to shore.

Cape Bird is an Adelie Penguin rookery. It is late in the season, and there are only about two thousand penguins here right now, as well as a flock of skuas. Earlier in the summer (January) there are many times that number but they have started their migration north. Winter is coming. The penguins that are left are still molting, so there are feathers all over the place. Most noticeable about Cape Bird is the smell. Penguins are very smelly and noisy. They seem to squawk all of the time.

Adelie Penguins, molting. The Akademik Shokalskiy is in the background.

The beach is littered with penguin carcasses in various stages of decay; some picked clean, others just weathering away. The skuas are circling, watching for dying penguins.

There are quite a few icebergs of interesting shapes and sizes in the water. We have become used to seeing the long, flat ones which broke off the Ross Ice Shelf, and we appreciate some irregular shaped ones. These have more character.

After lunch we start south again. Sea is smooth as glass. Temperature just above freezing. All afternoon and evening we cruise the ice edge between Cape Royds and north of Cape Bird. We see whales and a few Emperor Penguins. It looks like we are using up time, hoping for a dash into McMurdo Station tomorrow. The problem is to get permission. McMurdo Station is dependent on ships for the bulk of its supplies, and these ships are only able to get through in January and February. Even during these months, a U.S. Coast Guard icebreaker is required to keep the sea channel open the last five to ten miles into McMurdo. This year the ice has been especially bad and a second icebreaker had to be sent from Seattle. Even with this second icebreaker they are having trouble keeping the channel open. We need to receive permission to use the channel, and that is given to tourist ships only if supply ships are not using the channel.

News: The oil tanker we saw heading for McMurdo Station several days ago is still waiting to get into McMurdo Station. We are told to park a mile north of the oil tanker in an ice channel on the west side. There is talk that maybe in the morning Rodney will launch the Naiads with the sled runners and try to make it over the ice. It is about eight kilometers to McMurdo from where we are. There are significant risks crossing the ice that far from land and Mal and I conclude that this is too risky for us at our age. We will stay on the ship if Rodney decides to make an attempt over the ice.

The temperature is fifteen degrees and it is windy, in other words: cold. It is also the farthest south we have come—77 degrees 44 minutes South, and we are seven hundred thirty–seven nautical miles north of the South Pole. This is the farthest South we will get.

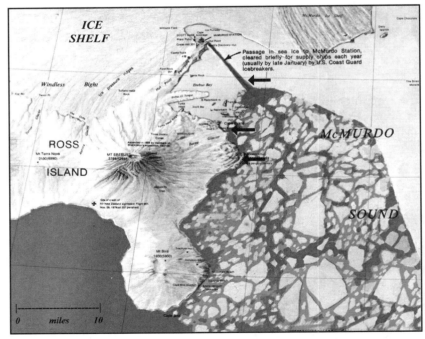

This map of the McMurdo Sound area shows Ross Island, Mt. Erebus, and McMurdo Station. It also shows the normal summer ice pack. We got as far south as the top arrow. You can see the channel that the icebreakers were trying to keep open. The middle arrow is the location of Scott's hut. The bottom arrow is Shackleton's hut.

Thursday, February 13—Ross Sea

The expedition leader, Rodney Russ, decides it is too risky to attempt to go over the ice to McMurdo Station. If the weather were to change—and it can and does very quickly here—a party out on the ice would be in serious trouble. Mal and I feel relieved that our decision the night before was a correct one.

The Akademik Shokalskiy leaves our overnight ice channel and "farthest south" point at about 7 a.m. It turns, and starts north. It is snowing tiny flakes, but hard enough to coat the decks and make them too slippery to walk. The Russian crewmen are shoveling snow and scraping ice. There are pretty little icicles hanging in front of our window. At 10 a.m. we cruise by Cape Bird. The whole beach is covered with snow where yesterday we had walked on gravelly surfaces.

Today's highlight is that we can see part of the Delaware–sized Iceberg C–19 in the distance as it glistens in the sunshine. Unbelievably spectacular! It is hard to visualize how big this iceberg is.

Mt. Erebus (12,450 feet) is an active volcano which dominates the scenery.

We cruise all day and twelve hours later we arrive at Franklin Island. After dinner, the Naiads take people to shore to see more penguins and go on a hike. For the younger passengers, there is also a climb up the steep mountain. To make that climb you would have to be an experienced mountain climber. I have a miserable cold and no energy to get all dressed up for cold weather so we, among others, stay on board. At midnight we continue cruising north.

Friday, February 14—At Sea

Steadily cruising north. Calm sea. Going through sea ice we see icebergs, then again nothing but water. It is constantly changing. Trying to reach Possession Island or Cape Adare by tomorrow afternoon. The calm sea is bad news. It is freezing over. It is fascinating to actually watch the water freeze right before our eyes.

Saturday, February 15—At Sea, and Frozen In!

We are still aiming for Cape Adare. At times the sea is completely free of ice; then suddenly there are again ice floes, icebergs, and pack ice.

At about 12:30 p.m. we get stuck in the ice. Totally frozen in. Many of us think it is fun, and it is, for about an hour. However, by the third hour we remember Shackleton's ill–fated trip and realize that it is possible to stay frozen in. His ship was frozen in for eleven months before it was crushed and sank, stranding the crew on the ice for another five months.

We start to wonder who would rescue us from here, it being nearly two thousand miles from New Zealand. There are no helicopters that can fly this far and still have fuel to fly back. Perhaps once the ice-breakers at McMurdo Station have finished their work getting the supply ships and oil tanker into McMurdo (maybe a month from now) they can open up a channel for us. But by then the sea will be solidly frozen. Summer is only two months long, and then winter arrives with no in–between season. This year winter is early.

We cheer when after five hours of hard work the captain is able to wiggle free. But it is a sobering experience. We are in a very inhospitable part of the world, and help is not just around the corner. This is not a cruise; this is an expedition, and there are risks.

We are trapped in pack ice for five hours. Everyone is aware of the Shackleton experience and it is a little frightening. We have only 2,500 hp vs. 75,000 hp of the U.S. Coast Guard icebreakers, but they are 300 miles away.

Intended stops at Possession Island and Cape Adare are canceled due to the ice pack being solid. We are now heading north towards the Auckland Islands, our next stop, five and a half days away.

There is snow all over the ship. It has been snowing most of the day. Our sunshine is gone, but we were lucky to have had it when it counted the most. We have heard stories about some trips where the sun never came out and there was one storm after another. We considered ourselves lucky.

Sunday, February 16—At Sea

It has been snowing during the night, and still is. Dark skies and there are huge waves. It is funny to see the crew shoveling two to three inches of snow off the deck.

Making good time, eleven to twelve knots, and are going with the waves, which are huge; and they look even more huge when viewed from the bridge. I am so pleased that the combination of the seasick-

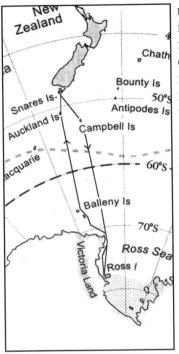

ness patch and the astronaut pills is working for me. The ship rolls fearfully and I feel fine. I have to get used to securing everything once again as nothing stays in place. It is interesting how, when walking, we have learned to compensate for the roll. Still, the safest place is in bed.

We are northbound for the Auckland Islands and will be there in four plus days. No more ice. I miss the beautiful icebergs. However, I do enjoy seeing the huge waves. They are unbelievable. It was still not totally dark last night, even though the solid overcast cut down on the light.

About 6 p.m., Rodney announces that we have to change course to the west to avoid pack ice between the coast and the upcoming Balleny Islands. We will be going far more to the west than the ship normally goes, but there have been reports of severe weather from another ship, and they expect extremely high seas for the next six hours. We were to secure everything in our cabins. The bar, which normally opened at 6 p.m. would remain closed, and dinner postponed until midnight—or canceled.

We prepare for the worst. The safest place being the bed, Rodney urges that we prepare to be there. Advises to take medications for motion sickness. It is a challenge to get ready for bed. Everything slides out of the closets when opened.

Monday, February 17—At Sea
Balleny Islands

Shortly after 5 a.m., Rodney comes on the intercom and tells us that we are just passing the middle one of the Balleny Islands and that it is a very rare occurrence for the Ballenys to be ice free and for a ship to be able to get close to them. We are cruising north, on the east side of the north–south string of islands.

I jump out of bed, put on my coat and hat, and go outside (port side). What a spectacular sight! We are cruising alongside mountains which rise thousands of feet straight out of the sea. They are shrouded in mist and look like Japanese paintings. There are huge, beautifully shaped icebergs in the water, and the mountains are capped with snow, five hundred to a thousand feet deep. It is not possible to judge the depth of the snow pack, the scale is just so large; but I have never seen anything like it before. The highest mountain is a little over seven thousand feet high but we cannot see it because there is a low overcast. Everyone is outside, and awestruck. "Fairyland" is not an adequate word to describe the view.

Coffee cups in hand, we spend the next four hours oh–ing and ah–ing, and taking pictures. What a grand finale to Antarctica; our last view of that fascinating, incomparable continent. Just nothing can ever top this experience.

At 7:30 a.m. we cross the Antarctic Circle. Now we are out in totally open sea until we get to the Auckland Islands, three days from now.

All day long, we still see an occasional iceberg. I love seeing them and shall miss them. They make the plain ocean journey so much more interesting.

The day turns sunny at about noon and the sea is not so rough. Rodney gives us more information on the big scare last night. The Kapitan Klebnikov, a ship we saw at Cape Royds, and the only other excursion ship we saw on the whole trip, had run into a cyclone on the southwest side of the Balleny Islands. They radioed us to stay away from the passage to the south of the Balleny Islands as they had encountered extremely violent rolling, had many injured people, and a

The Balleny Islands are seldom viewed because they are usually encased in pack ice, and battered by storms. The seas are rough and the overcast is probably 2,000 feet. Note the depth of the snow layer on the mountains. Awesome!

number of broken bones. Thanks to their warning we were able to avoid the storm by passing the Ballenys on the east side heading north.

Tuesday, February 18—At Sea

A violent sea! The sunny afternoon and evening turn into a rough night. Heavy overcast and several hours of darkness starting at midnight. I know it because it was not possible to sleep while being rolled—and not gently, either—from one side of the bed to the other.

In the morning, the ship is rolling so violently that I do not even consider getting out of bed. The announcement from Rodney is to stay in bed, if possible, for safety. I take my astronaut pills, as the patch

Heading north, the weather is rough. It is snowing, and the waves are much larger than this picture suggests. Time to be safely "in bed."

does not quite do it in this kind of sea. I hear reports that not many people were downstairs for breakfast, but I risk it for lunch. It is always comical how people stop at the dining room door, brace themselves against the door frame—the last handhold. They then decide on a place to aim for at one of the three long tables and wait for the correct motion of a wave to propel them towards the selected seat. The result is not always as intended. I lurched for one of the two empty chairs at the end of one table and crashed (literally) into the chair which swivelled full turn, and an already seated passenger stopped me from being propelled back out of the chair and into his lap, or more likely, to the floor.

I'm tired of spending so much time in bed. The sea has been so rough all day. At lunch, half of the time the dishes and glasses slid across the table and to the floor. In the kitchen it is mayhem. I don't know how they cope. One can watch the food just lift off the plate (become weightless), and slide downhill at a different speed than the plate.

6:15 p.m.—at 60 degrees South. At this speed of ten knots, it will be sixty hours to the Auckland Islands. We are about to leave the "screaming sixties" and cope with the "furious fifties."

Wednesday, February 19—At Sea

The "furious fifties" are acting according to reputation, but we are learning to cope with the motion again. Wandering Albatrosses pass the ship often now. Mal is getting quite restless. Now that we have seen the sights, he is anxious to get home.

I have trouble writing because of the extreme rolling. My left shoulder is quite painful, having been slammed against walls so often during the trip. Too cold, stormy, and rough to be outside.

Attend video lecture—"Life in the Freezer"—about penguins, as well as Melanie's lecture about penguins. They have evolved from birds rather than from sea animals.

I sleep a lot. Must need it. Afternoon—Rodney's lecture and video on saving bird species by poisoning rat populations on Campbell and other islands.

Dinner is always an especially interesting affair, requiring a lot of patience on the part of the passengers—not that anyone is in a hurry to go somewhere. There are two dining rooms with the galley in between.

Dinner is at 7:30 p.m. and, if we sit at the first table which is always served first, the appetizer is served at 7:45. Once all appetizer dishes are removed in both dining rooms, the orders for one of the two entrees are taken. It will be 8:15 before table one receives the meal and is usually finished eating before table three has been served.

After the main meal, dessert is served, but not until all dinner plates have been removed from both dining rooms, washed, and put away. Only then is the dessert served, which will be at 9 p.m. at the earliest for table one. Usually, a number of people have left by that time, not caring to wait so long. We always try to sit in Dining Room One at Table One.

There are two New Zealand cooks and two Russian waitresses. Each meal is beautifully presented in that the food on the plate looks like a piece of art. Trying to find reasons for the long delays, I come up with this: It takes time to decorate each plate so beautifully and they cannot do it ahead of time. Food gets cold, and the ship's motion often scrambles dishes and food so that three plates are done at a time, often with long delays between the next three servings. The dishes are washed by hand and I assume that it is necessary to clear the counters because the galley is so small and they don't have room for forty–eight dinner plates and dessert plates.

Food on board: We have experienced some unique combinations, especially at breakfast and lunch. Breakfast, for example, could be: sausage (not made of meat, as we know it), eggs, and spaghetti or bacon (sort of like Canadian style, but with lots of fat on it), and baked beans. Pancakes might be served with eggs or shredded pork. Mal and I stuck with cereal, toast, and fruit. There was always a huge basket of fresh fruits—apples, oranges, kiwis, bananas, apricots—on the buffet table and in the day lounge.

Lunch examples: Pizza, but instead of cheese there would be different vegetables on it, including squash, green peppers, and diced pork, and just sprinkles of shredded cheese. Every plate would be garnished with different fresh herbs and look like a picture.

Quiche consisted of eggs, bacon and diced vegetables with macaroni and raw vegetables.

Pumpkin soup was served frequently, and it was delicious. Lunches were always the biggest surprises. I was often not hungry, but went to lunch because I did not want to miss out on a unique treat.

At 9 p.m. we are at 54 degrees 34 minutes South and have slightly less than three hundred nautical miles to go to the Auckland Islands. The outside temperature during the day was twenty–five degrees, and this evening we are only rolling up to twenty degrees instead of the thirty–plus degrees, which has been the case most of the time.

It is easy to keep track of where we are thanks to the Global Positioning System. Mal has his small handheld unit he uses with the plane, and it works well. The ship also uses this same navigation system and Mal can cross check his readings with the ship's. They are always the same.

Thursday, February 20—Auckland Islands

After seven days of cruising, we are arriving at the Auckland Islands at 3:20 p.m. It has been rough at times. The Incline Meter—which measures how far the ship rolls—has shown anywhere from ten to forty–one degrees during the trip. We are promised a good night's sleep in a calm harbor, Carnley Harbor at Adams Island. When we leave here, we still have two days of cruising left before we reach Bluff. The outside temperature here is pleasantly above freezing.

The Auckland Islands are a group of volcanic islands that stretch from south to north over thirty–five miles. Like Campbell Island, these are also part of New Zealand, and tourists are allowed only if accompanied by a government representative. No one lives here, primarily because of the weather conditions.

After getting into the harbor this afternoon, we were invited to take a tour of the ship's engine rooms. Kosta, the chief engineer and our trusted Naiad pilot, offered to take three groups of fifteen each at different times. He speaks quite adequate English.

It is interesting to learn that the ship has only one propeller, run by two diesel engines, each producing twelve hundred horsepower. If the propeller gets damaged, which would seem like a possibility with our going through so much ice, it cannot be replaced at sea. In that case, the ship has to go into dry dock. Kosta dismisses damage as being unlikely because the propeller has a cage around it. They have made this trip many times over the last ten years without incident, so he is probably right. Still, I am glad they didn't tell us that until after we were out of the ice. The total power of the ship appears minimal and is certainly not strong enough to break through solid ice. By contrast the

U.S. Coast Guard icebreakers we saw had seventy–five thousand horse-power. The Shokalskiy was built in Finland, the engines in Russia. The engineer has a control room on the middle one of the three levels. A question was asked about the ship's stabilizers. Kosta explained that the way they work is that pumps transfer water from one side of the ship to the other to help offset the rolling. But, Kosta smiled and said: "No good. We need nine seconds for the water to shift from one side to another, but the ship rolls faster than that—four or five seconds. We have to turn the stabilizers off or they could actually make it worse." So much for stabilizers.

Friday, February 21—Auckland Islands

Breakfast is at 7:30 instead of 8:30 a.m. At 8:30, the Naiads (Zodiacs) take us out cruising the inner harbor coastline. It is a beautiful morning and everybody is in good spirits, having had a restful night's sleep without being tossed from side to side all night long.

Before dressing, we were told to be prepared to get wet. It rains often and without warning. With all the layers of clothing, it takes about forty–five minutes to get dressed. This includes the customary boot scrubbing. To avoid carrying foreign bacteria from one continent or island to another, we have to scrub footgear in a chemical solution, then rinse in another. Now we are dressed up warmly with layer upon layer of silk, wool, fleece, GoreTex, hats or hoods, scarves, gloves and mittens. Sunglasses are essential. One must get outside the warm room after dressing.

Near the shore is lots of huge kelp and there are dozens of sea lions. They love the wakes of our boats and follow us around like porpoises. We also see black winged seagulls, teal ducks, terns, and some skuas, which are rare this far north. The rata trees delight us with their red flowers. David Given tells us the rata trees can get to be a thousand years old. They have the habit of growing closely together, forming a solid canopy on the top with varied shades of green to brownish, depending on the age of the trees.

Along the shore there are lava tubes through which the sea water spouts up like geysers.

We are now wet and are thankful for GoreTex outer clothing. It is windy, raining, and we even had sleet for about ten minutes. Our gloves and mittens are soaked. By now we are quite chilled and are glad that

I am going through the boot cleaning exercise before going ashore at Enderby Island. We first clean our boots with a brush, as I am doing, then move to the next tub which is filled with disinfectant. This was required every time before we left the ship and after we returned.

the trip will be only an hour long. The warm room sounds better by the minute. Once again I think of the Antarctic Explorers who braved the coldest, windiest place on earth for months at a time, without the relief of a warm room, or even dry clothes, at the end of the day.

During lunch, our ship moves to Tagua Bay from where the Naiads take us to shore for a hike to Coast Watchers Hut #2 and the Lookout, which were used in World War II to watch for enemy ships entering the Auckland Islands. It is a great hike—the climate is quite wet and the mosses and lichens cover tree trunks and forest floor, much like our San Juan Islands.

It rains on and off while the sun shines, and forty–five people traipsing on the trail makes some places muddy and very slippery. We come across sea lion couples here and there in secluded spots. It is surprising to see them more than a mile from the shore and part way up a mountain.

The view from both cabins, especially from the Lookout, is spectacular in all directions, although I am particularly enchanted with the whole forest. The rata trees have beautifully gnarled trunks and are a never ending delight for the eye. Rata trees are closely related to the Australian gum tree, Botanist Dr. David tells us. We thoroughly enjoy the couple of hours of hiking. It is an easy hike, even uphill.

Soon after returning at 5 p.m., our ship moves along the sheltered east coast to Enderby Island where we will stay tomorrow.

Saturday, February 22 — Enderby Island Nature Reserve

Our ship is in Sandy Bay, but it is not a calm sea. Enderby Island is the northernmost island of the Auckland Islands group. It is a fairly small island, perhaps two by six miles and is completely exposed to the open sea on the north and east sides.

After breakfast we pack our lunches and get dressed for a day of hiking. We are far enough north now to have New Zealand summer temperatures, meaning it is in the low fifties. We dress for a wet landing. Mal's and my Wellingtons are reasonably comfortable for hiking, so we have no need to take along regular boots. We scrub footwear and are ready for Kosta to take us to Enderby Island, a nature preserve and a pristine island, which means there are no rats or other predatory animals. As always, our representative from the New Zealand Department of Conservation is with us.

We land on some rocks in a cave—an alcove at the bottom of a one hundred fifty foot high vertical cliff. Next we receive an orientation talk and a choice of either a short hike to a certain point, or all the way around the perimeter of the Island. We are told that we are going to see many varieties of mega–herbs, yellow–eyed penguins, and some of the three hundred twenty sea lions who breed on the Island. It is suggested that we stay at least fifteen feet away from sea lions as they do bite, if bothered. Well, we were to see all three hundred and twenty sea lions, and most likely more, on our eight–mile hike around the Island, and some from distances considerably closer than fifteen feet.

We do not realize that this would be an adventurous day. We are given a crude map of the outline of the Island and told to just keep the coast on our left and we'll automatically return to our starting position. There is no mention of approximate distances. The terrain, especially when covered with tussock grass, is very energy consuming to walk on. For this kind of hiking, the rubber boots do not give sturdy enough support. The terrain is also quite hilly, interlaced with countless tiny creeks in steep, narrow lava rock or sandy canyons which needed to be crossed.

Since we were told that we had all day for the hike, each person made his or her own pace, stopping to examine and explore as their impulse dictated. Mal and I are fast walkers, and pretty soon we are out of sight of everyone else, but keeping the sea on our left side as instructed. We see penguins, different birds, and everywhere the unbelievable displays of the mega–herbs. It is not until after having lunch on a grassy meadow that we see our first sea lion. He observes us until we put some distance between him and us. We had been told that sea lions can run by reversing their tail flippers and using them as legs. They are said to be able to run faster than a man can, but only for short distances. The males, who weigh close to four hundred fifty pounds, are territorial.

We are now in sea lion territory. While many of them, probably females, are on the rocky beaches, a number of males have climbed up into the area where we are walking and laid down to sleep. Because of the high grass tussocks they are hard to see when they are lying down. They are everywhere and we do not always have the recommended fifteen feet between them and us. We are scared. We have not seen any of our group for a couple of hours. At this time we do not know that we are way ahead of everyone else, and we wonder where they all went. We cope with the sea lions the best we can. Most of them are in pairs and sleeping. The male would sit up only if he had noticed our presence.

On one meadow there are sea lions everywhere. With a steep cliff down to the sea on our left and the impenetrable rata forest on the right, we have to carefully pick our way across the meadow. It is a very scary experience, especially when some of them sit up and make a menacing motion to follow us. We survive this ordeal.

At one point, close to sea level, there are many sea lions in the water, on the beach, and others sleeping in singles or groups, everywhere. We try to decide which would be the best way through this maze and start by trying to cross a benign looking, narrow creek. The water looks black and muddy and, still wearing tall boots, I step into the muddy water since it is too far to jump across, and it looks shallow. Surprise—my boot does not meet solid creek bottom, but instead starts sinking into mud that seems to be endlessly deep. I am already down in

A male sea lion can weigh 450 pounds and is able to run for short distances on his rear flippers as fast as a human being. Sea lions certainly appear meancing when they roar at you from five feet away.

it to my knee before Mal reacts to my screams and comes to my rescue. He has trouble pulling me out. The suction is so strong and I try to hold onto my boot, which becomes nearly impossible in this quicksand–like mud. We still have several miles of walking to do, and I need that boot. It is a scary experience, though not the last one.

The next scare is the surprise of a sea lion resting in between the very long tussock grasses. I struggle up an incline, doing all kinds of acrobatics to keep my balance on the uneven tussock terrain, when suddenly, about two feet from my outstretched right arm, I see a black face with a huge open jaw and two rows of ferocious–looking teeth. I jump to my left and yell for Mal to run. The sea lion had not even noticed when Mal passed by.

Next we get to a section of the dense rata forest and are happy to find a path cut through it. We had become quite worried when we saw the forest ahead of us and the coast being a steep cliff. At least there won't be any more sea lions, we thought. We had not seen any for about fifteen minutes. Then, on a tussock meadow between two sections of forest, hidden in the tall grasses, a sea lion suddenly rears up with a roar as we

Enderby Island is at the north end of the Auckland Islands. Here the growth of trees and vegetation is stunted by the severe winds and weather. The dense rata forest behind me is so thick it cannot be penetrated. Fortunately a path has been cut through this area close to the coast. We spend a day hiking on Enderby and see hundreds of sea lions, some of them too close for comfort.

pass within a foot of him. We run for our lives. Those teeth were too close for comfort. Later we compare notes, and it seems that this particular sea lion had fun scaring every single one of our people.

Finally we see our ship and feel like we are almost home, though the distance is still much greater than it looks. Even better is what happens next. Someone—a human being—calls to us. We turn and see Stan. What a relief. We are not alone! Stan tells us he had us in sight now and then for hours. He is a New Zealander, eighty years old, has traveled extensively all over the world, and took this particular hike eight years ago on a trip to the Subantarctic Islands. Now we feel we are in good hands and the rest of the hike is fun again. Stan tells us that he had been spooked by the same sea lion next to the trail a ways back. We laugh about it, though at the time it was not funny.

We are within half a mile of our destination when two sea lions decide they do not like our presence and start running after us. We feel so safe with Stan being with us that we do not even run until we see Stan starting to run. It takes only a couple of minutes for the lions to give up their pursuit. Perhaps we were out of their territory at that point. Rodney had pointed out that while sea lions can run faster than we can, they tire easily.

Back home on the Shokalskiy, we feel the fatigue of this long, eventful day.

Sunday, February 23 —At Sea

On this last full day of our trip to Antarctica, the "roaring forties" of the Southern Ocean are living up to their reputation. We will be happy to get onto stable ground tomorrow morning. No activity is possible on this severely rolling ship. At lunch, not even half of the people are present. The Shokalskiy is running at reduced speed to make it a little less uncomfortable.

Now it is 5:30 p.m. and I have been sitting in bed most of the day, for safety's sake. It would be a shame to break a bone on the last day, having survived until now. Trying to pack is impossible when everything that is not held on to goes flying through the cabin. Stan reports that our rolls are in the 30 degree range again, and Rodney announces for us to be extremely cautious when moving about the ship. In other words, if you don't have to go anywhere, stay put.

It is a long, boring day when one just sits in bed and tries to read while swaying from side to side. It is difficult to write this, too. For me, even the combination of a patch plus the astronaut pills has not completely done it. I don't get sick, but I just barely hang on. We hope to be by Stewart Island at dinner time and cruise in the lee of the Island so that people can come to the special farewell dinner.

Dinner is special, indeed. There is wine with the meal for those who want it, and chocolates afterwards, but we do not stay for the dessert. It usually is not served until 9 p.m. and I need to pack while the ship is nearly stopped and the wave action diminished. Still, it is a chore. The cabin is hot now that it is warm outside, and the ship still keeps rolling enough so that nothing can be left on the table and the suitcase keeps falling off the sofa until I put it on the bed. Both customs and breakfast are to start at seven o'clock in the morning., and debarkation between eight and eight–thirty.

Monday, February 24 —Bluff, New Zealand

I awake during the night and the engine has stopped. It is totally quiet. There are bright lights outside at 2:30 a.m. Looking out of the window, I am blinded by a row of spotlights and city lights beyond. We are in the harbor of Bluff—and in calm water.

The alarm rings at 5:15 a.m. It is wonderful to take a shower without having to worry about broken bones. Last minute things are packed.

Customs officials start their work at 7 a.m. They are mainly concerned about organisms brought into the country on hiking boots, since we had been tramping in the Auckland Islands and also in Antarctica. We tell them that we scrubbed our footgear and they are happy.

Last breakfast on the ship—a quiet one without dishes sliding off tables and people timing and coordinating a roll with a mad dash to a swivel chair; or the cereal becoming weightless and floating out of the bowls. All those are luxuries which we normally take for granted.

Our baggage has already been picked up from outside the door. Room No. 421 has been a nice location next to a door to the outside. It was also a central location near a set of stairs going down to the dining room and up to the bridge, two flights above us, which we did regularly.

We disembark at about eight–fifteen, pose for a group photo, and admire the big dents in the Shokalskiy's bow which the crashes of the huge waves did to us. She is running one more trip to the Subantarctic Islands and then will head for Vladivostok to go into dry dock.

When our bus is ready to leave, the Shokalskiy gives one long blast of the horn and the crew stands on deck and waves good–bye to us. It is a touching farewell to the greatest of trips. In total, we traveled five thousand and sixty–nine miles on the Shokalskiy.

After getting off the bus, I notice that I am still having sea legs. I really have trouble with dizziness and take another one of my astronaut pills, which does not help. All the rest of the day, the world is spinning around me and I keep losing my balance. I hang on to furniture and walls as I walk around the hotel room, and I don't want to go out into the street. This keeps up for several days, and at a gradually reduced rate for longer than two weeks. Still, I would take this trip again without any hesitation.

Postscript

In spite of the violence of the trip, and my subsequent shoulder surgery, I must tell you that Mal and I want to go back. I don't know what happened, but we have both fallen in love with the pristine beauty of the Antarctic.

In October 2003 we booked space on the Akademik Shokalskiy leaving Bluff in January 2005, for a 29–day trip. Unfortunately, as I said at the beginning of this chapter, I have now been told that my other shoulder has been damaged and I need another operation. We have had to cancel our reservations.

We are also becoming increasingly aware that we are not getting any younger and are starting to ask ourselves how much risk we should be taking. A broken hip on a month–long trip with no chance of serious medical treatment may not be totally wise.

Regardless, we have fallen in love with the Antarctic, and whether we can get back or not, that will not change.

16

Final Reflections

As I bring this autobiography to a close, I cannot help but sit back and reflect on the early years of my life and some of the influences that these experiences had on later years, and on raising my own family.

Parents

I can say that, except for the war, I had a good childhood. I grew up in a loving family. Peter and I were very much loved and nurtured by Mom and Papa. Since Papa's military duty required him to be absent from the family for long periods of time, most of the rearing of Peter and me fell to Mom. By circumstance she became the central figure in our lives. Mom did all that she could to prepare us for life, and even today I have to marvel at her philosophy and wisdom, and her loving and teaching ways. Her great sense of humor was extraordinary. With it she won many a friend as well as countless battles. Had Alzheimer's not been so mind–destroying, she would even have attacked that mean disease with humor and optimism.

Papa was also a kind and loving person with a good measure of humor. He loved his wife and his children with remarkable gentleness. I have often wondered how he must have felt in the military being ordered to shoot at other human beings in battle, rather than to love them and to be friends with them.

Religion

Between the ages of eight and ten I became quite interested in the church and in religion, and I started going to church services on Sundays. All I heard there was how bad and sinful people were, and how Jesus had to die a horrible death for our sins. I knew the Ten Commandments and knew that I had not broken any of them. Why was I so sinful? Perhaps God had sent that awful war down on us to punish us. This must have been why Mom did not go to church with me, I thought, but I found that she needed to catch up with the housework and laundry on Sundays, her only day off from her job. Mom said that Nature was her church, and she believed that if she was an honest and responsible person who respected others and did good deeds whenever possible, she did not need to go to church. "Living each day in good conscience" was Mom's motto. It was what she taught Peter and me.

Mom did encourage me to go to church since I felt inclined to, though she told me that I did not have to seek God in a church, but that I could find Him within my heart. In answer to some of my questions, Mom told me that the Bible is a book written by men. It tries to explain in stories the miracle of creation, and uses stories as examples to teach people to be honest and responsible. I was torn between respect for the Lutheran Church's interpretation of the Holy Bible and Mom's answers to my questions. If God was as loving as the Bible said, why was He consistently portrayed by the church as a God who will punish us for our sins, even though we were not told what those sins were. The minister would stand in the pulpit, shake his fist and point at the congregation while shouting that we will all be punished for our sins and go to hell. I remember wondering what sins, other than causing Mom to be angry at times, had I committed that were so terrible to deserve the wrath of this loving God. Church scared me. I received the clear impression that God was an angry and punishing God much more so than a loving one.

In church school we were told that God loves children; but adults were children once, and at what point did they get bad? Papa and Mom were good, loving people. Some adults may be doing bad things such as murdering people, but why did God have to punish all of us. This whole subject was very confusing and scary to me. I was obviously a sinful person and did not know why.

Mom kept telling me that I was not sinful and tried to direct my worship towards nature. For a time I still tried to find God in churches, but eventually I realized that organized religion did nothing for me.

When I came to America there was a choice of churches of many different denominations. For some reason I still felt that I needed to belong to a church, but with the countless new impressions coming at me in my new home country, I decided to leave the selection of a church for the future. My reasoning was practical. If I were to meet a man whom I wanted to marry and he was seriously affiliated with a particular church, I would be able to be flexible. I always felt that to give children a religious upbringing, it would be more successful if both parents belonged to the same church. When I met my future husband and we talked about marriage, we found that we both had an upbringing without strict religious orientation. For tradition's sake I wanted to be married in a church, and we selected the Unitarian Church, it being the least dogmatic.

Trying to give to our children the daily rituals which a religious upbringing requires and which had not been a part of my life all along, did not work. One cannot give something that one does not have. While l liked the Unitarian Church, was active in it, and took the children to Sunday school, I was still not totally satisfied.

Then I discovered God's Country—Utah and Arizona, the whole desert southwest with its extreme, incomprehensible, awesome beauty— and I was struck. There I felt at peace. Being alone out in the desert was infinitely better than being in church. With this conviction I had arrived where Mom had been all along. In nature I found the Supreme Being I had been searching for. The wonder of nature and the one who created it, and who created me—the Creator. I do not need big congregations of people around me—I love solitude—and spending time alone in the desert is what I love to do.

Teachers and Peers

A number of teachers stand out in my memory whom I thank for their teachings and the wisdom they bestowed on us children. I was doing very well in school and took this for granted. However, I could not sing, and I remember the whole class, including the teacher, breaking into laughter about my miserable attempts at a solo during year–end tests. This was extremely damaging to my self–esteem. In my own eyes I was a failure, and no good grades in the other subjects made up for the humiliating ordeal of the singing test I had to go through every year.

Perhaps the greatest impact on the destruction of my self–esteem at the time was during my early teen years. This was probably the most sensitive time in which a child tries to find his or her place in the adult world. During my three years in Business School, age thirteen to sixteen, I was shut out by my classmates with "you are too young, you wouldn't understand," and was sent away when they were talking about boys and dates; about silk stockings, and having a crush on the teacher. I was the youngest in the class of forty–seven girls because I had skipped a grade and had never adjusted socially. We had no counselors in our schools at that time. To this day I feel uncomfortable in social situations and I prefer to be alone.

Raising Children

During the years I was raising children, I noticed how much certain experiences from my childhood influenced my behavior.

Discipline was strict. While I grew up with a lot of love at home, rules were enforced. I would not have thought of disobeying Mom or Papa. With my children, once I said "no" to something, I stuck with it. It was how I was raised and it was all that I knew. In my time school had been structured and disciplined without compromise. There were loads of homework to do every day which was checked out and graded by the teachers. My children seldom had any homework to do when they attended public schools. I could not relate to what I saw in the schools, especially the lack of structure and discipline.

Food

There was no wasting of food. My children either ate what was being served or they were not hungry enough to eat. I considered their particular likes and dislikes, however, I felt they had to learn that other people in the family had different favorite dishes, and that we all shared everybody else's favorites. There was no dessert or a snack if a reasonable serving of the meal had not been eaten. To the dismay of visiting friends and cousins, there was no picking apart a sandwich and eating only choice parts of it, such as centers without crusts. I would get hysterical about wasting food, and their friends knew it and wondered about it. They then had to listen to my tirades about starving children in the world who would be more than happy to have good food such as this. Of course, they heard about some of my own experiences with hunger.

One of my stories made quite an impression on Michele who was a picky eater. One time I told her how my brother and I counted the noodles in the soup. When there were two noodles more in my soup than in Peter's, he thought that Mom loved me more because she gave me more food to eat.

How could I ever impress on the children what it felt like to be so hungry that we were fighting over every noodle, green pea or other scraps of food when they did not know what hunger really is like? I hope that they will never have to experience it.

I had no tolerance for waste of anything, and to this day I am plagued by extreme thriftiness. This is not just my problem, I have seen it in my German relatives and friends who have been conditioned by the same hard times. No bread crumb or tiny scrap of paper goes to waste. No leftover food is ever thrown out.

No apple peels go down the disposal to this day. I eat them. The first time one of our daughter's little friends had lunch with us, she wanted her apple peeled. Then she watched with dismay as I ate the peels. Later that afternoon I received a phone call from her mother asking me: "What is this I hear about Mrs. Gross eating garbage?"

Clothes and Peer Pressure

When the children grew older and became clothes conscious I found that I was totally unable to relate to them and their wishes. I could not understand why a pair of blue jeans had to have a label that said "Guess" on it. I knew nothing about peer pressure. It did not exist when I grew up. We were all in the same boat and wore what we had. It sure made it easier on our parents whose only problem with clothes at that time was that we outgrew them, and new ones were not available; or if the garment had a hole in it and there was no more thread of any color left to repair it, and none was available for purchase. It was difficult for me to understand why our children had to have certain items just because others had them.

There were many things that were so very important to our children, which I could not relate to at all. My life had been one of making do with what we had. We did not know any differently. We certainly were happier overall and appreciated what we did have. Every little gift, even as small as a scrap of colored paper, was a treasure and made us happy.

We did not know the feeling of "having to have because everybody else has," and it was a freedom which today's materialistic generations have lost.

Remembering "Blessings from the Sky"

As the years went by and I was living a good life in the United States, memories of the very difficult times during and after World War II returned often. One memory in particular was that of the incredible feat of the Berlin Airlift, which saved 2.2 million West Berliners from being forced to become Communists by trying to starve them into submission. Without West Berlin's freedom, it would have been impossible for me to ever come to the United States. The lives of Mom, Peter, and me would have taken quite a different course, and who knows if we would even be alive today.

It has always been a burning desire of mine to be able to thank personally just one of those brave pilots for what he and the Airlift did for us West Berliners. Seeing and hearing the airplanes fly into Berlin was reassuring because we knew they were bringing in food to keep us alive. But those planes were flown by "anonymous" people with whom we had no contact.

The first time I met a former Airlift pilot was in 1978, quite unexpectedly. We lived in the Washington, DC area and Mal was involved with the National Aviation Club. One evening we had dinner with Colonel Everett Langworthy. As he and I tried to get acquainted and I said I was from Berlin, he casually mentioned that he had been to Berlin many times. In answer to my question of "when," he told me that he flew in the Berlin Airlift. The next thing I knew was that I was in tears and hugging him. Ev has been a very special person to me. He was the first Airlift pilot whom I was able to thank personally for my freedom.

Years later while living on Orcas Island, Mal met Colonel Sam Burgess at an EAA meeting. In the course of discussion Sam mentioned he had been an Airlift pilot, and Mal, of course, told him I was one of those saved by that gallant effort. Subsequently I talked with Sam by telephone and thanked him for his part. Several years later he sent me his scrapbook on the Airlift, saying that he wanted to

Ev Langworthy, the first Airlift pilot whom I had a chance to personally thank for his part in keeping us alive and free.

leave it to someone who would appreciate it. He had no family. I was deeply moved by this, and his scrapbook is a treasured memento. Sam has since passed on.

One of the things Sam urged was that I join BAVA, the Berlin Airlift Veterans Association. Not being a veteran, I did not think I qualified, but he assured me that I was because I had been there, in Berlin, during the Airlift.

I attended my first BAVA Reunion in Washington, DC in September 1998. It was an incred-ible experience as I walked into a

roomful of pilots, mechanics, air traffic controllers and other airlift personnel who—fifty years earlier—had risked their lives to keep me alive and free. I did not know whom to hug and thank first. They were all precious.

Sam Burgess at the controls during the Airlift. I never met Sam, but he honored me by giving me his Airlift scrapbook.

Every five years BAVA members travel to Berlin to again visit the city they helped save from Russian rule more than fifty years ago. I attended the 2004 meeting in Berlin. The group of about 100 veterans traveled to Frankfurt afterwards to see for the last time their headquarters which are about to be torn down to make room for airport expansion. I am with Lorraine and Gail Halvorsen in this picture taken at Frankfurt with one of the C–54 Airlift aircraft in the background.

In 1951 the Berlin Airlift Monuments were built in Frankfurt and Berlin. The picture to the left is of the Frankfurt Monument and the picture on the opposite page is of the Berlin Monument. They are facing each other. The three prongs symbolize the three air corridors into Berlin during the Airlift. Each Monument is located at the respective airport used during the Airlift.

Seventy–six crew and ground personnel lost their lives during the Airlift, but 2.2 million West Berliners survived, including Mom, Peter and I.

The Frankfurt picture was taken during the BAVA visit in October, 2004. The white tents were put up for the Airlift veterans in case of rain.

The most special one of the pilots whom I met that day was Colonel Gail Halvorsen, the legendary "Berlin Candy Bomber." He became famous by putting the "Heart into the Airlift" and candy into the children's hands. When I met him, I saw *love* and *caring* in his eyes, and I knew that only he could have come up with such a daring idea as to make parachutes out of handkerchiefs, tie candy bars and gum to them, and throw them out of his airplane to the waiting Berlin children below.

I feel fortunate that fifty years later I had the opportunity to meet Colonel Halvorsen and to be able to thank him personally for his love and kindness towards the little Berliners, and for the hope that he and his comrades gave to all of the people in West Berlin. Today Mal and I consider the Halvorsens among our most precious friends.

Quite a few times I was surprised that, when thanking one of these men for helping to keep Berlin free, I was being thanked by him instead. "We had orders and were just doing our job," I was told, "but we thank the Berliners for being willing to get along on the smallest amounts of food in exchange for freedom." "The Berliners were the real heroes" one Airlift pilot told me.

The Airlift pilots could fly in only limited supplies of food, just enough for us to survive, but they brought us hope. It was the hope we needed more than the calories in order to survive; the hope to keep our freedom, and because of it to have a better life.

Without the Airlift to keep West Berlin free, I would not be here as a free person in the United States. My special, personal thanks go to all who were involved in making the Berlin Airlift a success, and to one unique person in particular, Colonel Gail Halvorsen, who put a personal touch of love on the operation.

"Hers was the Joy of Giving"

Conflicts we faced when our children were growing up were usually due to my inability to relate to their constant wishes and requests. I was always comparing the present world with the world that I grew up in.

Mom was my hero and my role model, and I wanted to follow in her footsteps. She would have been able to adjust to the different times and circumstances, whereas I seemed to measure everything against the time in which I grew up. I could not create the happy times of my childhood for my children because they had different needs in order to be happy. Being a perfectionist, I eternally worried about not doing the right thing and trusting my instinct. It seemed that Mom always knew what to do, and I admired her so much. I don't know where she got the energy to pull us through the difficult times and to cope with our growing up at the same time, but somehow she found the strength to keep going.

Johanna Stanneck in 1962—our Mom

Now our children are grown and have their own lives. They have turned out extremely well despite all of my doubts and worries.

Mom is buried in Northern Virginia where we lived at the time of her death on May 2, 1987. Peter and I had the following words engraved on her headstone: *Hers was the Joy of Giving*, which we found appropriate to sum up the essence of her being. Each time I stand at her grave I thank Mom for her unselfishness, and for her love and devotion.

Mom will always be my hero, for as I am growing old I still strive to be like her. She was positive, full of fun and laughter; had boundless energy, love for family and friends, and for life in general. Mom was totally unselfish and enjoyed giving to others, not only material things, but of herself. She has been a great influence in our lives, and because of her courage Peter and I survived. Never lost for a solution, Mom always knew what to do.

Peter and I stand in awe of her.

- The End -

Also by Inge Gross

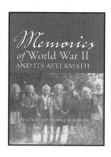

Memories
of
World War II and its Aftermath
1940-1954
An Autobiography
Volume I

(Hard cover, 320 pages, 100 pictures, $23.95)

The crashes and flashes of light in the dark of night sounded to the five year old child like a terrible thunderstorm. "No," said Inge's friend Reinhard, one year older and wiser. "It is an air raid.

Countless times after that night in late August of 1940, Inge fled with her mother and younger brother to improvised bomb shelters in cellars wherever they were living. The wail of the air raid siren became a plaintive cry echoing the plight of the lost and wounded. The city of her birth and childhood rocked with bombs and blazing fire as the war rumbled on.

In her first–hand account, Inge manages to transform herself back to those days of horror and fear combined with the innocence of a child growing up during war, and the even worse years immediately follow- ing World War II.

Inge tells her story as she remembers it. The resulting chronicle gives you, the reader, a fresh perspective as you watch a youngster growing up in war times, as she manages to forge strong relationships and maintains a cheerful outlook on life during very dark times.

Both Volume One and Volume Two are available directly from the publisher, Island In The Sky Publishing Co., PO Box 139, Eastsound, WA 98245. The price of each book including shipping via media mail is $23.95 if ordered directly from the publisher and paid by check. Readers preferring the use of priority mail or the use of a credit card should go on–line at: *www.MemoriesOfWWII.com, or Amazon.com.*